THE KING OF SPORTS

THE KING OF SPORTS

Football's Impact on America

GREGG EASTERBROOK

THOMAS DUNNE BOOKS

ST. MARTIN'S PRESS

NEW YORK

THOMAS DUNNE BOOKS.
An imprint of St. Martin's Press.

THE KING OF SPORTS. Copyright © 2013 by Gregg Easterbrook. All rights reserved.
Printed in the United States of America. For information, address St. Martin's Press,
175 Fifth Avenue, New York, N.Y. 10010.

www.thomasdunnebooks.com
www.stmartins.com

Design by Omar Chapa

ISBN 978-1-250-01171-8 (hardcover)
ISBN 978-1-250-01172-5 (e-book)

St. Martin's Press books may be purchased for educational, business, or promotional
use. For information on bulk purchases, please contact Macmillan Corporate and
Premium Sales Department at 1-800-221-7945, extension 5442, or write special
markets@macmillan.com.

796.332

First Edition: October 2013

10 9 8 7 6 5 4 3 2 1

To Charles Peters
As an editor and man of letters,
equal in accomplishments to
Harold Ross, Arnold Gingrich and Philip Rahv

CONTENTS

Sports do not build character. They reveal it.

—*Heywood Hale Broun*

THE KING OF SPORTS

PREFACE

"We want football! We want football!"

On a pleasant spring evening, a flash mob gathered at Radio City Music Hall to chant for the greatest sport of the greatest country in the world. Thousands were present to attend the 2011 National Football League draft, hoping to glimpse celebrity athletes, coaches and sportscasters. New York City police cordoned off an intersection to manage the crowd.

"We want football," the boisterous assembly chanted. "We want football! We want football!"

An earthquake followed by a tsunami had just struck Japan, killing sixteen thousand and causing leaks at a nuclear reactor. Hundreds had perished as an apocalyptic wave of tornadoes hit Alabama. Unemployment was high, the national debt increasing at an alarming pace. United States aircraft were bombing Libya, while the "Arab Spring" revolutions swept Egypt and the Persian Gulf. In Afghanistan, special forces were completing rehearsals for a commando raid to kill Osama bin Laden.

But to the crowd in Manhattan, something *really* important was happening—the National Football League had locked out its players. Come autumn, there might be no football on Sundays. The throng chanted, "We want football! We want football!"

The United States definitely wants football. Gridiron football is the king of sports—the biggest game in the strongest and richest of nations. Football rolls in money and popularity, and has taken command of that American shared experience, television. NBC's *Sunday Night Football* is the number-one network show: not the number-one sport, the number-one show. ESPN's *Monday Night Football* is the number-one cable show: not the number-one sport, the number-one show. In recent years, either nine or ten of the ten highest-rated television events were NFL contests, with football besting even the Academy Awards. The 2012 Super Bowl between the Giants and the Patriots was the most watched television broadcast in American history. And of the twenty most watched television broadcasts ever, both in the United States and internationally, all twenty were Super Bowls.

Each season of high school, college and professional football builds up to the Super Bowl, which in its zany excess—testosterone-pumped gladiators clashing, rock music at earsplitting decibels, buff cheerbabes dancing, military flyovers, encampments of motor homes, thousands of journalists from around the globe including reporters from North Korea—is the face the United States presents to the world.

I attend the Super Bowl annually. My first time, I arrived to find city streets packed with what seemed hundreds of thousands of revelers, far more than could possibly have tickets. Many did not, in fact, have tickets. They'd made the trip simply to be in the Super Bowl city, soaking up the party atmosphere, later able to tell friends, "I was at the Super Bowl," skipping that they watched on television from a hotel. When the Super Bowl was held in Dallas at the Cowboys' billion-dollar new stadium, some five thousand people paid $200 each just to stand outside the facility and watch on video screens, so they could say they'd been there.

Is it coincidence that America is the strongest, richest and most vibrant society, and also the sole country whose national sport is gridiron football?

Considering football's cost and over-the-top character, perhaps the United States is the only nation big enough, wealthy enough and crazy enough to have football as its national sport. But there is something deeper. Football both expresses the American spirit and plays a role in that spirit. Without football there would still be fifty stars on the flag and we'd still all be real live nephews of our Uncle Sam. But America wouldn't be quite the same.

The game offers many pluses. Football is the most complex of all sports on the basis of tactics: its sense of being a living chessboard is one reason play is so engaging. Football teaches young people self-discipline and teamwork, helps promote colleges and universities, can set positive examples for society. One of my children benefited tremendously from his years of high school and NCAA football, the sport helping him mature and gain self-confidence, in addition to granting him the thrill of being recruited by an important college. And football is fantastic entertainment: a well-played game is both exciting and aesthetically beautiful.

That athletics can teach valuable lessons, and be a fine diversion, are reasons even really smart people become sports nuts. Political columnist George Will and Supreme Court Justice Sandra Sotomayor are addicted to baseball. Albert Camus, the archetype of the French intellectual, preferred soccer to attending the theater or visiting museums. Former secretary of state Condoleezza Rice, now a professor at Stanford University, is an avid football fan and attends all Cardinal home games. Supreme Court justice Byron White, who died in 2002, was in youth a college football star and said of his lifelong love for athletics, "I read the sports pages first because they chronicle achievements. The news pages chronicle failures."

The pluses of football must be weighed against many negatives. They include concussions and other kinds of injuries, which occur more commonly to youth and high school players than to well-off professionals; public subsidies for NFL stadiums converted into private profit; young men who spend four or five years at major universities generating revenue but receiving no education; abuse of painkillers and other drugs. An unseen aspect of football is troubling, too. For every one young athlete who becomes a celebrated star, perhaps a hundred gain nothing, being used up and tossed aside.

It's bad enough that many universities clear $50 million per year or more on their football programs, with head coaches paid up to $5 million per year, while players get only meal money. Did you know that the National Football League, annual revenue around $10 billion, claims to be a not-for-profit enterprise in order to evade taxes? If you think that's an outrage—you're right.

Because football is a deep part of the nation's culture, its impact on the nation should be assessed. The two best books about football— *Friday Night Lights*, by H. G. Bissinger, and *The Blind Side*, by Michael Lewis—were not concerned with who wins games, rather with how the sport touches lives. Neither was conventional sportswriting, and both found a broad audience. These fine volumes made me think the football book that had not yet been written is the book about how the sport touches the entire nation. So this book asks what overall impact football has on American society.

Why me as author? I bring a moderate combination of intellectual and athletic experience. My writing includes eight books, a thirty-year association with *The Atlantic* as national correspondent and then contributing editor, contributing-editor roles at *Newsweek* and *The Washington Monthly,* and a political-columnist post at Reuters. I have been a fellow in economics and in government studies at the Brookings Institution, and a fellow in international affairs at the Fulbright Foundation. I played football in high school and at the small-college level. I have many years of youth-coaching experience, including as head coach of the middle school affiliate team for a large public high school. I write the "Tuesday Morning Quarterback" column for ESPN.com, have been an on-air football commentator for ESPN and for NFL Network, and have appeared in football documentaries produced by PBS and by NFL Films.

In the initial planning for this book, it became obvious that many pages would be devoted to faults of the sport—its negative impacts on health, education and use of public funds. To balance the reproach, I wanted to show that football can be done in a conscientious, ethical manner. So I decided to include an insider's account of a well-run team.

I considered focusing on one of the well-run NFL clubs. But there are fewer than two thousand NFL players, many with high incomes, making the pros' situations rarefied. Next I considered taking the reader inside a prep football team. But in its depiction of high school football, *Friday Night Lights* has already come close to perfection.

That led to college football. All the good and bad of the sport is on display in the major collegiate programs, and the college experience is familiar to large numbers of Americans. I decided to give it the old college try, and to seek a university whose football program met these qualifications: makes a major bowl most years, has a low rate of football scandals and a high graduation rate for African-American players.

The criteria cut the field to a distressingly small number: Boston College, Notre Dame, Stanford, Virginia Tech and Wisconsin. BYU, Duke, Northwestern and Vanderbilt would join the honor roll if the benchmark for winning were a little looser. That there are so few college-powerhouse programs that are not tainted would disturb the NCAA—if the NCAA cared about anything other than money.

I chose Virginia Tech. The head coach, Frank Beamer, is the winningest active coach in Division I. He's been at Virginia Tech for twenty-six years, spurning big-bucks offers from the pros. His program's twenty consecutive years with a bowl invitation shows that a team can win game after game after game without taking shortcuts in ethics or in the classroom. The engineering school of Virginia Tech is a leader in research into reducing sports-concussion risk. And Beamer represents an

Old South university with an African-American graduation rate many Northern colleges can only envy.

Beamer agreed to let me accompany the Virginia Tech team for the 2011 season, which would end with the Hokies ranked seventeenth. The intent was not to recount the season, but to see what high-level football looks like from the inside. There were no restrictions. I was at practices, in the locker room, on the sideline, traveled with the team, wandered into players' or coaches' meetings unannounced.

Public-relations "minders" have become nearly ubiquitous when writers are present at large institutions, but at Virginia Tech no one from the university followed me around and no one from the college's legal office approached me to sign anything. Beamer asked if he would have input into the finished product; I answered no, adding there were certain to be passages he wouldn't like. "Okay, that shows you are honest," he replied. Beamer and I made no written agreement: everything was done with handshakes. Which made me think, "Okay, that shows he is honest."

The Hokies were a breath of fresh air compared to the closed, paranoid style of the NFL. For the NFL sections of the book, I requested interview time with Commissioner Roger Goodell. He agreed; date and times were arranged. But when NFL headquarters staff learned that I planned to ask about the health effects and financial structure of football, the interview was immediately canceled. NFL spokesman Greg Aiello told me it was not "in our best interests" to discuss safety, subsidies or tax exemptions.

This book starts by profiling Beamer; then spends a chapter on what day-to-day life is like in the Virginia Tech football program; then shifts to the NFL, specifically its money; then looks at money and the NCAA; then examines the question of whether college football players are exploited; then examines concussions and other forms of health damage caused by football; then asks if football sends society the wrong messages on weight gain, pill-popping and other issues; then asks whether football has become uncomfortably like a cult; then profiles some of the many former players who have only ruined lives to show for their years in the sport; then asks why gridiron football is uniquely American. The penultimate chapter returns to the Virginia Tech Hokies, describing in detail the 2012 Sugar Bowl game. The book concludes by speculating on the future of football.

Because many of the pages that follow concern things wrong with football, it's important that the book begins and ends by showing what the sport looks like when you do it right.

Football needs to get its priorities in order. Up in the Blue Ridge Mountains of Virginia is a college where this has already happened.

NOTES

I have written the "Tuesday Morning Quarterback" column for fourteen years for Slate, NFL.com and ESPN.com, and shudder to think that project now exceeds two million total words. Some paragraph of his book reprise or expand upon research and ideas first presented in the column. All money figures have been converted into 2013 dollars. To avoid endlessly repeating "in an interview with me," when a quotation comes from the public record, I use constructions such as "said" or "has said"; when the quotation is from an interview with me, the speaker "says." For games with confusing dates—the 1981 Super Bowl was played in 1982, for instance—the text cites the year in which the game occurred.

Why Frank Beamer Decided to Follow the Rules

1

THE VIEW FROM FANCY GAP

Fancy Gap, Virginia, a postage-stamp town up in the cool air of the Blue Ridge escarpment, is only three hundred miles from the Ridley Circle Homes of Newport News, Virginia. Sociologically, they are worlds apart.

Frank Beamer, born 1946, grew up in Fancy Gap, an all-white hamlet where good folk attended church and high school football games, and the Mountain Top Motel was the closest thing to nightlife. The tranquil town represented an idyllic imagining of the American past—represents that still, today. Many people wish they could live in an idyllic version of the American past. Beamer did.

Michael Vick, born 1980, grew up in Ridley Circle Homes, a nearly all-black housing project where no one would wish to live. Ranks of town houses were squeezed between an eight-lane freeway and Langley Air Force Base. Military jets passing overhead regularly made windows in the Ridley Circle Homes shake. Garbage blew across the brown dirt spaces between the structures—there were no lawns, no shrubs.

Benzene fumes from a nearby petroleum tank farm could make the air sting the nostrils.

The general area was known to residents not as Newport News but as Bad News. In the Ridley Circle Homes, gunshots were common. Sometimes when there was a gunfight, mugging or rape, no one called the police, knowing gangs would retaliate after the officers departed. The crime-ridden Cabrini-Green project in Chicago had long been cited as the most inhumane public housing in the United States. Ridley Circle Homes was every bit as bad—it just didn't get as much press.

In 1997, Beamer drove across southern Virginia to meet Vick. Beamer was crossing a physical landscape of exit ramps and truck stops, but also the landscapes of American culture, sports and money.

When Beamer was born, the Army was not yet integrated; Jim Crow laws remained on the books, the Civil Rights Act not yet having passed; blacks in many states were effectively disenfranchised, the Voting Rights Act not yet having passed; no black person since Reconstruction had been a governor; no African-American had been on the Supreme Court or been secretary of state, to say nothing of in the Oval Office; no African-American had been admitted to Virginia Tech. Now a socially conservative white football coach raised in old-time Southern circumstances was on his way to meet a black teen raised in contemporary hip-hop pandemonium, and it was the white adult who would supplicate before the black teen.

FOOTBALL WAS CHANGING FROM SEGREGATED to largely African-American, a development both good (career opportunities and recognition for a minority group) and disquieting (what University of Georgia professor Billy Hawkins calls the "new plantation" of blacks harvesting not cotton but sports income for the nearly all-white NFL and NCAA power structures). Nowhere was the change more keenly felt than at quarterback, both the most important position in football and most visible. Quarterbacks are leaders, decision-makers and symbols. Old-timers accepted African-Americans playing the line or running back. But there was resistance to blacks taking the snap.

By the 1970s there were a few prominent African-American quarterbacks, including the University of Oklahoma's Julius Caesar Watts, later to represent the state's Fourth District in Congress. Black quarterbacks of the time tended to execute wishbone or option attacks built around simplistic tactics that made the quarterback a glorified running back. Then in 1988, the Washington Redskins, led by Doug Williams, became the first NFL team to win the Super Bowl with a black starting quarterback. Williams was a classic "pocket passer" who stood tall, scanning the field; that is, he played the position in the white style.

Not long after, Andre Ware of the University of Houston become the first African-American quarterback to win the Heisman Trophy. Ware too played as a pocket passer in a complex system. Just after Ware's success, Syracuse University recruited Donovan McNabb, a high school star from a rough neighborhood in Chicago. He had an offer from Nebraska to be a glorified running back in the school's simplified offense, and an offer from Syracuse to be a pro-style passer in a sophisticated offense. McNabb, later the third player selected in the NFL draft, chose Syracuse. From McNabb on, African-Americans could compete evenly with whites to be not just runners but decision-makers who lead teams.

Sports in the early postwar era were, to Americans, a pleasant diversion; by late in the twentieth century, as Beamer made his trip, sports were a national obsession. In the 1960s, one NFL game per week was nationally televised, along with one or two college games. Those numbers would rise to six NFL and forty or more college football games shown nationally each week. In the early 1950s, when sports first were shown on television, annual network fees to all of college football totaled about $8 million, in today's dollars. By 2012, the twelve universities of the Pac-12 Conference would divide $250 million annually in television sports income from football, plus apparel and licensing income—more than twice as much per school, annually, as all colleges combined realized in the 1950s. In 2012, ESPN signed a contract to telecast the three games of the major-college football playoff bracket that is expected to commence in 2015. The deal will pay an average of about $155 million per contest—twenty times as much, for individual college football games, as all colleges combined received from football TV rights in an entire year, when Beamer was a boy.

NFL revenue was headed off the charts. From 1998 to 2013 alone, NFL television revenue doubled, from about $2 billion to about $4 billion. *Forbes* estimated the Dallas Cowboys to be worth $1.8 billion, the New England Patriots worth $1.4 billion. The great US sports spectacle of the early-twentieth century, the 1932 Los Angeles Olympics, had cost $40 million. By 2012, annual NFL total revenue of around $10 billion was 250 times the number for the 1932 Olympics. Licensing income was growing exponentially too. In 2011, Gatorade signed a ten-year, $2.3 billion contract with the NFL to ensure that it would be a bucket of Gatorade, not some other drink, poured over the victorious coach's head as the scoreboard clock reached all-naughts. That is an awful lot of money to get announcers to say the words "Gatorade shower." But football had become the gold standard of promotion. And who plays quarterback is essential to the promotion of a college football team.

Changes in society, sports and money all were factors in Beamer's hope to recruit Michael Vick. So was a change in the way football was being played. The drop-back pocket passer then favored by the NFL almost always throws, while the option quarterback then favored by many colleges usually runs. At Warwick High School in Newport News, a third type of quarterback was drawing notice—one who could throw or run, unpredictably. Michael Vick would take the snap, sprint left or right, double back, spin, then suddenly run or, just as suddenly, stop and throw. The young man from Newport News was demonstrating a new style of playing the quarterback position.

Eventually, the way Vick played would mutate into the "spread option" offense used by Tim Tebow and Urban Meyer at the University of Florida to win a college national title in 2009; then into the "zone read option" used by Cam Newton to win a college national title at Auburn University in 2011, and by the San Francisco 49ers, Seattle Seahawks and Washington Redskins in the 2013 NFL playoffs. Thousands of hours of game-planning by many college and pro coaches would be required for Vick's manic run-around quarterbacking style to evolve into the highly disciplined zone-read offense. But anyone watching Vick perform in high school could see that he was onto something.

Vick was torn between Virginia Tech and Syracuse, which wanted him to surrender his street-ball style and perform as a conventional pocket passer. After all, this had just worked with McNabb. The conventional pocket-passer role was seen as higher status, as being a "real" quarterback. When Tebow reached the NFL, sports touts would complain that he was not a real quarterback because he refused to stand in the pocket. Syracuse was telling Vick: come to our school, be a real quarterback. Beamer knew he could win this prized recruit only by promising to let Vick be Vick.

At that point, Beamer was already an accomplished coach in the nation's favorite sport. But Virginia Tech football was followed mainly by its alums, while Virginia Tech, the institution, longed to break out from regional status to achieve a national profile. Perhaps recruiting a gifted, unorthodox figure such as Vick might place both coach and college into the limelight. Football could only get bigger.

ALL PERSONAL STORIES BEGIN IN youth, though not all have a defining moment. Beamer's does. At the age of seven, parents not present, Beamer and his eleven-year-old brother played with fire. There is a reason children are told not to play with fire. The burns left part of Beamer's face disfigured, despite three years in a hospital and some thirty skin grafts endured by a child under conditions of 1950s medicine. The burns would not prevent Beamer from becoming a public figure, nor from wedding a college beauty and having a long, successful marriage. The challenge of surviving the burns and the childhood years of hospitalization brought out something in his personality. Beamer seemed born determined.

His father was a highway engineer, his mother a schoolteacher. Both taught old-fashioned values. "My family environment growing up stressed that that if you followed the rules and worked hard, success would come," Beamer says. "I am not gullible, I know that is not always true. But it's what I was raised to believe, and it is how I chose to lead my life."

Beamer was a three-sport letterman in high school, a feat almost impossible today, as youth and prep football have become year-round pursuits. Graduating, he enrolled at Virginia Tech, which was expanding and hoped to grow from a regional engineering school into a national research-center university. The University of Virginia, the state's prestige campus, emphasized the humanities. Virginia Tech's leaders correctly guessed that research would be the wave of the future for large public universities, and moved the school in that direction. They likewise correctly guessed that hosting major football games would cause millions of people to hear the words *Virginia Tech*. Winning major football games would cause millions of people to associate the words *Virginia Tech* with success.

For a century, college presidents and trustees have seen football as a way to promote their institutional brands, while giving alumni a reason to keep paying attention to the school, and mailing donations, long after they have flung their graduation caps into the air. The first game in which the gridiron version of the sport diverged from rugby was played between Princeton and Rutgers in 1869. Stanford and Cal, the elite universities of California, have played each other at football since 1892; until roughly World War II, Harvard, Yale, Princeton, Penn, Cornell University and the University of Chicago were among the country's football powers. For more than a century, victory at football has associated the name of a college with success. Virginia Tech sought the same association.

For a century, the sport has also been viewed as detrimental to, or at best a distraction from, a university's core educational mission. In 1905, Teddy Roosevelt called college presidents to the White House to discuss public anger about the effect of football on higher education: whether this meeting led to meaningful reform or merely to agreement to outlaw the dangerous flying-wedge formation is a question historians debate to this day. By 1929, a Carnegie Foundation report would slam college football for distorting campus values, to say nothing of wasting educational funds on "costly varsity sweaters and extensive journeys in special Pullman cars." The 1932 Marx Brothers movie *Horse Feathers* would present college football as corrupt to the point of rigged. In 1939, the University of Chicago would drop football while the University of Pittsburgh, a power, joined other colleges in deemphasizing the sport.

Then as now, the fundamental objection was to college football as a business. But fundamentally, colleges *are* businesses. Faculty members certainly do not protest the charging of tuition. Twenty-year-olds receive nothing of clear monetary value while adults at the college live well—this does not describe NCAA athletics, this describes the situation for all students enrolled in universities. Professors of medieval poetry expect students to pay through the nose to attend their classes, with no assurance this will lead to enlightenment, much less a job. Colleges are businesses that must sustain themselves. That football is used as an enticement for students to enroll in colleges, and for alumni to make donations, should not in itself trouble any lover of higher education.

Attending Virginia Tech, Beamer started at cornerback, appearing in the 1966 and 1968 Liberty Bowl games. He was known as a tenacious player whose work ethic and hard hitting compensated for average stature and speed. When Beamer played NCAA football, concussions were laughed off as "getting your bell rung," torn knee ligaments were career-ending disasters, many coaches refused to allow players to drink water during hot-weather practice, and poor-quality helmets caused a palpable risk of death by skull fracture. During the four years that Beamer was a college athlete, ninety-one football players died as a direct result of skull fractures sustained during games or practices, according to the American Football Coaches Association, which since 1931 has kept statistics on harm caused by the game. The arrival in the 1970s of the polycarbonate helmet would nearly eliminate skull-fracture risk; today, risk of death from college football is about the same as risk of death from college hazing.

After flinging his own graduation cap into the air, Beamer had no illusions about the NFL. College players may dream of "the league," and college coaches may inveigle them with a fantasy that they can concentrate on football, skipping the classroom, because a million-dollar NFL bonus awaits. But even many star college players never take a snap at the professional level, and for those who do make the NFL, a career is a few seasons.

Knowing the NFL to be a long shot, Beamer enrolled in master's program at Radford University, located in the same corner of Virginia as Fancy Gap, thinking he might study to become a guidance counselor. Beamer passed his free time coaching high school football in the town of Radford, and found he enjoyed coaching. Soon he was a graduate assistant—a coaching intern—at the big-deal program of the University of Maryland, then a football powerhouse. Beamer moved on to salaried coaching positions at The Citadel in South Carolina and at Murray State in Kentucky, neither important galaxies in the football universe. In 1986, the Virginia Tech job came open. He applied.

A MURAL PHOTOGRAPH IN THE football coaches' office complex at Virginia Tech—as at all Top 25 programs, the coaches enjoy offices and conference-room facilities many Fortune 500 firms would envy—depicts a game from 1926. Thousands of spectators crowd Miles Stadium. The referee wears dress slacks and a collared white shirt, as if he stopped by on his way to church. Hundreds of Model Ts are parked in ranks in the distance. Considering the year, a significant fraction of the population of downstate Virginia had come to attend the game.

Before there was television entertainment and before professional sports were ubiquitous, large numbers undertook relatively arduous journeys for the excitement of a college football contest. Traversing the 225 miles from Richmond to Blacksburg on old two-lane blacktops in a Model T with a top speed of thirty-five miles per hour, and crude suspension, was no joyride. In 1935, some ninety-four thousand spectators attended the Cal-Stanford football clash. Not only did this dwarf the thirty-three thousand present for the Bears-Giants professional football title game of 1933, compared to California's population of the time, ninety-four thousand spectators was as if a million people attended a Cal-Stanford game today.

In 1965, Miles Stadium would be razed and replaced by Lane Stadium, offering 66,233 seats—quite substantial for an isolated college hard to reach whether by automobile, train or commercial airline. In 1982, Virginia Tech would play football on national television for the first time. Even in 1982, nationally televised college football games were rare. That would change when, in 1984, a Supreme Court decision essentially deregulated the broadcasting of college football, leading to its nearly round-the-clock presence on today's television in autumn.

Up through the 1982 game, Virginia Tech sports squads bore the not-quite-inspirational nickname Fighting Gobblers. Feeling it was ridiculous to chant "Go Fighting Gobblers!" on national television, Tech students voted to change their athletic teams' nickname. To what? In the late-nineteenth century, Tech cadets yelled "hokie!" as school-spirit cry, the same way Georgetown University students of the period yelled "hoya!" Both are nonsense words with a nice ring. Virginia Tech teams became the Hokies, though keeping a turkey-mascot image, causing sportscasters to this day to assume that a hokie is a species of wild turkey. The Blue Hose of Presbyterian College and the Ichabods of Washburn University are perhaps the most amusing nicknames in collegiate sports; Blue Hose refers to stockings, not to melancholy courtesans.

The magnificent stadium where the Hokies now perform sits at 2,057 feet, its Blue Ridge setting part of the school's lore. The Appalachians are glorious, but also have long been synonymous with rural isolation and lack of awareness of the larger world. As Virginia Tech grew from enrollment of six thousand in the year Beamer was born, to thirty-one thousand today; from a regional land-grant institution with the clunky name Virginia Polytechnic Institute and State University to a national research-center university that styles itself on the Internet as VT; from a safety school to selective admission—more than one Virginia Tech faculty member has a child attending nearby Radford because he or she couldn't get into Virginia Tech—the Blacksburg campus became the capital of downstate Virginia. On dates of football home games, Lane Stadium is the most important location in the mid-Atlantic.

Beamer applied for the Virginia Tech job and won it. "If you had told me when I was a boy that I would play football at Virginia Tech and then return to be the coach there, I would have said my life was going to be perfect," he says.

Others felt quite differently. The school's boosters were crushed when Beamer was chosen. Bobby Ross, a famous coach, had been expected to take the position. Beamer was a who-dat from Murray State, itself hardly a sparkling name—though a cradle of college coaches, including Mike Gottfried, Ralph Friedgen, Houston Nutt, Ron Zook and Beamer assistant Bud Foster. It was widely believed Beamer got the job because he was willing to accept a salary of $150,000, about half what head football coaches at large universities earned at the time. Since Beamer took over at Virginia Tech, the colleges of the Atlantic Coast Conference, to which the school belongs, have had a total of sixty head football coaches, while the Hokies have had one. And by 2012, Beamer would possess the most victories of any active major-college football coach.

THE COACH'S TENURE DID NOT begin well, his charges going 22-32-1 in Beamer's initial seasons, while receiving no bowl invitations. Then in 1992, the Hokies finished 2-8-1. The boosters wanted Beamer's head. "Today, I would not have gotten another year," Beamer says. "There's so much more money at stake now. The more money involved, the more quickly people want results."

At the end of the 2011 football season, fired college head football coaches included Zook (at Illinois), Dennis Erickson (at Arizona State), Turner Gill (at Kansas), Larry Porter (at Memphis), Rob Ianello (at Akron), Neil Callaway (at the University of Alabama–Birmingham), Rick Neuheisel (at UCLA), Paul Wulff (at Washington State), Pat Hill (at Fresno State), Mike Sherman (at Texas A&M) and David Bennett (at Coastal Carolina). All were fired not for ethical lapses nor low graduation rates, rather, for not winning enough. Bennett had a career 63-39 record at the school that fired him, but had just failed to deliver a postseason invitation. Gill and Ianello were each cashiered after just two seasons on the job—their sin was not winning instantly. At the end of the 2012 season, eight of the NFL's thirty-two head coaches were fired, including Lovie Smith of the Chicago Bears. The Bears had just finished 10-6, but missed the playoffs. Get rid of the bum!

Granted six seasons of modest on-field results, a honeymoon no major-college coach would receive today, in his seventh season Beamer led the Hokies to a 9-3 finish and a win in the Independence Bowl. The season began Beamer's incredible streaks: twenty consecutive winning seasons, twenty consecutive bowl seasons, eight consecutive seasons with at least ten victories.

During his honeymoon, Beamer was learning to coach: no one is born knowing how. Also he was ironing out the tactical innovations for which he would become known—using complex, choreographed plays to block punts and field-goal attempts, plus choreography on kick-return plays. At the time, most football teams, including in the NFL, did not have complex kick-blocking strategies nor choreographed kick runbacks. Punt and kickoff return calls tended to be simply "return right" or "return left." Beamer's method of coaching special teams differed from the traditional too. Not only did his teams expend considerable practice time on kicking plays, but there was no special-teams coordinator. Typically in football, a special-teams coordinator runs the kicking plays and is viewed by the offensive and defensive staffs as a lower-status coach. At Virginia Tech, Beamer assigned each of his assistants, including the offensive and defensive coordinators, one aspect of the kicking game, and graded them on it. That gave everyone on the coaching staff an incentive to create blocked kicks or kick-return touchdowns.

This package of tactics, dubbed Beamer Ball, allowed the Hokies to average five blocked kicks per season from 1991 to 2010, while other big-college teams were averaging one blocked kick per season, and to average four touchdowns per season on kicking plays, against a big-college average of one per season.

Blocked kicks and kick-return touchdowns are among the game-changer plays in the sport. The blocked kick typically gives the defending team a bonus of about forty yards in field position, plus the psychological impact of the other team's being embarrassed by failing to execute an action regarded as routine. On a kick-return touchdown, one team has worked, worked, worked for a few yards of advantage, and suddenly a skinny guy from the opposition is sprinting the length of the field untouched.

Beamer Ball would prove among the most important innovations in football of the 1990s and was a factor in leading the Hokies to the 1999 national title game. Gradually the edge diminished as others learned to imitate Beamer's tactics. Since 2011, Virginia Tech's kicking statistics have differed little from the kicking stats of other big-college teams, and Beamer is a bit glum about this. But Beamer Ball helped Virginia Tech gain a national reputation and become a recruiting power—the latter sustaining the program once the special-teams edge faded.

BEAMER ALSO NEEDED THE EARLY, losing seasons to develop his quixotic philosophy: that graduation rates and sportsmanship are more important than wins. All college coaches say education and sportsmanship matter, but few act as though they believe this. If Nick Saban, head coach of the Alabama Crimson Tide that won the 2012 and 2013 college football titles, said, "At Alabama, our players are students first and athletes second," his own staff would burst out laughing. In the 2012 championship season, the University of Alabama graduated just 62 percent of its African-American football players. That's progress, since five years before, Alabama football graduated just 46 percent.

While all college coaches mouth the right words about education and sportsmanship, Beamer means what he says. His teams' graduation rates for African-American players consistently are at the top for major-college football, and it is black graduation rates that matter most. White athletes have been taken advantage of too, but exploitation of black players is the deepest worry regarding college football. As Hawkins says, "Teen and young-adult black males have few role models for intellectual or business success. Their role models are in sports and music. But the number of people who can make livings in professional sports or in the entertainment industry is very small compared to the number of positions available in the business world and in education for people with college degrees. Because of this, creating for African-American college athletes a delusion of grandeur about the odds of professional success, while distracting them from completing their college degrees, is extremely cynical."

Some may assume a major-college football program cannot excel without taking educational or recruiting shortcuts. But consider that quarterbacks from Notre Dame or Stanford, colleges with strict academic standards for athletes, have started in the Super Bowl on fourteen occassions. No quarterback from an Oklahoma or Texas university has ever started in the Super Bowl. Nor has any quarterback from Ohio State or USC, big-money programs infamous for NCAA violations, ever started in the Super Bowl.

Consider the 2011 Orange Bowl. The contest was one of the five BCS bowls held that year—the very top of college football competition. Stanford and Virginia Tech entered the Orange Bowl as highly ranked teams, featuring numerous players who would be top NFL draft choices, including Andrew Luck of Stanford, first overall selection in 2012, and David Wilson of Virginia Tech, 2012 first draft pick of the New York Giants. The Stanford–Virginia Tech Orange Bowl pairing had the highest combined graduation rate for football of any game in the annals of the Bowl Championship Series.

You'd think the BCS organizers and the network broadcasters would have touted the status of that Orange Bowl as the best-ever BCS contest in educational terms. But the high graduation rates went unmentioned. Lauding the schools that succeed in combining football with education, the NCAA and the big conferences seem to feel, only draws attention to the fact that many big-college programs don't even try to educate players.

How BEAMER COULD WIN A record number of games, achieve his twenty-year streak of bowl appearances, and still run a program with integrity, is the subject of the next chapter. First, let's finish his 1997 trip across Virginia to recruit Vick.

Arriving at the Ridley Circle Homes, Beamer told Vick, his mother and Vick's high school coach that Virginia Tech could not offer the glamour found at colleges such as USC or the University of Miami: The Hokies could offer only football and schoolwork, in an isolated location with no limos or house-party scene, but a lot of emphasis on personal responsibility. The reverse-psychology pitch appealed to Vick, who wanted to get away from the stress and dangers of his youth, and also appealed to Vick's mother.

In 1999, Michael Vick would lead Virginia Tech to college football's national championship game. Though the Hokies lost, the game put the school and its coach on the map. Later Vick would become the second Virginia Tech player selected number one in the NFL draft— defensive end Bruce Smith went first in 1985—and consequentially, the first African-American quarterback to be the first selected. Chosen by the Atlanta Falcons, Vick would reach stardom and the NFL's Pro Bowl, go to prison, emerge repentant and become a star again.

As the years passed, Beamer stayed in touch with Vick, even when he was disgraced—jailed, suspended by the NFL and all but run out of town on a rail by Arthur Blank, the Falcons' owner. Beamer continued to think kindly about Vick when his second star turn went sour in the 2012 season. Starting for the Philadelphia Eagles, with expectations high, Vick turned the ball over fifteen times in ten games—a dismal stat—and was benched as the Eagles had a losing season. Afterward Beamer said, "I feel about him now what I felt about him when he was here, that he is a good person with a good heart. He made mistakes—not just dogfighting, which is against the law, but lying, which is wrong in all circumstances. Now think of the good he can accomplish by showing young people that breaking the law and telling lies are terrible acts—but that doing what's right allows a person to bounce back. Young people will listen to Michael Vick in a way they would never listen to you or me. By talking about his mistakes, he is having a positive impact."

In 1999, Beamer had welcomed Vick into football's Brigadoon, and that sense of welcome remained long after Vick had departed and could no longer help the school win games. Over his long tenure as Virginia Tech coach, Beamer has welcomed many young men, plus adults who staff the program, into one of the few places in big-deal football where friendship is real, integrity means more than final scores and there are no conveniently fuzzy lines between right and wrong.

Transiting the mountain passes and divides that guard Blacksburg gives an air of entering a place cast out of time. The digitized chaos of modern urban society seems far away, though satellite uplink vans are present in the school's sports complex on game weekends. As in Brigadoon, *old-fashioned* is not an insult. Though one must be prepared to travel to the bustling, sinful cities and defeat their men-at-arms at football.

The next chapter: what Virginia Tech football is like today.

2

IF THE CALL IS GUN WEAK TREY DALLAS

BLAAAAAATTTTTTTTTT!

Every few minutes, an earsplitting horn sounds at Virginia Tech practices, informing coaches to move on to the next item. Each day's timetable is broken down into hyperspecific increments: punt-coverage drills at 5:23 p.m., punt-return drills at 5:29 p.m., and so on. At the center of the practice field is a tower from which assistants videotape every aspect of each run-through; coaches will then stay at the football office far too late, reviewing not just game film but practice film. A student volunteer controls the horn; being a student volunteer for a ranked college football program is quite prestigious. More than a hundred players are on the practice field, joined by a dozen coaches and a coterie of trainers, graduate and undergraduate assistants, journalists, academic tutors, sports-medicine majors, "compliance" officers and boosters.

Not all present are men: most of the tutors and sports-medicine majors are female, and they blend in without apparent gender tension. On the tower, a bright digital clock shows the countdown to the conclusion of the NCAA-approved amount of time the Hokies may be on the field that day.

BLAAAAAATTTTTTTTTT! Practice is over. Most of the players sprint toward the locker room, knowing an appealing "training table" meal awaits, along with Gatorade. College football players drink Gatorade at breakfast, lunch and dinner. They down several bottles a day, including in cold weather, in the belief that having Gatorade in your system at all times reduces the odds of muscle cramps.

Even if you're thirsty, the thrill of yet another Gatorade can wear off. Want a Frost Ripetide Rush? Some Rain Tangerine, perhaps? The players also quaff Gatorade protein shakes and munch Gatorade "energy bites," basically high-tech candy. Candy is the exception to the otherwise impressively health-conscious diet of today's NFL and NCAA football players: most locker rooms have a bowl of Snickers and 3 Musketeers bars, for a sugar rush before practice. In the halls of the Virginia Tech football facility, hundreds of cases of Gatorade sit shrink-wrapped on shipping pallets.

As practice ends, a few players are taken aside for interviews by assorted sports media, from ESPN to a college-owned house channel, all catering to the insatiable American desire for information about football. A few hear their names called out by their position coaches—like all college programs, Virginia Tech has not only a head coach, offensive coordinator and defensive coordinator, but coaches for each position, including a coach for inside linebackers and a coach for outside linebackers. Your name called out at the end of practice is not good. This means you are in minor trouble: missed a class, didn't hustle. (Players in major trouble would not be practicing.) As everyone else leaves to relax and grab some ice-cold Fierce Wild Berry Gatorade, the players whose names were called are marched by their position coaches to Beamer, who leads them through up-downs.

Of the many drills football players detest, up-downs might head the list. Chop the knees high for fast running in place; then drop to the grass and do push-ups; then leap high and resume chopping. Beamer doesn't say anything as he works his whistle to govern the up-downs. He doesn't need to. No player wants to be left on the field with a sixty-six-year-old coaching legend while everyone else heads to dinner. That Beamer does the miscreants' drill himself makes players really, really want to stay on their coaches' good sides.

"Life is ten percent what happens to you, ninety percent how you react," Beamer says to the chastised players as their up-downs end. "Young people make mistakes. Sometimes it's okay to make a mistake. It is never okay to repeat a mistake." He waves, and they trot off. Beamer muses, "It's so important to bear in mind that these are not professional athletes. They are college students. They are here first to learn, second for sports." At more than one big-college athletic department, this statement would be considered hopelessly naïve.

THE SCHOOL YEAR STARTS EARLY for Division I football players. Typically they report to campus in early summer to begin conditioning sessions and take one or two courses—picking up credits over the summer allows players to carry light course loads during football season. This only matters to colleges, such as Virginia Tech, that enforce strict academic rules for athletes. Auburn's undefeated 2004 team was marred by the revelation that many members "remained eligible through independent-study-style courses that required little or no work," *The New York Times* reported in 2006.

An NCAA athlete must carry six credits per semester—at most universities, this defines part-time attendance. "Six credits per semester is not being a college student," says Cory Byrd, a former Hokie who is now an athletic tutor. Virginia Tech requires football players to carry at least twelve credits per semester, with the team average being fifteen.

Whether athletes excel in the classroom is a matter of a college's own rules, and of the expectations set by coaches and the college's administration. NCAA rules govern whether an athlete can receive a sports scholarship, but once that happens, colleges self-certify academic eligibility. That was how Auburn could declare players eligible based on "little or no work"—all too often, when it comes to football or men's basketball, "little or no work" is fine to the college, so long as games are won.

When the University of Connecticut men's basketball team met Bucknell University in the 2011 March Madness tournament, Connecticut entered the game with a 31 percent graduation rate, Bucknell with a 91 percent graduation rate. Victories was all the UConn Board of Trustees seemed to care about, since they did not enforce any GPA standard on athletes: if the men's basketball players were flunking out, that was perfectly fine with UConn administration. Bucknell felt differently, not allowing athletes to practice unless they were making regular progress toward graduation. Bucknell imposed a strict internal GPA standard on its athletes, though the NCAA requires only a token standard. Virginia Tech has a similar policy. To many big-university athletic departments, requiring the football and men's basketball teams to be in class makes about as much sense as requiring water to flow uphill.

The NCAA allows a Division I college to have eighty-five attending on football scholarship, so the scholarship players who spend summers with their football programs have their tuition and living expenses paid. Players who are not on scholarship—often, ten to twenty are in this situation—must pay their own summer costs, unless they receive regular financial aid. Those who are not on NCAA scholarship are not required to attend summer drills, but know their chances of playing are minimal if they don't.

Occasionally a college has an unused scholarship slot and awards it to a walk-on. Leftover scholarships are intensely desired—in a sense, representing a second chance to be recruited for the boy who did not receive a Division I offer out of high school. Jim Leonhard, eventually a star with the New York Jets, went to the University of Wisconsin in 2001 and played as a walk-on, not receiving an athletic scholarship until his senior year—he had been named All Big Ten before he had an athletic scholarship. At Virginia Tech in 2011, a walk-on named Martin

Scales, who was attending the school as a history major, planned to drop out of college when his father lost his job. Beamer awarded him an unused scholarship. Scales occasionally played as a reserve running back and went on to graduate.

Until 1977, there was no limit on the number of football scholarships. The result was that a few programs—Texas, Oklahoma, USC—dominated the Top 10 every year. Armed with booster money, they would award scholarships to a hundred to two hundred top high school seniors, far more than would ever take the field in college, just to keep them away from competitors. As the NCAA began to impose scholarship ceilings, fixed at eighty-five in 1994, college football became democratized. Players who a generation before would have been fourth string at Michigan became starters for Appalachian State, which would defeat Michigan, on its home turf, in 2007 in one of the greatest upsets in sports annals. Spreading the football talent helped induce more colleges to compete in top-level football—from 239 schools playing Division I football in 1980 to 260 Division I programs in 2010.

The universities competing in the NCAA's Division I (big school) and Division II (medium-size school) have about twenty-five thousand scholarship players in any given year. (Many liberal-arts colleges field teams in Division III, but this classification forbids athletic scholarships.) That means about twenty-five thousand young men each year attend college essentially free, owing to football—one of the leading pluses of the sport.

There is a hidden benefit—a Division I football scholarship can last five years. Many players redshirt as freshmen, taking classes and attending practice but not dressing for games. Those college programs that care only about winning have players focus on lifting weights in their redshirt year, so they are physically magnificent when they step onto the field. Conscientious programs such as at Virginia Tech, Boston College or Northwestern use the redshirt year to acclimate eighteen-year-old starstruck athletic prodigies to classroom routines, setting them on course to a diploma.

"A major-university football player gets five years in college instead of four, and all kinds of personal tutoring," notes Bruce Garnes, deputy director of football operations at Virginia Tech. The Hokies have seven academic tutors who work exclusively with athletes, a resource that regular students at any university might long for. When potential recruits come to Blacksburg to visit, their first meeting is with an academic counselor. The Hokies' graduation focus is laid out to recruits, and to their parents, before they get to see the NFL-like football facility, before they see the awards hall with jerseys of retired stars, before a coach shows them the majesty of Lane Stadium. Garnes continues, "With an extra year of college and extra academic support, there is just no excuse for not graduating."

Some defenders of low graduation numbers for major-college programs say football players don't perform notably worse, in terms of walking across the stage wearing gowns, than the student body as a whole at their schools. For example, the University of South Carolina, one of the SEC colleges that is synonymous with great football and lax academics, finished ninth in the football polls in 2011, while graduating just 45 percent of its African-American players. Since the university as a whole graduated 55 percent of black students, the apology goes, was the football team's classroom performance really so bad?

It was—because Division I football players ought to graduate at a higher rate than the student body as a whole. Scholarship football players get an extra year of instruction, extra tutoring—and don't pay for college. The latter is crucial. Running out of money is the primary reason university students fail to complete degrees. NCAA football players don't run out of money.

In the five most recent years at Virginia Tech, an average of 77 percent of football players have graduated, versus an average of 75 percent of all students; an average of 73 percent of African American football players have graduated, versus an average of 61 percent of all African American students. This is what could happen at every big-money university, if thinking that education matters more than victories was not hopelessly naïve.

• • •

ABOVE TWO THOUSAND FEET IN rolling mountains, Blacksburg is pleasant in the summertime—dry air, rarely hot. If one must run hills to prepare for a football season, few places are more welcoming.

Through the summer months, Hokies endure grueling conditioning sessions, plus supervised weight lifting, *lifting* to athletes. As recently as when Bart Starr and Fuzzy Thurston performed for the Green Bay Packers team that won the first Super Bowl, football players trained with push-ups, sit-ups and jumping jacks. The dreaded training-camp trial was the twelve-minute run: a generation ago, many linemen could not jog for twelve minutes without stopping.

Football has evolved to reward speed and endurance. Today even three-hundred-pound linemen run strapped into small parachutes to improve their quickness, while spending hours weekly on treadmills. Scientific use of barbells and dumbbells now entails timing of different types of lifts involving different body areas and types of muscle fibers, along with timing of protein consumption. "The game is won in the fourth quarter," coaches say, when both teams are tired and the one that still possesses spark will prevail. Today the backups on the Virginia Tech roster, or the roster of any major-college program, are stronger and more fit than starters for the 1966 Packers. Conditioning and supervised lifting in the NFL have even more dramatic effects, since by the time they are professionals, players are in their midtwenties, the years of physical peak. "Today's worst NFL team would defeat the 1966 Green Bay Packers by fifty points, based solely on size, strength and conditioning," says Chris Sprow, a senior editor of the *ESPN Insider* scouting service.

When the academic year begins, Virginia Tech turns into a bustling small city, with crowded sidewalks and lines to board shuttle buses that ply the campus. The main bus-marshaling area fronts the school's magnificent formal lawn—both Virginia Tech and the University of Virginia boast the sort of long lawns that Thomas Jefferson thought visually signaled the word *academia*—and is within view of the memorial to the thirty-two innocents murdered in the 2007 massacre.

The memorial is a semicircle with thirty-two blocks of dolomite limestone, each block bearing only a name, nothing more. Quarried nearby, the limestone is known locally as Hokie stone and is employed as facing on most of Virginia Tech's classroom buildings. Norris Hall, where the worst occurred, was not torn down; renovated, it remains in use as the school's Center for Peace Studies. Virginia Tech decided not to erase what happened, rather, to incorporate the memory into what the college is—though the event is invariably referred to as "April sixteenth," not as "the murders" or "the massacre." The ghoulish killer was Korean by birth. Five years later, I wandered through Norris Hall and saw many Asian faces, plus Korean names on classroom doors. No grudges are held; this is not in Virginia Tech's nature.

ONCE SCHOOL IS IN SESSION, a typical Virginia Tech player's day would be like this:

6:00 a.m.—report to the football complex for treatment if rehabilitating an injury. By Halloween, half the team is rehabilitating. Sitting in an ice bath at 6:00 a.m. is loads of fun.

Morning—breakfast, attend class, lunch.

2:00 p.m.—individual meetings with coaches by position; press interviews.

3:00 p.m.—overall team meeting.

3:30 p.m.—tape up for practice.

4:00–6:00 p.m.—practice

Afterward dinner, study hall (sometimes mandatory), homework, snack, bed.

The NCAA limits the amount of time athletes may spend preparing for sports. Virginia Tech abides strictly to NCAA time limits; other colleges laugh at them. When Tim Tebow was the star quarterback at the University of Florida, he and his position coach, Dan Mullen—later head coach at Mississippi State—gave *The New York Times* an interview in which they described in detail the twenty hours per week Tebow spends reviewing film during the off-season. The relevant NCAA rule reads, "During the offseason, a student-athlete's participation shall be limited to a maximum of eight hours per week, of which no more than two hours per week may be spent on the viewing of film." Mullen knew the rule of course and also knew the NCAA never enforces rules like this. Even during the off-season, at many college programs, players spend more time on football than on classwork.

NCAA regulations limit colleges to ten football coaches, a number that itself seems high. This is another rule widely ignored. Clemson University's 2011 football media guide listed ten regular coaches plus nine "strength and conditioning" coaches whose sole responsibility is football. Job description for one of the people the NCAA does not view as a football coach: "Works with the centers and offensive guards from a strength and conditioning standpoint." Clemson further has a "director of football programs" and a "director of football player personnel," plus two assistant athletic directors for football and an associate athletic director for football. That sounds awfully like twenty-four football coaches.

Clemson can publish this information in a media guide because it knows there is no chance the NCAA will take action. Other big-money programs go unchallenged with similar affronts. In 2011, Ole Miss listed eleven football coaches and seven men with coachlike titles such as "assistant athletic director for player development." Virginia Tech has 14 football staffers with coach- or coach-like titles. Following the rules to the letter causes, for the Hokies, a competitive disadvantage.

No restrictions apply to the time spent on football by coaches, who are in the football complex at all hours nearly year-round. In the off-season they pour over film of the hundreds of high school players to whom Virginia Tech might extend the maximum of twenty-five scholarship offers it can make annually. A coaches' conference room, where they pass many hours, has a table suitable for King Arthur and his knights.

Football is in some ways a junior imitation of military life; coaches—the officers—exhibit military mannerisms. The assistants address or refer to each other as "Coach" under all circumstances. If one is speaking of a fellow coach not present, it isn't "Curt said" or "Jim thinks," it's "Coach Newsome said" or "Coach Cavanaugh thinks," in the same way an officer would not say "Rasheed thinks" but rather "Major Wright thinks." *Coach* is a male-world honorific. Men volunteer to help with youth league programs in part for the satisfaction of being addressed as "Coach."

Being in the military analogy the flag-rank officer, Beamer invariably is addressed as "sir," including by his peers. At one meeting Beamer said to his defensive coordinator, "I need last week's defensive statistics." The fifty-three-year-old Bud Foster replied, "Yes sir!"—and jogged, rather than walked, to his office for the papers.

Because Virginia Tech has a stable program with a family atmosphere, assistants rarely depart. Foster has worked for Beamer since 1981. "A lot has changed in that time," Foster says. "When I played college football, we were excited if the final score was listed in the newspaper. Now everything we do goes out on television and the Web. When we walk into a hotel lobby, if ESPN doesn't have cameras there to film our arrival, the players think something is terribly wrong." Beamer's right-hand men Billy Hite and John Ballein have been with him since the late 1980s, essentially since he was handed the head coach's whistle. Offensive assistant Bryan Stinespring has worked for Beamer in various capacities since 1993.

By football standards, this is remarkable little turnover. Going into the 2012 NFL season, the Oakland Raiders had their fifth head coach in eight years, including three consecutive seasons with a different head coach. The Miami Dolphins were on their tenth offensive coordinator in twelve years, the Denver Broncos on their ninth defensive coordinator in ten years. In 2010, the University of Maryland fired its coaches. One year later the new head coach fired his new offensive and defensive coordinators. Turmoil of this sort is the norm in college and NFL football. When a head coach wants to shift blame, his assistants are ready scapegoats. NFL owners cannot fire their teams, and athletic directors know it takes two to three years to turn over a college roster. So if a season goes poorly, firing coaches is something quick and dramatic that a pro owner or college administration can do to placate the fan base.

Beamer doesn't operate this way. Following the 2-8-1 season of 1992, Beamer fired several assistants. Twenty-one years would pass, to 2013, before Beamer again dismissed more than one staff member; in January 2013, he fired three assistants after a 7-6 record. The ever-rising emphasis on win-win-win is shown by how, in 1992, it took a two-victory season to cause college boosters to demand a football housecleaning. By 2013, when Virginia Tech finished above .500 and won a bowl game, the season was viewed by the school's supporters and donors as a calamity because Virginia Tech football failed to reach the Top 20! Beamer agonized for weeks over his 2013 decision to let go three assistants, plus demote Stinespring from offensive coordinator to tight-ends coach, a major step down in status.

Most coaches fire assistants without hesitation to shift blame for any season perceived as less than triumphant—hang the assistants out to dry in the press too. Beamer craves stability, and unlike coaches who preach loyalty then throw staff overboard, Beamer actually believes in loyalty. To avoid criticizing former assistants in public, Beamer spun the 2013 dismissals as a move to bring in younger coaches with a grasp of evolving football tactics and youth culture.

COACHES' MEETING INCLUDE A WEEKLY Bible-study session, often at the crack of dawn, run by team chaplain Johnny Shelton. The atmosphere is fundamentalist. A typical comment, from a coaches' Bible-study session: "If you want to lead your wives as the Bible instructs, then you must first show your wives love."

Before games Shelton leads players in prayers for strength, endurance, or safety, but never for victory. Few things can shake faith more than an unctuous clergyman offering a pregame prayer that boils down to "God, crush our opponents." The divine, Shelton says, cares whether Virginia Tech players exhibit admirable behavior, but does not care who wins at football. In parts of the United States, the second half of that sentence is radical theology.

One of the coaches' meetings is a weekly session in which academic advisers review, course by course, the classroom situations of each player. Each position coach—the wide-receivers coach is responsible for the wide receivers, and so on—gets a readout of what the players under his aegis must accomplish academically that week. If the list is not completed, the player does not practice; and every football player knows if you're not allowed to practice, you're not going to play. Those who are completing their coursework but have low grades are assigned Sunday study sessions, even on the Sundays following away games.

During one of the sessions the school's chief tutor for football, Sarah Armstrong, informed the coaches several players were not taking seriously a class about gay and lesbian issues. From the course catalog: "2314, HUMAN SEXUALITY. Explores the diversity of human sexuality using global perspectives. Biological, historical, developmental, psychological and sociological approaches frame this interdisciplinary examination of the social constructions of sexuality." A room full of old-school football coaches was being lectured by a young woman about "social constructions of sexuality." The coaches listened respectfully, then Beamer told his assistants he did not want players cracking wise in the sex class. A good guess is that did not occur again.

Virginia Tech football academic reviews are so detailed and serious, I wondered if the one I attended as part of an itinerary was staged for my benefit. So later in the season I walked into the main conference room unannounced, on a day I'd said I would be absent, at the time normally employed for academic review. The same was happening when no observer was expected: an hour-long accounting of what every player needed to accomplish in the classroom that week. Graduation statistics don't fall out of the sky.

•   •   •

BEAMER HAS A REPUTATION FOR being low voltage in public; his private demeanor is the same. Strictly business, never upset. Mike Goforth, the Hokies' athletic director for sports medicine—he runs the trainers' room—says he has never seen Beamer lose his composure. "Once I forgot an assignment," Goforth says. "He called me into his office and stared at me for a moment. Then he said, 'Michael, this surprises me.' I squirmed. I would have much rather been yelled at." Though Beamer rarely jokes in public, he shows wit in private. During a coaches' meeting discussion of a high school star who wasn't performing well in college, Beamer quipped, "This kid's light needs to come on, and I'm not sure he even has a switch."

Prominent in the conference room is a depth chart, with magnetic tags representing each player. The starters know who they are, of course; the backups are nervous about whether they are second-, third- or fourth-string. Second-string is fine: you travel to away games, you'll get in and get your jersey dirty when the starter—and football people still say this even in an era of rampant profanity—"needs a blow" (meaning needs to go to the sideline and breathe deeply). Third- or fourth-string is not good. Your jersey will not get dirty, so as you trot off from a home game after the double whistle, it will be obvious to your friends, family and girlfriend that you did not play. You won't be on the travel squad—like most colleges, Virginia Tech dresses its full squad only for home games, not taking along for away dates players with no chance of entering the contest. Coaches post a travel-squad list in the locker room the day before each away-game departure; it varies a bit, depending on who's injured and who practiced well that week. For the player who is poised between second- and third-string, checking the travel roster is an unpleasant moment.

The locker room is wood-paneled, with a dozen flatscreen TVs set to ESPN, ESPN2, ESPNU and ESPN Classic. The joke in the 2004 movie *DodgeBall* about a sports event airing on "ESPN8" may not be a punch line much longer. Each player has a large locker with a personal nameplate, stocked with freshly washed gear and a range of Nike apparel—tracksuits, hoodies, T's, shorts, casual wear. Virginia Tech's apparel-marketing arrangement is with the company, which competes with Under Armour and Reebok to be exclusive supplier for high-profile teams in football and basketball. "Everything I wear is Nike. I try to feel grateful and not take this for granted when I meet friends who are only wearing Hanes," says Kyle Fuller, a defensive back.

Virginia Tech renovated the football locker room in 2006, seeking conspicuous stylishness. High schoolers on recruiting visits are impressed by fancy locker rooms. Other schools that Virginia Tech jockeys with for recruits were renovating their locker rooms, so in arms-race style, the Hokies had to, as well. Locker rooms that resemble exclusive health clubs have spread broadly across college athletics, including to women's sports.

Beyond the offices and coaches' conference area are an extensive weight floor just for football players; and a training area shared by all Virginia Tech varsity members, where it is standard for male and female athletes to mingle in shorts and T's. Young men and young women with fantastic physiques, nearly naked in close proximity to each other, would have shocked polite society a generation ago. Today this is common in collegiate athletics and almost never leads to issues because acting blasé under these circumstances is important to athletes of both genders. There is also a football players' lounge, where the walls display large headshots not of stars but of the team members with the highest GPAs, and a study hall adjacent to the lounge, with forty computer workstations and a tutor always on duty.

Next is the football hall, itself a sizable building. An exhibit area displays memorabilia of famed Virginia Tech players and of great victories. Nearby is a theater that seats 150, named for Michael Vick, used when everyone watches game film together. Each position has a classroom all its own—a quarterbacks' room, a tight ends' room, a linebackers' room and so on. A long mural shows the names of Virginia Tech players who achieved all-American status or performed in the NFL.

One memento on display in the Hokies' exhibit hall is a quarter-back wristband from 1964. Written on the wristband are two formations and fourteen plays—a game plan for that era. Today the offensive coaches' conference room at Virginia Tech has an entire wall devoted to whiteboard diagrams of the team's twenty-six formations, from which hundreds of plays are possible.

PLAYERS ENDLESSLY REVIEW THE FORMATIONS, calls, checks and audibles of modern football. Terminology ingrained during summer months must be reinforced to prevent mistakes under game pressure, especially since the no-huddle fad that swept football beginning around the year 2005 can mean a player gets only a few seconds between hearing the call and the snap of the ball.

One day in the quarterbacks' classroom, coach Mike O'Cain was reviewing the "sims"—decoy signals intended to confuse the defense—that Virginia Tech's six quarterbacks were expected to know by heart. Over in the defensive-line classroom, coach Charley Wiles was reviewing the "fronts," or alignments. A defense of the 1960s had two fronts, one for short-yardage downs and one for long-yardage. The contemporary Virginia Tech defense has a dozen fronts, each with multiple variations. "Guys, if the call is Gun Weak Trey Dallas, what do you do?" Wiles asked the defensive linemen. Obviously the correct answer was "Double eagle."

A generation ago, a rushing call sounded like 65 Toss Power Trap, the play the Kansas City Chiefs used to score the decisive touchdown in their 1970 Super Bowl victory over the Minnesota Vikings. Chiefs head coach Hank Stram called 65 Toss Power Trap although the team had not practiced it in months. The nomenclature was simple enough that in the huddle, players told quarterback Len Dawson they remembered what to do. A passing call a generation ago sounded like Red Right Tight Sprint Right Option, the play the San Francisco 49ers used to stage "The Catch," defeating the Dallas Cowboys in the 1982 NFC championship, one of the memorable upsets of sports lore.

These designations had simple meanings. Red Right Tight meant the Red formation with the tight end on the right and "backs in a divide," the standard NFL set of the period. Blue, Green and Brown were the other basic formations of the West Coast Offense under head coach Bill Walsh. Sprint Right Option meant quarterback Joe Montana would take off right with the option to pass or run, getting outside the "tackle box" before looking downfield. (That makes it a sprint-out rather than a rollout; on a rollout, the quarterback looks downfield the entire time.) The play was called in the huddle, as nearly all plays were then. Montana actually said only "Sprint Right Option" because the 49ers used Red Right Tight so often the formation was assumed.

By 2008, when I was an assistant coach at Churchill High School in Potomac, Maryland, a call would sound like Lobo Roll 25 Wheel. High school kids would need to remember what that meant. They would need to remember the meaning of all the codes such as Rodeo 23 Omaha or Wing Left 34 Boot or Blast Green 88 Cross Seam. Churchill's playbook was a little much, but not out of step with the complexity ascending at all levels of football. By the twenty-first century, even at a high school, Sprint Right Option would have sounded too simple.

By 2011, a Virginia Tech play would sound like Pro Flip Sail Louie Y Choice. The operative part of the call is Y Choice, which means the tight end does not decide what pass pattern to run until he starts down the field. If a linebacker covers him, then he chooses a deep seam, because a tight end should outrun a linebacker. If a defensive back covers him, then he chooses a dig, going ten yards and slamming to a halt, because a tight end cannot outrun a defensive back, but is stronger and so should make the catch despite the defensive back's slamming into him as the pass arrives.

Not only must the Virginia Tech players remember the codes for twenty-six formations, a hundred or so actions and multiple variations—many big-college and NFL teams now employ similarly complex play-calling—but they don't get much time to think about assignments because most play calls are not given in the huddle. They're called at a line of scrimmage, as part of the fad for no-huddle tactics.

In the no-huddle systems used by Virginia Tech, to signal in the call, three players on the sideline—three backup quarterbacks—make elaborate, rhythmic hand motions that resemble poorly performed dancing at a rave concert. Only one is the live signaler; the other two are dummies, so that even if the opposing team watches the signals, it won't know which signal to take seriously and which to ignore. Before each quarter, coaches tell the offensive players which signaler is live.

As the hurry-up offense was changing from a rare tactic to common, "at first we tried to send the plays in by substituting a player, who told the call to the quarterback," O'Cain says. But sending in signals by substitution didn't work as it once did. "Some of the calls have become so long, inevitably the guys forget one of the words." A player rushing onto the field could remember 65 Toss Power Trap. Now calls sound like Rip Frostee 28 Cross Hummer Box. O'Cain explains, "If the player forgot one word, and said Rip Frostee 28 Cross Box, everyone on the field would go 'Huh?'"

Like many coaches experimenting with quick-snap tactics, O'Cain found visual signals worked better than verbal ones. "Ours is a visual society," he says. "Today's young people grow up spending more time looking at images than reading words. It turned out even complex play calls could be sent in accurately if we used visuals." By 2010, the University of Oregon would be signaling plays by holding up, on the sideline, large poster boards, each of which had four bright images: whimsical choices like Big Bird, Jennifer Aniston, a Lamborghini. Players knew which image to check—say, the lower right—ignoring the rest. The images corresponded to a wristband code.

By the time the University of Oregon reached the 2011 BCS title game with very-quick-snap tactics dubbed the Blur Offense, the Ducks needed just sixteen seconds between downs. Virginia Tech couldn't quite reach that pace. But like everything else in our world, college football was speeding up.

•   •   •

BEYOND THE PRACTICE FIELDS IS the tunnel that leads into Lane Stadium. The moment of emerging from the tunnel to seventy thousand roaring spectators tingles the spines of all but the jaded. A piece of limestone from the Virginia Tech quarry is above the tunnel exit. Players reach high to tap the stone as they run into the stadium.

Lining the length of the tunnel are the names, from all past years, of football players who graduated. Not who were stars—who graduated. DeAngelo Hall, a Virginia Tech star who was the eighth choice of the 2004 NFL draft, years later was back at school taking courses, seeking his diploma. Otherwise, even as the Hokies' highest NFL draft choice in a decade, his name would not be inscribed in the tunnel.

BEAMER IS A CREATURE OF habit, so most regular days follow a script—if you know what day of the week it is, you know what the Hokies are doing. On game weekends, the pace of team life changes.

If the game is away, the Hokies leave the afternoon before, so players can be in class the morning the trip begins. Some big colleges leave two days before an away game, to give players' bodies time to recover from travel weariness. That means skipping class, which is okay at many colleges—and not just for football, also for women's sports—but not okay at Virginia Tech. The Hokies travel early only to bowl games, which occur when school is not in session.

Most home games are on Saturdays. On the Friday night before, the team has dinner at a steak house, then stays in the best hotel in Roanoke, half an hour from school, to get away from campus distractions. The Friday-night feast, at the Farmhouse, in the perfectly named Christiansburg, Virginia, follows a strict routine. Ballein calls the players up to a buffet table in order of their GPAs. Star players may sit feeling hungry as they watch third-stringers who are doing well in the classroom get first choice of the steaks and prime rib. Simply by observing the order in which players walk up, everyone knows who is excelling academically and who is bringing up the rear.

A police escort accompanies team buses to the steak house, to the hotel, then back to campus the next morning. Police cruisers flank the buses; motorcycle officers race ahead to close intersections so the convoy can pass without stopping for lights.

The absurd touch of police escorts for football is common. NFL teams at the Super Bowl always have police escorts, including when shuttling to practices and meals; most NFL teams have police escorts for regular-season games. The buses bearing the LSU football squad were surrounded by state-police cruisers with flashing lights as they traveled to New Orleans for the 2012 college championship; by the time the Tigers' buses arrived at their hotel, eighteen police cars and motorcycles were accompanying them. CBS, ESPN, Fox and NBC broadcasters sometimes get police escorts to games, allowing them to roar past gridlocked traffic as if they were a summit-meeting delegation. When NFL commissioner Roger Goodell attended the 2011 Pittsburgh-at-Baltimore contest, he had a police escort bracketing his car front and back.

College teams don't need police escorts; that they get them is a measure of the over-the-top nature of contemporary football. Football broadcasters or the NFL commissioner are private businessmen. Why should they receive special treatment?

Of Goodell's traffic-stopping police escort, the *Baltimore Sun* quoted a police official as saying, "The National Football League had security concerns given Goodell's rank." The notion that hooded assassins were shadowing Goodell is beyond parody. President George W. Bush's National Commission on Terrorist Attacks Upon the United States concluded that no specific American individual had ever been targeted by terrorists. Nevertheless, if the NFL had "security concerns" regarding Goodell, it could have hired private bodyguards at its own expense. Later the *Sun* reported a Baltimore police official admitted the "terrorism" claim was always nonsense—the escort was for Goodell's convenience, so he could cut through game-day traffic, rather than wait his turn like the riffraff.

Waste of taxpayer money on police escorts for football—coupled to inconvenience for average people, who must pull over while the football royalty passes—is a minor issue, low on the list of skewed priorities associated with today's athletics. But if society cannot think clearly about a minor question such as whether people involved in football should get special treatment, how can society think clearly about the big issues of football, such as health and education? As for the Hokies, voters around Blacksburg probably approve of the police escorts, which add a feel of excitement to a quiet area.

TEAM BUSES ARRIVING AT LANE Stadium for a home game do not disappear into a cordoned-off access area, as with buses bringing an NFL team to a contest. Instead the buses park at the formal arched entrance of the stadium, where await thousands of spectators, the cheerleaders, the dance squad and the regimental marching band, a cadets' organization. The team then stages a slow walk to the entrance to the athletic complex where they will dress. As this happens, cheerleaders somersault, brass instruments oompah a few familiar ostinatos, and adoring supporters clap while calling out players' names.

Many college programs stage some variation of The Walk prior to football home games. Those who look carefully at the throng present for The Walk at Virginia Tech will notice most of those cheering are at least middle-aged—long since graduated from the institution, if they ever attended. This is broadly true across collegiate athletics. At a USC football game, a Duke basketball game, there are students in the stands, but the majority of the paying customers are older, either boosters or simply enthusiasts of the sport being played.

In autumn of 2011, I watched from the Hokies' sideline as Virginia Tech lost in Lane Stadium to Clemson, ending hopes of an undefeated season. Star defender James Gayle twisted an ankle early and had to leave the game; quarterback Logan Thomas had an off day; the normally stout Hokie defense was confounded by Clemson's Sammy Watkins, an eighteen-year-old phenom. In the locker room immediately afterward, Virginia Tech tailback David Wilson, soon to be named ACC Player of the Year, rhythmically pounded his fist against a table repeating, "No, no, no, no."

Beamer stood on a chair to address the team. Everyone is gracious in victory—well, almost everyone. You learn more about a person's character when he loses than when he wins.

"Clemson won because they played better than we did, so they deserve the credit," Beamer said. "Tonight was just one day in your life. There will be better days. We will work to improve. The important thing is that you stay together and not point fingers." Then Beamer called on Ballein, who read the list of players required to report to study hall on Sunday morning—mere hours after a nationally televised game—because their GPAs weren't satisfactory.

Beamer wasn't angry or red-faced, didn't criticize or embarrass any player, and did not use profanity. Many football coaches talk such a blue streak that their language looks like cartoon swear words: "#@&!!@#+!" Many football coaches are lividly angry in the locker room after a loss, screaming denunciation at the opponent, the officials, their own players.

In a season with Beamer, I observed him:

- Teach freshmen how to rush a punt by aiming not for the punter but for a spot in front of him and exactly nine yards past the line of scrimmage—where the kick would be as it left the punter's foot.

- Read to kindergarteners.

- Say in a postgame interview that a false-start penalty that cost Virginia Tech a first-and-goal on the opponents' 1 was caused by the student band's beginning to play as the Hokies called signals. When videotape showed the student band had been silent, Beamer apologized profusely. Students bands at big-college programs pride themselves on knowing when to play and when not to.

- Fail to notice the clock advancing with Virginia Tech in goal-to-go with a few seconds remaining in the first half, a mistake that forced the Hokies to use their final time-out and settle for a field goal. "That was my fault," Beamer said immediately to his assistants along the sideline.

- Often tell his players, "Go, man, go," a phrase not much uttered since maybe 1975.

Though I observed Beamer do these and many other things, I never heard him use profanity in public and only once heard him mutter "damn" during a private meeting.

Much more important, I never saw Beamer lose his temper or denigrate a player, assistant or staffer. Far too many coaches are unable to control their anger, or think that screaming is motivating. Iron law of athletics: a coach who screams is wasting everyone's time, including his own. When an NFL coach screams at a millionaire professional, that may be poor form, but a professional can look after himself. When a youth-league or high school coach screams at a quaking child, this is another matter.

Beamer is among the small number of NCAA and NFL coaches to practice "positive coaching," whose mantra is simple: never demean, only challenge others to improve. In 2009, TCU head coach Gary Patterson told National Public Radio that he had caught himself screaming at a player, felt ashamed, and resolved to become a better person by switching to positive coaching. If only society's leaders would take a look into the mirror and resolve to become better people! Many from the football old school would say that treating players with kindness and respect would backfire. Two years after Patterson's conversion to positive coaching, TCU won the Rose Bowl.

THE WEEK FOLLOWING THE CLEMSON loss, Virginia Tech trailed the University of Miami in the fourth quarter, at home. The faithful were restless and even booed, which does not happen much during big-college home games. On fourth down with seconds remaining, Thomas faked a handoff to Wilson, kept the ball, and bulled forward for a 19-yard touchdown and the win. Quarterback Tyrod Taylor of the Baltimore Ravens, a former Hokie, was on the Virginia Tech sideline shouting, "This is where the Logan Thomas legend begins!" That night the sports press was thick with Thomas's name.

Because of the dramatic win, the stadium did not clear as usual—Hokie supporters were still rollicking long after the comeback concluded. On his chair in the locker room, Beamer praised the University of Miami and then said to his own players, "This is the kind of night that turns a team into a family. We are going to be behind again. When that happens, remember what this felt like." Wilson asked if he could stand on the chair and said to his jubilant teammates, "Guys, the whole campus is going to be a big party. Don't do anything stupid tonight." Everyone knew what he meant. Then Ballein stood on the chair and, saying nothing about the game, recited the names of players due in study hall Sunday morning.

A few months later, Wilson would leave Virginia Tech as a junior, declaring early for the NFL draft. Even at college programs such as Notre Dame, Stanford or Virginia Tech, where there is genuine emphasis on education, if a football player is likely to be "first or second day" in the NFL draft—meaning a high selection—there is wide support for a decision to go pro. Beamer accompanied Wilson to the press conference at which he announced he was leaving early and wished him well: the defending Super Bowl champion New York Giants would chose Wilson in the first round. There was nothing but good vibrations for Wilson, though his leaving deprived the school of the senior year of a talented player in whom the Hokies had a substantial investment.

Being a high NFL draft choice means cashing an enormous bonus check. Any college player who can grab that brass ring should do so, whether or not it means leaving college too soon. Who knows what the future holds? Perhaps a disabling injury. Players who will be high NFL draft choices don't urgently need diplomas—nice if they get them, but not urgent. It's the NCAA players who will never take a snap in the NFL who must graduate. And that describes nearly all NCAA players.

VIRGINIA TECH FINISHED THE 2011 regular season 11-1, ranked tenth in the nation. The next step was the ACC title game, played on a neutral field in Charlotte, North Carolina. Once again the opponent was Clemson, once again on national television.

There was a lot of downtime in the hotel before the 8:00 p.m. kickoff—players and coaches sitting around in tracksuits, feeling bored or anxious. Most players and coaches prefer the early-afternoon kickoff: waiting around all day is nerve-racking. For high school games played on Friday nights, school takes your mind off things. For a college away game on Saturday night, there's nothing but waiting.

The team hotel was across from First Presbyterian Church, built two centuries ago, after Europeans settled in what is now Charlotte. Outside the church was the ever-changing clamor of contemporary life—Internet, helicopters, rap, fashion, national obsession with football. Inside the church, in two hundred years hardly anything had changed.

Virginia Tech and Clemson played even in the first half, but after intermission Watkins ran wild again, and again the Hokies lost. That dropped the team to 11-2 and out of contention for BCS bowls, the high-prestige events for which invitations would be announced the following day. Though an 11-2 record is impressive—many megabucks, win-at-all-costs programs only dream of going 11-2—BCS invites never are extended to colleges that just lost. Bowl committees want teams that enter on a winning streak.

The ACC title contest was played at the stadium where the Carolina Panthers perform, and after the loss, Beamer needed no chair to stand on in the Panthers' expansive locker room. Virginia Tech had just lost on national television, yet the head coach said nothing about that. Nor did he criticize the defense, which again had no answer for

Watkins, or the offensive linemen, who had their worst outing of the season. Here is the entirety of what Beamer said to the team:

"I was very unhappy that some of you did not shake hands at midfield after the game. That's not who were are. Clemson earned the win, so we should have shaken their hands. I do not ever want to see poor sportsmanship on our part again." Beamer stopped speaking, and there was a long silence as players looked at their feet. Then he continued, "Now we are unlikely to get a BCS invitation. But we have won more than ten games and will go to a bowl, and tonight only a handful of teams in college football can say those words. So no sour faces. Back to work."

That was it. There was no yelling by Beamer or by any of his assistants. The team showered and boarded its five buses, each person in the travel party handed a box of chicken at midnight. Just try figuring out what to do with your elbows when eating a chicken dinner on a bus next to a six-foot-four-inch, 320-pound football player. En route back to Blacksburg, one of the buses broke down; passengers from that bus crow-barred into the others, making for an uncomfortable ride. The four operating carriages were back on the Virginia Tech campus at 4:00 a.m. Sunday, wheeling up to the stadium gate with all else silent. Players with low GPAs were required to be in study hall after breakfast.

Through that Sunday, the coaches were at the football facility, awaiting the bowl-invitation announcements. Beamer was hoping for a consolation-prize event with status, such as the Chick-fil-A Bowl in Atlanta, a city with a reputation for hosting events well. Virginia Tech's sports-media personnel were practicing their spin in case the Hokies found themselves invited to one of the games that are butts of late-night comedians' jokes, such as the Meineke Car Care Bowl or the Beef 'O'Brady's Bowl.

Beamer was unperturbed, saying, "We will still go to a bowl game, and a bowl week in a nice hotel is a great reward for the players and for spouses of the staff, a pleasant way to conclude the season. Something they'll always remember."

At 7:00 p.m., war whoops went up throughout the Virginia Tech football facility. The phone had rung—and Virginia Tech was invited to face Michigan in the Sugar Bowl, one of the max-prestige BCS events. Despite losing the ACC title contest, Virginia Tech would make its second consecutive BCS appearance and once again play on prime-time national television.

The invitation was an indicator of respect for what Beamer and his straitlaced, old-fashioned program has accomplished. The penultimate chapter will describe the Sugar Bowl game in detail.

Now the book changes course from Virginia Tech to the questions of football in American society. Virginia Tech's program is in many respects an ideal—run about as well as can be imagined. Many aspects of football fall far short of ideal. America's favorite sport causes health harm, interferes with education, relies on public subsidies and has other defects that must be fixed. The next series of chapters addresses these issues.

3

HOW THE NFL PRETENDS TO BE
THE NONPROFIT FOOTBALL LEAGUE

The New Orleans Superdome—known to international audiences for scary images of thousands huddled there in 2005, during Hurricane Katrina—has hosted seven Super Bowls. Opened in 1975, the Superdome cost Louisiana taxpayers $580 million to construct. Its anchor tenant was the NFL's New Orleans Saints, whose majority owner at the time was a wealthy oilman named John Mecom. In 1985, Mecom and his investors sold the franchise to Tom Benson, an equally wealthy businessman with holdings in real estate and auto dealerships.

After acquiring the team, Benson raised periodic alarms about moving the Saints to another city, which would deprive the publicly financed Superdome of its tenant. In 2001, the Louisiana state legislature voted to give $8.5 million in taxpayers' money each year to Benson as an "inducement payment"—the actual term used—to keep the Saints in New Orleans.

Louisiana conferred the annual gift on Benson although his statements about moving appeared to be empty threats. The Cleveland Browns had departed Ohio, becoming the Baltimore Ravens (later a second Cleveland Browns franchise was created). The move caused a political backlash against the NFL; to placate Congress, the league adopted internal rules that make it difficult for franchises to change cities. Even knowing this, Louisiana gave pubic money each year to Benson. The Saints' owner paid no taxes on the $8.5 million annual "inducement payment," essentially contending to the Internal Revenue Service that money received from taxpayers cannot be considered income—a view that would puzzle any government employee filling out a Form 1040. The IRS filed a lawsuit against Benson for failure to pay taxes; wealthy tax evaders know such litigation often takes years to resolve.

In the cleanup from Katrina, federal and state taxpayers put another $335 million into two phases of renovation of the Superdome, including adding more seats for NFL games and enlarging the cupholders to increase concession sales by allowing pricey supersize drinks. Despite more public subsidies, in 2009, Benson again threatened to move the Saints. When the first demand is met, a shakedown artist may come back to the well. Louisiana governor Bobby Jindal, who boasts of being a fiscal conservative opposed to government spending, mollified the Saints' owner anew by agreeing to compel taxpayers to spend about $5 million annually leasing vacant New Orleans office space from Benson. Considering the New Orleans office-space market was at the time glutted, leasing vacant space from Benson was a Christmas present.

In sum, neither set of owners of the New Orleans Saints put up any of the nearly $1 billion in capital to build and renovate the Superdome, while the NFL contributed a token $16 million to post-Katrina repairs, 0.2 percent of league revenues in the year the donation was made. But though taxpayers covered the costs of building and improving the facility, and though taxpayers give $13.5 million annually in gifts to the Saints, Benson keeps all profits from ticket sales, concessions and parking. More significantly, all revenue from television broadcasts of football games staged in the publicly financed Superdome belongs to Benson or to the NFL.

In 2011, Mercedes-Benz purchased naming rights to the building, now called the Mercedes-Benz Superdome, at $5 million annually. Benson demanded this money. The demand was too much even by the low standards of backroom Louisiana politics: naming rights revenue went to offset some public costs. By then, taxpayer-financed renovations had added luxury boxes to the Superdome. NFL owners especially like such boxes because while regular ticket revenue is shared with visiting teams, the home team keeps all luxury-box income. Louisiana taxpayers paid for luxury boxes few could afford to sit in, and Benson kept all income the boxes generated.

In 2012, Benson's net worth would be estimated by *Forbes* magazine at $1.1 billion, with nearly all that from football. Real estate and auto sales are volatile businesses that involve risk and depend on consumers' free-market choices; subsidized pro sports are a risk-free mechanism for converting taxpayers' money into private gain—using politicians as middlemen to compel taxpayers to make choices about money they would never make voluntarily.

Stadium-construction subsidies have been rationalized as creating economic activity. Studies by Judith Grant Long, a professor of urban planning at Harvard University, show that stadium building adds less to local economies than promised—and at any rate the subsidies merely replace money NFL owners would have paid on their own, since without stadia, there is no product to sell.

Long calculates that 87 percent of the total capital cost of NFL stadia is provided by taxpayers, not by the NFL or its ownership class. When operating costs are added, Long's research finds, the Buffalo Bills, Cleveland Browns, Houston Texans, Kansas City Chiefs, Jacksonville Jaguars, New Orleans Saints, San Diego Chargers, St. Louis Rams and Tampa Bay Buccaneers turn a profit on stadium subsidies alone—receiving more money from the public than they need to build and operate their facilities. Long's numbers suggest that just three NFL franchises, the New England Patriots, New York Giants and New York Jets, behave honorably with the public purse, paying at least three-quarters of stadium capital and operating costs. The other 29 NFL teams are busily robbing the public blind.

PUBLIC SUBSIDIES CONVERTED TO PRIVATE profit happen in too many arenas of contemporary life. Sometimes, such as with the bailout of General Motors, once the subsidies end, society is better off. In the modern business of football, the subsidies never end. College football sometimes misuses money, but colleges also advance the common good. The National Football League is strictly a profit-making entertainment endeavor, yet is subsidized up one side and down the other. Imagine if Hollywood's studios, sets and costumes were funded by taxpayers, then movie companies kept all the profit and dodged taxes to boot. That's the situation with professional football.

CenturyLink Field, where the Seattle Seahawks perform, opened in 2002, with Washington State taxpayers providing $370 million of the $500 million construction cost. The Seahawks pay Washington State about $1 million annually in rent—this simplifies a shell-corporation arrangement intended to confuse voters—in return for the revenue from ticket sales, concessions and parking. Taking into account that visiting teams receive a share of the gate, the revenue-to-rent calculation suggests the Seahawks realize about $100 million in revenue from ten NFL dates per year, while paying $1 million in rent—a 100-to-1 advantage for the Seahawks. The Seattle Seahawks are owned by former Microsoft executive Paul Allen, who in 2012 was ranked by *Forbes* as the forty-eighth-richest person in the world, net worth $14.5 billion. Average people are taxed to fund Allen's private-jet lifestyle.

M&T Bank Stadium in Baltimore, where the 2013 Super Bowl champion Ravens perform, cost Maryland taxpayers at least $350 million. The Ravens are owned by Steve Bisciotti, who made his fortune in the temp-staffing business and now has an estimated net worth of $1.5 billion. The billionaire receives nearly all the revenue generated by Baltimore's publicly subsidized NFL facility.

Cleveland Browns Stadium, where the second iteration of the Browns perform, cost the taxpayers of Cuyahoga County $400 million to construct; the county also pays for repairs and upgrades and paid to improve parking and light-rail access to games. In exchange, nearly all football and concession revenues go to owner Jimmy Haslam III, who made his fortune with Pilot Flying J, a chain of truck stops. *Forbes* estimates the Haslam family net worth at $3 billion. Average Ohio residents are taxed to increase the luxury in which the Haslams live.

The stadium where the Miami Dolphins play, whose name has changed many times, cost about $600 million to build and later renovate, with Florida taxpayers providing about half that amount. The Dolphins' ownership has changed many times. Nearly all revenue from pro football contests played in the stadium is kept by the current majority owner, real-estate developer Stephen Ross. In 2013, Ross asked Florida taxpayers for $350 million to improve the stadium. *Forbes* estimates Ross's net worth at $4 billion. Norman Braman, former owner of the Philadelphia Eagles, and a Miami resident, called the proposal "welfare for a multibillionaire."

Looking back on the Middle Ages, today's commentators express disgust that aristocrats lived in extravagance at the expense of average people. Public subsidies for billionaire NFL owners are not of course exactly the same. But they're the same general thing.

THE BILLION-DOLLAR NFL STADIUM is a badge of civic status. Santa Clara Stadium, where the San Francisco 49ers are expected to perform beginning in 2014, will cost well north of $1 billion. With California a budget-deficit mess, there was voter opposition to public financing: Why should the NFL receive a major subsidy when education budgets were being cut? The deal announced in 2011 was that the stadium would cost the city of Santa Clara about $155 million, with the bulk of the capital, about $1 billion, from private sources.

At least, that's how the deal was announced. Here's the catch. A new government entity, the Santa Clara Stadium Authority, is borrowing $850 million from a consortium led by Goldman Sachs, to provide the "private" financing. Who are the members of the Santa Clara Stadium Authority? The members of the Santa Clara City Council. The 49ers did not borrow the construction money—indeed, though the entire project is in California, the NFL team created a Delaware-chartered entity, Forty Niners Stadium LLC, to insulate itself from financial accountability. The City of Santa Clara agreed to this legal ruse, then signed the notes; should something go wrong, taxpayers will take the hit. If recent economic history is any guide, the arrangement is a recipe for profuse management bonuses at Goldman Sachs, high living by the family that owns the 49ers and bankruptcy for the City of Santa Clara—followed by demands for a federal bailout.

The 49ers have agreed to pay Santa Clara $30 million annually in rent for four decades, which makes the deal, from the team's standpoint, a forty-year loan at 2 percent. These are spectacularly favorable terms that no commercial lender would dream of offering to the best client. At the time of the agreement, thirty-year Treasury bonds were selling for 3 percent, meaning the Santa Clara contract values the NFL as a better risk than the United States government.

While almost all capital obligation for the new stadium is being carried by the public, almost all football revenue from the facility will be kept by owner Denise DeBartolo York, whose net worth is estimated at $900 million. York took control of the team in 2000 from her brother, Edward DeBartolo Jr., after he pleaded guilty to bribery charges involving the governor of Louisiana. Brother and sister inherited their money from father Edward DeBartolo Sr., a department-store developer who on his death in 1994 was described by *Forbes* as one of the nation's richest men. A generation ago, the DeBartolos made their money the old-fashioned way, by hard work in the free market. Today the family's wealth rests on political-insider influence and California tax subsidies.

ACROSS THE NATIONAL FOOTBALL LEAGUE, the story is the same. The stadiums where the New York Giants, New York Jets, Dallas Cowboys,

Washington Redskins and New England Patriots play were mostly privately funded, though they benefited from generous public subsidies for land and infrastructure, plus tax favors. The bulk of NFL stadiums, along with almost all related development such as parking lots, power, sewer connections and transit, are underwritten by taxpayers—then the revenue generated becomes private gain hoarded by the super-rich.

The Pittsburgh Steelers, winners of six Super Bowls, most of any franchise, perform at Heinz Field, a glorious stadium that opens to a view of the serenely flowing Ohio River. Pennsylvania taxpayers contributed $365 million to construction of Heinz Field, and to retire debt from the Steelers' previous stadium. The Steelers put up $100 million.

To raise their share, the Steelers sold "personal seat licenses," a financial arrangement sometimes found in stadium financing. Steelers supporters paid an average of $1,600 for the right to buy future season tickets at a specific seat—that is, paid $1,600 up front in order to pay more in the future, with Steelers' season tickets currently averaging about $900 per year. Buying a PSL turned out to be a smart investment. With the Steelers popular and usually reaching the playoffs, today Heinz Field PSLs trade on the secondary market for an average of $9,000. That represents a 465 percent return on a late-1990s investment—better than gold!

The arrangement was solid gold for Steelers' ownership, the Rooney family. Taxpayers supplied most of the capital for the stadium; income from PSL sales went entirely to the Rooneys. Most game-day and television revenues, also made possible at public expense, go to the Rooneys. When the Heinz corporation purchased stadium-naming rights for $57 million—get the number?—the Rooneys kept that too.

In 2012, the Rooney family reached into the pockets of Pennsylvania taxpayers again. The Sports & Exhibition Authority of Pittsburgh and Allegheny County agreed to offer a $20 million bond and impose new taxes on downtown parking garages, in order to add three thousand seats to Heinz Field. Average people will make the bond payments and pay the parking tax; most revenue from the seats will be kept by the Rooney family.

Rooney is a magical name in Pittsburgh politics, and the Rooneys are admired for pressuring the NFL to hire African-American coaches. The Rooney family consists of numerous brothers, with Dan and Art II each owning 30 percent of the Steelers and other family members, plus unrelated investors, owning smaller blocs. A 30 percent share of the Steelers would set Dan's and Art II's net worth at around $300 million apiece. Despite astronomical personal wealth, the Rooneys demand genuflection from Pennsylvania taxpayers. In 2008, with Pennsylvania a battleground state, Dan campaigned for Barack Obama and donated generously to organizations supporting him; Obama rewarded Dan with the US ambassadorship to Ireland. Rooney had the cash and time to be a player in national politics because his NFL franchise is supported by money forcibly taken from taxpayers.

THE PITTSBURGH–ALLEGHENY COUNTY SPORTS & Exhibition Authority is not unusual. In many cases, NFL stadia are owned or financed by government-chartered authorities that issue bonds and impose taxes, and that exist for the purpose of converting public funds to private profit. The Seahawks' field, for example, is owned by the Washington State Public Stadium Authority, which compels taxpayers on the eastern side of Washington, such as those in the city of Spokane, nearly three hundred miles from Seattle, to subsidize entertainment for those in the Emerald City. Typically, public authorities that build NFL stadiums draw their income from "dedicated" taxes. For example, half of 1 percent of Cincinnati sales taxes are funneled to debt service for construction of Paul Brown Stadium, where the Bengals play; parking, hotel and rental-car taxes in Houston are used to repay bonds from construction of Reliant Stadium, where the NFL's Texans perform.

Usually the bonds issued by special stadium authorities are tax-exempt—meaning that to divert funds to a football facility, a city, county or state must either increase taxes on average people or cut spending that benefits society broadly, such as on schools and green space. More than once, an NFL star has gone back to the old neighborhood where he grew up and lamented the lack of libraries and public-recreation facilities to help steer young people in a positive direction. Money that might have been spent on such amenities instead went to subsidize pro sports.

Though issuing tax-free bonds erodes the local tax base, mayors, city councils, and county governments have a long-standing love of such bonds; the deals underwrite impressive construction in the present, while costs do not fall due until after the politicians responsible have left office. City and state politicians in New York, for example, allowed Bank of America $1 billion in tax-exempt bonds for its new fifty-five-story tower in Manhattan. Funds that might have gone to New York public schools instead further inflate bonuses to bankers, whose children attend private schools. For pols, the venal motive in tax-exempt bonds is that they generate funny money that may end up as campaign donations, sweetheart "consulting" deals, or payoffs. In 2012, Jimmy Dimora, a Cuyahoga County, Ohio, commissioner, was sentenced to twenty-eight years in prison for accepting bribes. One of his roles was to oversee public-bond issues in the county where the Cleveland Browns play.

Sometimes the bonds outlive the stadiums, meaning taxpayers continue to pay while the civic sphere receives literally nothing—as if having to keep up mortgage payments after moving out of the house. Philadelphia and Seattle taxpayers continue to pay on bonds for NFL stadia demolished years ago. New Jersey's sports authority issued hundreds of millions of dollars in tax-free bonds for the old Giants Stadium, opened in 1976—considerably more bond value than the stadium was worth. Though the facility has been razed, New Jersey taxpayers still cover about $35 million in annual subsidies on Giants Stadium bonds, which were used as a cookie jar by a generation of corrupt Garden State politicians.

It might seem refreshing that the Giants' and Jets' new $1.7 billion MetLife Stadium, the most expensive football field ever built, was constructed with private capital—$700 million in bonds issued by the New York Jets through Citicorp, $700 million in bonds issued by the New York Giants through Goldman Sachs, and $300 million provided by the NFL. Yet the political arrangements still strongly favor football. The two teams received zoning exemptions, potentially worth more than a billion dollars, for developing land around the new stadium; the teams are likely although not certain to come out ahead on raising private capital for the stadium, while taxpayers are certain to lose income that might have been realized by auctions of the legal permissions. The two clubs are expected to clear about $200 million annually from stadium revenue, while the State of New Jersey must pay $30 million annually for power and sewer service to the facility. The wealthy owners of the Jets and Giants prosper—the Jets are owned by Woody Johnson, scion of the Johnson & Johnson fortune—while average New Jersey taxpayers cover the costs.

A hidden goody bag for NFL teams is that cities and counties may accept "payments in lieu of taxes" for NFL stadia. The State of New Jersey and East Rutherford, New Jersey, essentially agreed to a $6.3 million per year "payment in lieu of taxes" for MetLife Stadium and environs. "Payment in lieu of taxes" can sound like mere semantics, and many organizations, including museums and colleges, ask local governments for this favor. The operative distinction is that while real-estate taxes are dictated by assessment laws, payment in lieu of taxes is a negotiated amount, whatever government officials agree upon—perhaps, with kickbacks on the side.

If *Forbes* is correct, the Jets and Giants combined are worth roughly $3 billion, making the $6.3 million annual payment in lieu of taxes the equivalent of a two-tenths of 1 percent property tax. Typically in the Northeast, businesses pay property taxes that equate to one-half of 1 percent of their value. Individuals pay more. A homeowner in Essex County, New Jersey, a few miles from the new Jets-Giants stadium, is assessed 1.5 percent annually of the value of his or her home. If the Jets and Giants facility were assessed like other nearby businesses, the annual property tax payment would be perhaps twice as much. Payment in lieu of taxes assures that taxes on small businesses and average households are much higher than taxes on NFL stadia. Typical people are taxed more to channel additional wealth to the ruling-class families who own the Jets and the Giants.

That's if an NFL stadium is taxed at all. The futuristic new field where the Dallas Cowboys perform, with its 105,000 seats, go-go dancers on every level, and built-in nightclubs, is appraised at nearly a billion dollars—yet pays no property taxes. At the basic property-tax rate of Fort Worth, Texas, nearest city in the same county as the stadium, Cowboys' owner Jerry Jones would pay about $8 million per year in property taxes. Instead he pays nothing—an $8 million annual public handout—while Tarrant County taxes the property of average people more than it otherwise would.

THE NFL BENEFITS FROM PUBLIC subsidies, tax favors and antirust waivers—more on the latter in a moment. The result is a form of feudalism. Because many NFL teams are family owned, the taxpayer-subsidized, government-protected nature of NFL economics allows entire family groups to live as pashas at the average person's expense. The feudal lords and ladies of European history, or of Pakistan today, collected public payments while contributing little or nothing productive to society. An NFL franchise has become a license to collect public payments, in return for contributing nothing productive to society.

The Chicago Bears play in Soldier Field, renovated about a decade ago. Illinois taxpayers put up $475 million for the renovation, while the league and club combined to add about $250 million. The legislation giving Illinois's $475 million gift to the Bears was signed by Governor George Ryan, who a few years later went to prison for accepting kickbacks. Today the Bears pay just $6 million annually for rent on the $475 million gift, while keeping almost all ticket, television and concession revenues from Soldier Field.

Let's strike a few zeros to make the economics of the Bears' situation easier to understand. Suppose you purchased a house that cost $475,000. Would you expect to pay just $6,000 annually on the mortgage? Your mortgage should be around $25,000 annually. Now suppose you paid nothing for utilities, upkeep or property taxes on your home—those costs were passed along to your neighbors. That is the Bears' situation relative to Soldier Field.

The principal owner of the Bears is Virginia McCaskey, net worth estimated by *Forbes* at $1.3 billion. The eldest child of former Bears owner George Halas, she and her offspring are believed to control about 80 percent of the team. In 2012, the Bears' masthead listed in senior management positions Virginia McCaskey, George McCaskey, Pat McCaskey and Brian McCaskey. Could they all, entirely by chance, be the most qualified persons for their positions?

The top officers of the Cincinnati Bengals are Mike Brown, Pete Brown, Paul Brown, Katie Blackburn (daughter of Mike) and Troy Blackburn (Katie's husband). The top officers of the Tampa Bay Buccaneers are Malcolm Glazer, Bryan Glazer, Joel Glazer and Edward Glazer. The top officers of the Indianapolis Colts are James Irsay, Carlie Irsay-Gordon, Casey Irsay Foyt and Kalen Irsay. The top officers of the Minnesota Vikings are Zygmunt Wilf, Mark Wilf and Leonard Wilf. If a true free-enterprise corporation wants family members in cushy jobs, that is the company's choice. But NFL franchises are government-subsidized and protected by government against economic competition—the paradigm of feudalism.

Historically, feudal families lavished themselves with acclaim for offering crumbs to average people. For Veterans Day 2012, the NFL announced its owners would donate, to veterans' groups, $300 for each point scored in designated games. During CBS, ESPN, Fox and NBC broadcasts that weekend, the NFL was extensively praised for grand generosity. Not mentioned was the total donation, which would come to $432,000. Because scoring averages don't vary much, the total donation could have been predicted within a small range. Annualized, NFL stadium subsidies and tax favors total perhaps a billion dollars. So the NFL took a billion dollars from the public, then praised itself for giving back $432,000—less than a tenth of 1 percent.

•   •   •

THE NFL's OWNERS HARDLY ARE the only ones to benefit from favorable government treatment of football. CBS, ESPN, Fox and NBC, which broadcast NFL games, privatize programming created in public-funded facilities—the companies keep all after-tax advertising revenue and cable-carrier fees, though the revenues and cable fees could not happen without public funding of stadia. A fundamental reason these networks rarely mention the subsidized nature of the NFL, and venerate the NFL's owners rather than air exposés on their subsidized wealth, is that any emphasis on fair compensation to the public for its investments in the NFL would inevitably call attention to the networks' own bag-of-candy arrangements.

ABC does not broadcast the NFL, and so would seem to have no reason not to report on NFL subsidies. But Disney owns ABC and most of ESPN; the two networks coordinate sport programming, effectively giving ABC a stake in the NFL status quo. Thus all of the nation's major networks—ABC, CBS, ESPN, Fox and NBC—benefit financially from subsidies to professional football. Then by the strangest and most amazing coincidence, their news divisions shy away from the issue.

Players benefit too. The public subsidies for the NFL leave more money for players than would be available if NFL teams paid their own way. Today, NFL players average $2.1 million annually in salary and benefits. A few receive very handsome contracts; quarterback Drew Brees cashed a $37 million bonus in 2012. It's great that magnificent athletes are well paid. But the NFL has only about two thousand players in any year. In a winner-take-all arrangement, a small number of athletes do extremely well from football, while the overwhelming majority of good football players never earn a dime from sports.

THE YEAR 2012 WAS A busy one for public giveaways to the NFL.

In Virginia, Republican governor Bob McDonnell, who styles himself as a budget-slashing conservative crusader, took $6.4 million forcibly extracted from taxpayers' pockets and gave the money to the Washington Redskins, for the team to spend upgrading a workout facility. Hoping to avoid public notice, McDonnell wrote an executive order for the gift, signing the order when the state legislature was out of session. Redskins owner Daniel Snyder has a net worth estimated by *Forbes* at $1.1 billion. But even billionaires like to receive expensive gifts!

Hamilton County, Ohio, the governing body for Cincinnati, was cutting its budget for schools, yet taxpayers were paying $26 million annually for debt service on construction of the field where the NFL's Bengals perform. Press materials distributed by the team declare that the Bengals donate $1 million annually to Ohio community groups. Sound generous? That's about 4 percent of the public subsidy the team receives each year.

In Missouri, Rams owner Stan Kroenke was threatening to move his team to Los Angeles unless taxpayers provided $700 million for a stadium refurbishment. Kroenke's net worth is estimated by *Forbes* at $4.4 billion. He came into his money by marrying Ann Walton, daughter of Walmart cofounder James Walton. Their forebears stood on their own in the free market; Stan and Ann have become specialists in using sports franchises to reach into taxpayers' pockets, owning the Rams, the Denver Nuggets of the NBA, the Colorado Avalanche of the NHL and other teams that perform in publicly subsidized facilities.

In Minnesota, the Vikings were asking for a new stadium, at a time of a $1.1 billion state deficit. The Minnesota legislature extracted $498 million from taxpayers' pockets as a gift to the NFL, covering roughly half the cost of building a new stadium, with the Vikings to pay $477 million. Initially the Minnesota legislature said it would not provide any funding unless given an audited statement of the Vikings' finances. Privately held like most NFL teams, the Vikings receive public funding yet are not required to disclose financial data to the public. When the Vikings refused the request for an audited statement—which likely would have shown the owning family to be extremely wealthy, yet crying poor mouth—the Minnesota legislature folded.

The Vikings will pay $13 million annually to Minnesota for use of the new stadium, but keep all ticket, concession and parking revenues. Thirteen million a year for $498 million in capital is, essentially, a forty-year no-interest loan. Vikings owners Zygmunt and Mark Wilf have a net worth estimated at $1.3 billion.

A $498 handout to a welfare mother would cause outrage. After approving the $498 million handout to billionaires, Minnesota governor Mark Dayton said, "I'm not one to defend the economics of professional sports. Any deal you make in that world doesn't make sense." To appease a football owner, the governor of a major state did something he knew full well "doesn't make sense." Even by the standards of political pandering, Dayton's negligence was breathtaking.

Ink dried on the deal, the Vikings casually said they would sell Minnesotans personal seat licenses to help raise the $477 million the team previously told the state legislature it would pay. Residents would be taxed to give $498 million to the Wilf family, then pay a second time for a license allowing them to pay a third time for game tickets.

Minnesota politicians were terrified they would be blamed for causing the Vikings to move to another city, always highly unlikely. Suppose this happened. It would have been a sad day for football fans; many pleasant traditions are attached to the Vikings' presence in Minnesota. But can keeping an NFL franchise in City A as opposed to City B really be more important than providing education and health care, combating poverty, reducing taxes or controlling the national debt? The sports establishment has skewed priorities. The skewed priorities of society can be just as bad.

In his office at 345 Park Avenue in Manhattan, NFL commissioner Roger Goodell must have smiled when the governor of Minnesota bowed low to kiss the feet of the NFL. The National Football League is about two things: producing high-quality sports entertainment, which it does very well, and exploiting taxpayers, which it also does very well. Goodell should know—his $29.5 million annual income comes from an organization that dodges taxes by pretending, on paper, to be a philanthropy.

• • •

THE SOCIAL CRITIC MICHAEL KINSLEY memorably said, "The scandal is not what people do in violation of the law, the scandal is what's legal." The Park Avenue headquarters of the National Football League is a tax-exempt not-for-profit. And the sham of the NFL nonprofit status is entirely legal.

This situation came into being in the 1960s. Two competing alliances, the National Football League and American Football League, were going head-to-head to sign players and attract television audiences. They wanted to merge. The NFL-AFL merger was good for the sport, stabilizing pro football while ensuring quality of competition through a common draft and revenue-sharing that allows small-market franchises such as the Jacksonville Jaguars to have roughly the same budget as big boys such as the Dallas Cowboys. In the 1960s, the question was, under what conditions could the two leagues merge?

A tedious legal dispute exists regarding whether professional football is a single entity with operating divisions called teams, or a collective of independent businesses with a marketing arm called the NFL. This matter has gone to the Supreme Court as recently as 2010. Common sense says the NFL is a single entity, despite that the people who run individual clubs have the title *owner*. NFL teams are not attempting to put each other out of business. The Chicago Bears want to defeat the Detroit Lions but do not want to drive the Lions out of business. Indeed, the Bears hope the Lions have a profitable season. Other teams regard each other similarly.

The single-entity conception of the NFL allows for a neutral schedule, which is good for quality of competition. Otherwise the Tampa Bay Buccaneers, say, could call the Miami Dolphins and challenge them to several games each year, but refuse to play, say, the Arizona Cardinals. That's the way professional football was in the 1920s, when the Kenosha Maroons or Providence Steam Roller drew up their schedules by issuing challenges. Since the NFL-AFL merger, finalized in 1970, a neutral schedule formula dictates pairings, preventing NFL teams from gimmicking their schedules.

For pro football teams to cooperate not just in scheduling but in the pricing of television rights, the merger required antitrust waivers; otherwise, teams discussing with each other how to price television-rights fees would be price collusion.

Congress granted antitrust waivers to the NFL in two stages. The first was the 1961 Sports Broadcasting Act, which conferred legal permission for NFL headquarters to negotiate television deals as if the NFL were a single entity.

Then in 1966, Congress enacted Public Law 89-800, which granted the NFL a general antitrust exclusion. Unlike carmakers or beer breweries or restaurant chains or electronics manufacturers, the NFL is exempt from antitrust rules—making it much, much easier for the league's feudal families to rake in money. Public Law 89-800 had no name—the way laws have names such as Patriot Act or Patient Protection and Affordable Care Act—in order to keep the bill as low-profile as possible. Congress wanted the bill to be low-profile since the purpose of the legislation was to increase NFL owners' wealth at the expense of average people.

While Public Law 89-800 was being negotiated with congressional leaders, NFL lobbyists tossed in the sort of obscure provision that is the essence of the lobbyist's art. The phrase "professional football leagues" was added to Section 501(c)6 of 26 U.S.C., the Internal Revenue Code. Surely you've heard of Section 501(c)6 of 26 U.S.C.! Previously, a sentence in Section 501(c)6 granted not-for-profit status to "chambers of commerce, real-estate boards and boards of trade." Since 1966, the sentence has read "chambers of commerce, real-estate boards, boards of trade or professional football leagues."

The insertion of "professional football leagues" into the Internal Revenue Code definition of not-for-profit organizations was a transparent sellout of the public interest. This lobbyist-written phrase has saved the NFL hundreds of millions of dollars in tax obligations, which means either that average people must pay higher taxes or the national debt must be increased.

•   •   •

NONPROFIT STATUS APPLIES TO THE NFL's headquarters, which adminis-ters the league and its all-important television contracts, and to the NFL Management Council, which conducts pro football's labor ne-gotiations. The Form 990 of the NFL Management Council covering 2010 shows the NFL used that organization's nonprofit fiction to shield $35 million from taxation, while donating $850,000 to charity—meaning 2 percent of the money exempted from taxes was given away. Individual teams are for-profit and pay income taxes.

In addition to allowing NFL headquarters to evade taxes on itself, the phrase slipped into Section 501(c)6 of 26 U.S.C. helps give the league a powerful tool for claiming another favor: tax-free bonds. Lucas Oil Stadium, the gleaming new field where the Colts perform, cost Indiana taxpayers $615 million in subsidies plus another $200 million in tax exemptions. That dwarfed a $100 million NFL capital contribution—and the icing on the cake was that the borrowing was tax-free.

Tax-free bonds have been used to underwrite construction of many NFL stadia, including the ones where the Browns, Cowboys and Ravens perform. The NFL's ability to obtain tax exemptions for inves-tors represents a huge hidden subsidy to professional football's landed families, to say nothing of the Wall Street investment-bank houses that structure the deals. Tax-free bonds were originally devised to aid local governments and public-service organizations: as recently as 1986, Congress said they should not be employed for business ventures such as professional sports. Lobbyists for the NFL (and for profes-sional basketball and baseball) have quietly arranged with legislators to alter key words of state and federal laws to keep tax-free financing available to the wealthy—while average people pay full boat for loans, then subsidize Wall Street bailouts.

If only the NFL stopped at subsidies, tax favors and masquerading as a sponsor of public service: through its NFL Ventures subsidiary, the league goes out of its way to harm average people, by selling team logos to lotteries.

The Virginia state lottery has a Redskins-branded ticket, the Texas state lottery has a Houston Texans–branded ticket, and so on. Though lotteries claim they exist to fund education, a study by the Federal Reserve Bank of St. Louis found that only a third of the $58 billion wagered on lottos in 2010 went to education; most of the money went to prizes, fees for management companies and payments to local politicians. People foolish enough to buy a lotto ticket know their money will disappear. But most state lotteries, including the ones the NFL endorses, are marketed to prey on the poor—sold in convenience stores and liquor stores, from machines concentrated in low-income zip codes. The Federal Reserve study showed that 62 percent of the most common form of government-lotto tickets are purchased by the disadvantaged.

The NFL opposes wagering on sports, officially because the integrity of competition would be undermined; the real reason may be that the NFL receives no cut. Lotteries are another matter. Because the league receives a cut, the NFL backs lottos enthusiastically. The misanthropy here is overflowing: use flashy pictures of football stars to trick the poor into surrendering money, then hide the gain behind tax exemptions.

NONPROFIT STATUS HELPS THE NFL enrich top management while evading taxes. According to the league's annual Form 990, in 2011 the NFL paid Goodell $29.5 million; that figure is more than earned that year by Jeffrey Immelt, CEO of General Electric. Earlier Form 990s show that in 2010, the league paid NFL Network president Steve Bornstein $12.2 million; paid former commissioner Paul Tagliabue $8.7 million; spent $7.5 million on travel and expenses for its ten top executives; and paid no corporate taxes. In 2009, the NFL had the temerity to claim to the IRS to have lost $42 million, while reporting $48 million conferred on top management. No entity that was losing money in the bona fide sense would exist long if raining such largess on executives.

Perhaps it is spitting into the wind to ask the men who run the National Football League to show a sense of decency regarding the lucrative public trust they hold. For Goodell to take $29.5 million from an enterprise that is so profitable in part because it hides behind a tax-exemption fiction does not seem meaningfully different from, say, the CEO of Fannie Mae awarding himself a gigantic bonus while taxpayers were bailing out his company. Goodell's $29.5 million, and the high pay of other top NFL officers, was made possible by increasing taxes on average people, or by increasing the national debt. Goodell's windfall was legal—but the scandal is what's legal.

Perhaps it is spitting into the wind to expect a son to be half of what his father was. Goodell's father Charles, a member of the House of Representatives and the Senate from 1959 to 1971, was renowned as a man of conscience—one of the first members of Congress to oppose the Vietnam War, and one of the first Republicans to fight for environmental protection. In youth, my initial experience with politics was campaigning for Charles Goodell, who was among my boyhood heroes. Were Charles Goodell around today, what would he say of Roger Goodell's avarice? Roger has become the sort of person his father once opposed—a powerful insider who uses his position to double-cross average people.

Perhaps Roger Goodell would say in his own defense that since the NFL's owners are pigs at the trough, he might as well get the largest share he can. But two wrongs don't make a right. I wanted to put these questions to Goodell to learn what he would say. But as the preface notes, he canceled our scheduled interview when he learned that my topics included the NFL's tax exemptions.

THE NUMBERS IN THE PREVIOUS paragraphs are known because in 2008, the IRS moved to require 501(c)6 organizations to disclose, on their Form 990s, payments to top officers. The reasoning was that nonprofit status should not be employed as a subterfuge for personal enrichment. The NFL lobbied Congress to grant pro football a waiver from the disclosure rule, so that it need not reveal top-management salaries—since employing nonprofit status as a subterfuge for personal enrichment is precisely what Roger Goodell, Paul Tagliabue and others in the NFL's headquarters suite are doing.

During the lobbying battle, Joe Browne, the league's vice president for public affairs, told *The New York Times*, "I finally get to the point where I'm making one hundred and fifty grand, and they want to put my name and address on the [disclosure] form so the lawyer next door who makes a million dollars a year can laugh at me." Browne added that his "hundred and fifty thousand" salary is not as much as it sounds because that amount does not buy in the New York area what it would in "Dubuque, Iowa." The Form 990 disclosures do not include home addresses, so it's unclear what Browne was speaking of there. At any rate, Congress denied the waiver—and then, left no option, the NFL disclosed that Browne made $2 million annually.

The National Football League's top officer for public affairs lied about a public-policy matter the NFL wanted kept quiet. Maybe it's spitting into the wind to ask the men who run the National Football League to exhibit character. By the time of the Penn State child-rape scandal, it was evident that many who enjoy insider status derived from football do not hesitate to deceive or simply to lie in order to protect the flow of money and privilege from which they benefit. Of course Bernard Madoff, Kenneth Lay of Enron and others enriched themselves by deceit. But most powerful liars don't have not-for-profit status, as does the NFL.

ONE MIGHT THINK THAT WITH football so phenomenally popular, politicians could win votes by assuming populist stances regarding the NFL subsidies and exemptions. Instead, in almost every instance, Congress and state legislatures roll over and play dead for pro football. Politicians seem to want to cozy up to the NFL's wealthy owners, in order to receive campaign donations and invitations to luxury boxes.

For a while Senator Arlen Specter of Pennsylvania, an influential Republican moderate who served thirty years in the Senate, was on pro football's case. He told me in 2007, "The NFL owners are arrogant people who have abused the public trust and act like they can get away with anything."

They act that way because usually they can get away with anything. Few members of the House or Senate criticize NFL subsidies or monopoly arrangements. Congress has in the last decade expressed concern about football concussions and sports drugs such as HGH, though it has taken no concrete action, just held hearings seeking television exposure. Otherwise members of Congress praise their home teams and angle to rub shoulders with the owners, whose feudal status makes them desirable political backers.

A rare instance of the NFL's not getting its way came roughly from 2005 to 2010, when the league and Comcast engaged in a rights dispute. The NFL wanted to charge Comcast about $20 per year per subscriber for its house channel, NFL Network. When Comcast said no, the NFL essentially asked Congress to rig the situation in its favor by declaring that football belonged in basic-cable packages. After being rebuffed by Congress, the league settled for about $10 per year—Comcast has lobbyists too.

But in dealings with the NFL, Congress usually gives away the store. Antitrust exemption—almost priceless to a large business—was granted to the NFL in exchange only for its promise not to schedule games on Friday nights, when most high school football occurs. Perhaps the NFL should have received an antitrust exemption. But rather than drive a hard bargain for the public, Congress simply handed the NFL what it wanted.

The most basic public giveaway to the NFL is the league's ability to create images in public facilities, then sell exclusive licenses to the images and keep all revenue—broadcasting the images over public airwaves to boot. Football fans know the warning intoned during each NFL contest—that "unauthorized use" of the game's images without "express written consent" of the league is prohibited. Thanks to inaction by Congress, entertainment created in publicly funded stadia is treated by law as the private property of the NFL.

When for example Fox broadcasts an NFL game of the Tampa Bay Buccaneers from Raymond James Stadium, built entirely at public expense, the NFL owns the rights, which it sells to Fox. If the network filmed children playing touch football on the National Mall in Washington, DC, built at public expense, no one would believe that meant Fox had acquired an exclusive right to images from the National Mall. Yet this is how sales of NFL game images are structured. Typically, a city or county government agency signs a contract with an NFL team, granting it exclusive control over football images created in the stadium. No federal law, nor any state law, prevents images created at public expense from being privatized in this manner.

Baseball, basketball, ice hockey and other sports also benefit from entertainment images created in publicly funded facilities being converted into private property. That others take advantage of the public too is no justification. The NFL's sweetheart deal is by far the most valuable, owing to the sums involved. And the sums have become majestic.

In 2013, WHAT ARE NOW charmingly called the "terrestrial networks"—CBS, ESPN, Fox and NBC—pay the NFL about $3 billion for license rights to broadcast games. Satellite carrier DirecTV pays another $1 billion.

Beginning in 2014, the group will pay the NFL about $6 billion annually for broadcast rights. Beginning that year, ESPN alone will remit to the NFL a staggering $1.9 billion—about twice what NBC will pay—to broadcast *Monday Night Football,* and for that sum ESPN doesn't even receive a place in the Super Bowl rotation, which alternates annually among CBS, Fox and NBC. Airing a Super Bowl not only is prestigious. CBS, which carried the 2013 Super Bowl, realized about $250 million from in-game advertising at $3.7 million per thirty seconds, plus millions more from pregame and postgame ads. A measure of football's vise grip on American sports is that in 2014, ESPN will spend $1.9 billion for seventeen NFL games, compared to $700 million for ninety Major League Baseball outings—$112 million per NFL game, $8 million per MLB contest.

Why would ESPN pay roughly twice as much as NBC, though receiving no Super Bowl broadcast? Because not just live-game images but highlights of games played in publicly funded facilities have value, and these too become the property of NFL owners. ESPN airs football talk and football news round the clock on several channels for 365 days of the year, along with continuous NFL coverage and commentary on a popular website, ESPN.com—whereas NBC covers the NFL only on Sunday evenings during the season.

Licensing rights to extensive use of NFL highlights are beneficial to ESPN because the organization's many all-sports "platforms" allow advertising to be sold, and cable fees realized, year-round, while studio-based talking-heads sports programming costs far less to produce than on-location game coverage. Comparison of the ESPN and NBC agreements that begin in 2014 suggests NFL highlights alone are worth about $900 million a year. Pro football is so lucrative, its highlights are worth more than an entire slate of MLB live-game broadcasts.

ALLOWING THE NFL TO CONVERT images from public facilities into private profit, Congress also allows the NFL to prohibit the taxpayers who fund most NFL facilities from watching the best games.

The 1961 Sports Broadcasting Act contained a clause authorizing pro football to "regionalize" coverage. What does that innocuous word mean? It means the NFL can require that a television station broadcasting within seventy-five miles of an NFL team to show only that team, if it is playing. Normally, requiring a publicly regulated local broadcaster to show Programming A, while forbidding it to show Programming B, would be restraint of trade. The production company of, say, *Wheel of Fortune* could not forbid a local affiliate from, say, showing old movies. Yet the 1961 legislation authorized the NFL to require local network affiliates to air local or regional teams when a more important national game was what viewers wanted to watch. NFL regionalized coverage means viewers who live with seventy-five miles of Cleveland must watch Browns games, even if they'd rather see some other contest, and so on in other cities throughout the country.

Consider that on December 16, 2012, the important early-Sunday game was Denver at Baltimore, pitting Peyton Manning, the year's comeback story, against a Ravens team that would reach the Super Bowl. Much of the nation saw Denver at Baltimore, while Texas and Indiana saw the equally exciting Colts versus Texans contest. But "regionalized" rules required all local affiliates in Florida to show Jacksonville at Miami, a laffer between two losing teams already eliminated from the playoffs. The important late-afternoon game that day was Pittsburgh at Dallas, pairing perennial contenders. Regionalized rules forbid local affiliates in California and the lower Midwest from showing the game. Viewers there beheld a total woofer, 2-11 Kansas City at 3-10 Oakland.

In places where NFL teams are close together—for example the Eagles, Ravens and Redskins are proximate—the NFL draws crazy-quilt maps of what zip codes are required to watch which team. Parts of western Pennsylvania may be compelled to watch Buffalo Bills games, even if the Pittsburgh Steelers, the hands-down viewer choice, are playing at the same time. There are other examples.

The notion of forcing audiences to watch the closest NFL team dates to the period when the NFL was dependent on ticket sales and when—no DVRs, broadband or narrowcasting to smartphones or tablets—viewing habits were very different from today's. The regional-coverage concept is obsolete, but NFL owners don't want to change the policy because they like controlling what viewers see. A television or movie studio that raised its middle finger to customers in this way would lose business. But television and movie studios are not protected by a moat of antitrust exemptions.

WHY DO NFL OWNERS OPENLY abuse the public trust? There is a three-word answer: Because they can.

In all walks of life, men and women tend to get away with whatever they can, until stopped by law or social pressure. NFL owners have found they can demand special treatment from a sports-crazed public, from supine legislators and from big-media companies—CBS, ESPN/ABC, Fox and NBC—that are NFL broadcast partners benefiting financially by presenting pro football in glowing terms. Like a defense contractor putting subcontracts in every state to head off political oversight, the NFL has parceled out some rights to every major broadcast corporation. Maybe that was a coincidence of negotiations. But surely the NFL knew that giving every major broadcaster a monetary stake in pro football also gives each a stake in the pretense that government subsidies and special exemptions for the NFL are sound public policy.

In 2009, the National Football League threatened to move its annual Pro Bowl game away from Honolulu. At the very time the State of Hawaii was cutting its budget for public schools, Hawaii lawmakers gave the NFL a $4 million annual gift to keep the event in their capital city. The lawmakers' action was bad enough. What was disgraceful was that the rich, subsidized owners of the NFL accepted.

They took the money because they could. Until public attitudes change, those at the top of the pro football pyramid will keep getting away with whatever they can.

This is troubling not just because average people are taxed to provide subsidies, and special government favors are granted so a small number of NFL owners and their families can live in great wealth, as modern feudal lords and ladies. It is troubling because athletics are supposed to set an example—and the example being set is one of selfishness. Football is America's game. Should the favorite sport of the greatest nation on Earth really be one whose economic structure is based on inequality and greed?

The next chapter: college football also misuses taxpayers' money—and students' tuition too.

Money and College Football

4

TOO BAD YOU WEREN'T INVITED TO THE FIESTA FROLIC

By a quirk of their nearly century-long history, the Green Bay Packers are the sole major US professional sports franchise that offers shares for sale to the public. All other major US pro sports franchises are either family owned or closely held private concerns. Because they sell public shares, the Packers are the sole major pro sports franchise that discloses financial data.

In the 2010 football season, the Packers won the Super Bowl—can't improve on that—and did well financially, clearing $43 million in net income. The Packers had $302 million in revenue, with the leading source being national-television income, which the league splits into thirty-two equal portions. This arrangement keeps competition even—unlike, say, in Major League Baseball, where the New York, Los Angeles and Boston teams have far more money to work with than do their peers. That National Football League coaches and owners talk rock-ribbed conservatism, but model their business finances along socialist lines, is an obvious irony. That a socialist business structure is tremendously successful—terrific games, high level of competition, incredible popularity—is a less obvious irony in a country where the public so often is told that sink-or-swim is the only kind of economics that works.

Green Bay's biggest cost of doing business was $159 million for players: mostly salary and benefits for current performers, but also pensions for athletes who left the game before 1993, when the current collective-bargaining structure went into effect.

In 1993, NFL teams spent an average of $48 million annually on players. By 2013, the average would be $123 million—a 160 percent increase in two decades, a faster rate of increase than enjoyed by professional basketball or baseball players in the same period, or for those in nearly any other profession. Average annual pay and perks per NFL player rose from about $800,000 in 1993 to the roughly $2.1 million of 2013. Just as the NFL benefited from a socialist revenue-sharing agreement that gave the same amount each season to losing teams as to winning ones, players benefited from their 1993 decision to switch from confrontational labor relations to cooperative bargaining.

Some in the press, their minds stuck at the 1952 steel strike, failed to understand the concept of cooperative bargaining. In 2006, HBO's Bryant Gumbel called NFLPA leader Eugene Upshaw the "personal pet" of the NFL Commissioner, because Upshaw wanted to resolve a contract dispute in a civil manner, while Gumbel wanted bricks thrown through windows—that's a more exciting story!

Friendly negotiations left NFL players better off than they would otherwise have been because labor peace raised the value of professional football as a television product. The NFL has not missed a game for labor reasons since 1987. Baseball and basketball experienced crippling strikes during the period, while the National Hockey League canceled an entire season plus locked out players for half a season.

The knowledge that owners and players were on the same page, and that games would be played, raised the rights market for NFL broadcasts—networks began to offer stratospheric dollar figures because they knew pro football programming would not be disrupted.

This increased income to current players and also to older retirees, who by the 2011 NFL-NFLPA collective-bargaining agreement were receiving $62 million annually in pensions. That amount was sheer magnanimity, considering players who retired before 1993 never won any pension rights for themselves when they were in charge of the union, and chose confrontational tactics.

Beyond the $159 million the Green Bay Packers paid in 2010 to current and former players, the team spent an additional $100 million on coaches, front-office staff, travel, trainers, medical care and overhead. That left $43 million as the net, and a 14 percent return on revenue would leave any businessperson quite pleased. The Packers' board voted to use some of the net to purchase land near Lambeau Field, where the Packers perform, holding the acreage for future expansion—on the theory that NFL franchises can only get more valuable.

The same 2010 season that ended with the professional football title bestowed on Green Bay ended with the college football championship won by Auburn University. The Auburn Tigers football program had $76 million in revenue, with the lion's share coming, just as with an NFL team, from television-rights fees. The $76 million paled before the $302 million in revenue enjoyed by the Packers. But while Green Bay had operating expenses of $259 million, Auburn had football operating expense of just $39 million—after all, Auburn's players are unpaid. For the season, Auburn enjoyed a football net income of $37 million, amazingly similar to the Green Bay Packers' net income of $43 million.

Big-college football programs can make nearly as much profit as NFL programs. And while individual NFL franchises pay corporate taxes, college football income is almost entirely tax-sheltered.

THOUGH AUBURN'S FOOTBALL PLAYERS RECEIVED no pay, money flowed to Auburn coaches and athletic officials. In 2010 the college's athletic director, Jay Jacobs, received $600,000, for a middle-management position. Auburn paid a total of $15.9 million to the coaches of its men's teams, football dominating this outlay. Head football coach Gene Chizik received a $3.5 million salary, plus perks such as club memberships. Gus Malzahn, the offensive coordinator, earned $1 million. Jacobs declared that the head coach's impressive pay was justified because "Coach Chizik is a great mentor to our student-athletes."

That year, 52 percent of African-American football players at Auburn graduated. What Auburn meant in saying Chizik was "a great mentor" was that he was good at getting players to win games. Auburn's athletic department could not have cared less that nearly half its black players did not graduate, and apparently the Auburn board of trustees and the Alabama state legislature—Auburn is a public university—could not have cared less, either. Had the athletic department, board of trustees or state legislature cared, priorities would have been different. Two years later, after the Tigers went 3-9, Chizik was fired. When Auburn lost, magically he ceased being a "great mentor."

As Chizik was shown the door, he received a $7.5 million buyout, a severance guarantee that had been added to his deal after the national title win. His many assistants, also cashiered, received a total of $3.5 million in severance; to clear the way for hiring Chizik in 2009, Auburn had given about $5 million to the previous head coach it fired. That's $16 million, paid by a public university, just to get rid of football coaches who angered the boosters by failing to go undefeated. Jacobs, the Auburn athletic director, made the decision to hire Chizik and to grant him extravagant contract guarantees. If Chizik is a bad coach, Auburn's athletic director doesn't know what he is going. Yet Jacobs kept his high-paying, taxpayer-subsidized job.

Auburn's example is not an isolated one. The previous collegiate season ended with Ohio State University and the University of Texas, the top two colleges for sports revenue, meeting in the Fiesta Bowl. That year, Ohio State graduated 49 percent of its black football players. Did the school feel ashamed? Its president, Gordon Gee, received a raise, to $2 million annually, while its athletic director, Gene Smith, received a raise, to $1.1 million annually. Texas graduated 37 percent of its African-American football players. Did the school feel ashamed? Its head coach, Mack Brown, received a raise, to $5 million.

AUBURN BELONGS TO THE SOUTHEASTERN Conference, which has won seven consecutive BCS football titles. The Knight Commission on Intercollegiate Athletics is a private organization that critiques college sports. In 2010, a study sponsored by the Knight Commission found that universities of the SEC spend an annual median of $164,000 per NCAA athlete, versus $13,000 on academics per regular undergraduate student. Measured by money, in the SEC sports are twelve times more important than academics. Not only do these numbers mean spending per athlete is outrageous in the Southeastern Conference; they mean spending for the education of typical SEC undergraduates is less than the per capita spending at most of the nation's public high schools. And they mean spending academic per typical SEC undergraduate is well below the $23,000 to $28,000 per year that SEC member institutions charge to out-of-state students as tuition.

Other conferences are nearly as bad. The Knight Commission found that member institutions of the Big 12, which enfolds most large universities of Texas, Oklahoma and Kansas, spend a median of $131,000 annually per NCAA athlete, versus $14,000 on academics per regular undergraduate. Thus in the Big 12, sports are nine times more important than academics. Members of the Atlantic Coast Conference, to which Virginia Tech belongs, spend a median of $103,000 per athlete versus $15,000 on academics per regular undergraduate— seven times as much per athlete as other types of students. Members of the Pacific-12 Conference, which includes Stanford and the University of California at Berkeley, also spend seven times as much per NCAA athlete as on academics per regular undergraduate.

Sporting events are inherently more expensive than classroom lectures; colleges that play football in the less costly Division IAA spend about three times as much per NCAA athlete as per regular undergraduate. But spending in the big conferences shows total lack of perspective, and football drives the distortion.

In 2012, the NCAA fined Penn State $60 million, over four years, as punishment for an institutional cover-up of child rapes by a football coach. The NCAA's explanation was that $60 million represented a year's football revenue at the university. Yet Department of Education statistics say the correct total for Penn State's most recent reported year was $73 million. Be that as it may, the $60 million assessment against Penn State was not, as NCAA president Mark Emmert pretended, a grave judgment. Considering the amount of money at the big-program level of college football, the fine was strictly symbolic.

Penn State will lose $15 million a year for four years against a football revenue base four to five times that amount. Had Penn State been banned from NCAA football, the money consequences would have been painful to the institution. As is, even after the penalty, Penn State football will remain a cash cow. Football is not a cash cow to every university. But at the football-factory schools—moo!

MOST COLLEGES LOSE MONEY ON athletics. Of the hundreds of universities and colleges that field teams in Division I, participating in sports from football to Nordic skiing and "mixed rifle," only twenty-three reported "positive net generated revenues" from athletics in 2011, NCAA data show. Different schools emphasize different sports. High Point University of North Carolina, with no football team, is a soccer power; Cornell University is both Ivy League and a wrestling power; the University of Maryland Eastern Shore is the Boston Celtics of women's bowling. But whatever sports a college chooses to emphasize, the majority of colleges lose money through their athletic departments. If there were no collegiate athletics, college overall could cost somewhat less—a restive proposition as students and parents struggle with the price of higher education continuing to rise much faster than inflation.

Football and men's basketball are known in collegiate athletics as "revenue sports" because they alone bring in more than they cost. For instance, in 2010 the University of Georgia cleared $53 million on its football program—$75 million in revenue against $22 million in costs—and also cleared $3.4 million on men's basketball. All other sports at the university were money pits. Men's sports such as track and baseball operated in the red. Women's teams at Georgia lost prodigiously—a $8.4 million net loss, on $12.5 million in expenses against $4.1 million in revenue.

Saying most colleges lose money on athletics is, at one level, like saying most colleges lose money on Shakespeare. At many institutions of higher learning only dorm rooms, whose fees typically work out to a rent of $1,500 a month for a tiny space with no kitchen or bath, are pure profit. If a college tried to determine what aspects of collegiate life were remunerative and then jettison the rest, not much would remain.

Every university should have a classics department, whether there is demand for classics in any given academic year or not. Every university should stage operas, symphony concerts and theater whether this makes economic sense or not. Classics and the arts are part of the life of a college. By the same token, every university should have basketball games at a field house, should have women's lacrosse on a freshly mowed field. Athletics are part of the life of a college, part of what makes such institutions Shangri-las of learning and contemplation.

Colleges without sports are easy to imagine—just visit Europe. The Universities of Oxford and Cambridge hold a celebrated annual boat race, and some European colleges have gyms and tracks. But there's nothing like the intercollegiate athletic scene in the United States. Basketball and soccer are either professional or run by clubs that are unaffiliated with universities.

The association of team sports with higher education is a uniquely American innovation. That association has been controversial for a long time—in 1905, the faculty of the University of Wisconsin passed a resolution demanding an end to college football, which it declared "has become a business supported by levies on the public." That is, the faculty wanted the University of Wisconsin to be like a European university—all lecture halls, no locker rooms. Would the University of Wisconsin have been better off if this had happened?

FOOTBALL HELPED AMERICAN HIGHER EDUCATION by raising enthusiasm about college. The dramatic postwar expansion of American higher education synced directly with the growing popularity of the gridiron sport. In 1940, just 6 million Americans held a bachelor's degree; by 2012, 96 million did. Higher education would have expanded whether athletics existed or not. But college attendance and college football grew at the same time, each amplifying the other.

By 2012, the total number of college graduates in the United States exceeded the total population of the United States when Teddy Roosevelt was president. This remarkable rise in numbers of graduates occurred not at private liberal arts colleges, which have grown surprisingly little, but at public universities intended to serve average students. Simultaneously, large public universities displaced, as football powers, the private colleges that ruled the sport in the first half of the twentieth century. After World War II, funding for public universities grew dramatically, as did the size and scope of these schools. As public universities were expanding, the sense of excitement generated by football helped make the college campus a desirable place to be.

At any university, what happens in the English or engineering or biology department is more important than what happens on the sports field. But the academic departments do not generate public enthusiasm and media attention: football reliably produces both. In the last quarter century, for instance, Brandeis University has developed one of the leading schools of public health, both an accomplishment in itself and one relevant to pressing global needs. But Brandeis does not field a football team, and so remains little known outside Massachusetts. Contrast this with Boise State, once little known outside Idaho, which in 1986 installed blue turf at its football stadium, then invested in a winning football team with a whimsical preference for trick plays. Boise State University now commands national attention.

On-campus football and basketball games make colleges exciting places to be, raising interest among the young. Sports events induce state legislatures to fund colleges, put donors in the mood to give to schools, make alumni want to stay in touch with their old colleges, place the names of colleges in newspapers daily. Many major American universities are built around football stadia, which serve as electric hubs of the campus. At Virginia Tech, for example, the engineering department and the formal lawn are impressive, but Lane Stadium generates the sense of campus buzz.

Suppose football vanished—would Virginia Tech, or any other university, be better off *as a school?* Almost surely not. In a 2012 paper, professors Michael Sauder of the University of Iowa, and Arik Lifschitz and Mitchell Stevens of Stanford University, argued that football confers "status markers" on college, making the public more willing to support spending for higher education. The he-man nature of football also provides balance for left-wing college subjects such as gender studies. A century ago, some felt that universities, where men wore robes and studied Latin and Greek, were effete domains; football made college seem manly. Today, with the student body of US colleges overall at 56 percent women, American universities might be perceived by the public as too female. Football solves that perception problem many times over.

These are among the reasons even elite US colleges—Yale, Penn, Williams, Bowdoin, the University of Chicago, the Massachusetts Institute of Technology, Duke, Northwestern—field football teams. They do so because they believe it makes them better *as schools.*

My 2009 book about globalization, *Sonic Boom,* lists the world's one hundred best colleges and universities. Eighty-nine are in the United States, eleven in the rest of the world combined. *The Great Brain Race,* a 2010 book by Ben Wildavsky about the global college scene, comes to the same conclusion. And of those eighty-nine great US colleges and universities, most field teams of boys and men in plastic armor slamming into each other as autumn leaves fall. They don't do this because some nefarious force has pulled the wool over their eyes. They do this because they think athletic excitement makes them better *as schools.*

The enthusiasm generated by sports events on campus surely is one reason that in 2011, 50 percent of US eighteen- and nineteen-year-olds were enrolled in college, the highest such figure in American history. According to a 2010 study by the College Board, 40 percent of US citizens hold at least an associate degree, compared to 32 percent in the United Kingdom, the nation most similar to the United States. Broadly across the European Union, college achievement is lower than in the United States—32 percent of Danes held at least an associate degree, 27 percent of French citizens and 24 percent of Germans. American success with spreading higher education to large numbers of people—to "the masses," as a European professor would say—is especially striking when one bears in mind that college costs more in the United States than anywhere else in the world. Yet, large numbers of Americans are inspired to attend. The campus excitement generated by sports is among the reasons.

Florian Ederer, an economist at UCLA's Anderson School of Management, says, "Football has a positive overall impact on American universities, by drawing support for higher-education spending and by making college attractive to young men. The irony is that the main benefits of football may be to college women. They enjoy the advantages of the money and public attention that football brings to their campuses, but don't lose time at football practice, don't run concussion risks, don't fail to graduate like so many football players, and are not as wrapped up in football success or failure as men." By this way of thinking, football is a male warrior sport where, at the college level, many of the spoils go to women.

•   •   •

IF FOOTBALL IS MAINLY A plus for higher education, this hardly means colleges have the sport in perspective.

In the 2010–11 academic year, the University of Texas had a $150 million athletic-department budget; Ohio State University's athletic-department budget was $132 million. Ohio State listed 458 staff members in its athletic department. In addition to dozens of coaches and trainers, athletic director Gene Smith supervised two "executive associate" athletic directors, two "senior associate athletic directors," twelve associate athletic directors, a "senior associate legal counsel for athletics," and a nine-person NCAA compliance office. In all, sixty-eight people had titles reading *associate* or *assistant* director—and every one of them failed to detect the 2011 scandal that led to the resignation of Ohio State head football coach Jim Tressel.

Broadly across collegiate athletics, coaches are not teachers who also coach: they do nothing all year long but their sport. The twelve football coaches at USC, the four men's basketball coaches plus "director of basketball operations" at the University of North Carolina—they don't teach classes, just run a business enterprise that bears the school's insignia. Even at a Division III college, in most cases the head football coach, and men's and women's basketball coaches, do not teach, just coach.

The nine people at Ohio State who did nothing all day long but administer NCAA compliance surely enforced with intense vigor petty rules about cheeseburgers, but when it came to corruption at the top of the football program, they saw nothing, nothing! Before resigning, Tressel would state he had known about the violations for years but did not inform the athletic department because "I just didn't know who to contact." Using Google, it took me forty-five seconds to get the names and phone numbers of the school's compliance officers. Despite doing a horrible job of administering the Ohio State athletic department, Smith kept his $1.1 million per year post. Or perhaps Smith did a great job. Ohio State athletics may have broken rules left and right, but money kept rolling in. Which do you suppose the Ohio State board of trustees cared about, ethics or money?

In the same year that Ohio State had 458 staff members in its athletic department, the school's English Department had 242 staff members. Sports at Ohio State received significantly more staffing than English though nearly all Ohio State students take a course through the English Department, while only about 1 percent of the student body participates in NCAA athletics. And sports received more staffing than English despite the wide consensus that young Americans are inadequately educated in subjects such as English, while not a single person in the entire United States believes there isn't enough emphasis on football.

Sports-money numbers at other universities are not as extreme as at Texas or Ohio State, but still high: an average $77 million athletic-department annual budget in 2010–11 for the schools whose football teams have appeared in a Bowl Championship Series game.

Consider the University of Florida, a perennial powerhouse. For the 2010–11 school year, football brought the University of Florida $17.5 million in ticket sales and $48 million in television-rights fees. Football expenses were about $12 million, leaving a football net of $53.5 million. Overall, Florida's athletic department took in $108 million and spent $94 million, netting $14 million. Six million dollars of the $14 million was "donated" by the athletic department to the university's academic budget. The athletic department kept the rest.

At the University of Florida, as at many big-college sports programs, the athletic department is structured as an independent organization that leases campus space and school logos, then operates a tax-exempt business over which the school's president and board of trustees have little control.

Florida's sports subsidiary, called the University Athletic Association, Inc., did pay for all NCAA scholarships the school awarded, sparing Florida taxpayers that expense. But the association spent roughly three times as much on coaches' and administrators' salaries as on educational costs for all scholarship athletes in all sports. And the athletic department is structured such that if it has an off year, the university must cover any red ink; if the athletic department has a profitable year, it is not required to "donate" anything to the school.

This arrangement is not an outlier. In 2012, the University of Tennessee fired its head football coach for the unspeakable sin of consecutive losing seasons. The college gave Derek Dooley a $5 million severance payment, simultaneously announcing the athletic department's scheduled $6 million annual contribution to academics would be waived for three years. "We will do the things required to return our team to national prominence," UT chancellor Jimmy Cheek announced. The University of Tennessee athletic department, with more than $70 million in annual revenue, gets a three-year exemption from contributing anything at all to education at its sponsoring university. Cheek might as well have said, "As the chancellor of a major university, I care far more about football than about education."

In 2012, athletic director Joe Alleva of LSU, one of the nation's powerhouse football programs, announced the athletic department had agreed to "transfer" $7.2 million annually to the university. "Why will do we do it? Simply put, Tiger athletics is a part of LSU and should play a role in the broader mission of the institution," Alleva said, as if this were a novel concept. The most recent data show LSU's athletic department has $48 million more revenue than expenses. Thus LSU athletics agreed to give 15 percent of its profit to the university, keeping the rest for itself. Essentially LSU football is leasing the school's tax exemptions, land and brands for a fraction of their value, and expecting praise for giving back anything at all.

ORIGINALLY, COLLEGE SPORTS EVENTS WERE for the entertainment of students, alumni and the local community. As sports passion has taken hold on the United States, increasingly the marketing department rules.

Cameron Indoor Stadium, the wonderful 1940s-era arena where Duke plays basketball, has 9,314 seats. Only 1,200 are allocated to students. Undergraduates whose parents pay $59,000 annually for them to attend Duke may camp out overnight at the box office in hopes of snagging student tickets. Most seats go to boosters, corporate buyers, and well-to-do basketball lovers with no personal attachment to the college started in 1838 as Brown's Schoolhouse.

Big-college football stadia have "student sections," which sound like a fun place to sit with your friends. The student section always comprises the least desirable seats: off-campus customers sit in the good seats or the luxury boxes. The University of Tennessee plays its home games at 102,000-seat Neyland Stadium. Student tickets are a bargain at $10, but there are only 13,500 student tickets. Eighty-seven percent of the ducats for Neyland Stadium are reserved for nonstudents. That is, those not already paying $22,000 to $39,000 annually to the university are the focus of game-day ticket sales. Students—the school's core customers—are ignored, to market tickets to expense-account types.

One of the reasons big public universities want winning football programs is that the excitement generated helps draw out-of-state students, who pay higher tuition rates than in-state residents. The big public universities immediately shaft those students by saving most of the football tickets for someone else.

Virginia Tech prides itself on reserving nineteen thousand football tickets for students, meaning almost all undergraduates can attend a home game. About 30 percent of those at a Hokies game at Lane Stadium are actual college students—this is among the highest percentages of actual-student attendance in Division I. At most of the nation's monster football programs, 80 to 90 percent of those in the stadium don't attend the university. They are just sports customers.

At banks, at credit-card companies and in other parts of commerce, an aspect of marketing is "sell-up"—get the customer to buy extras. Sell-up is big in college football. Want seats along the prestigious Tech Terrace at a Georgia Tech home football game? Donate $800. Want first choice of any bowl-game seats for Kansas State? Donate $50,000.

Want good seats for home basketball games at Duke? Donate $8,000 per season, which works out to roughly $500 per game. Give $10,000 to the Virginia Tech football program and you'll receive Hokie Points, which can be exchanged for the chance to purchase 50-yard-line seats, or for premium parking near the stadium.

Large donations at any college program may get you lunch with the coaches, a pass to attend practices or to stand on the sidelines during warm-ups, invitations to an annual team gala. Really large donations allow a booster to travel with the team: being on the team plane to a bowl game is high status. At the end of 2012, oilman Boone Pickens had accumulated 6,090,941 "Athletic Priority Points" at Oklahoma State, almost a hundred times as many as held by the number-two booster. Perhaps Pickens could cash in these points to live at the university president's house.

GENERATIONS AGO, SINCLAIR LEWIS DENOUNCED college-sports boosters as "rah-rah boys." Today's rah-rah boys tend to be well-heeled business-people who want to feel important by hanging around with a big-college football team. In many places, there is tremendous cachet to having rubbed shoulders with the university's football coach or knowing some tidbit of inside information, such as which star looked good in practice and which spent the week with his knee iced. Today's rah-rah boys can buy that access perfectly legally.

In the NFL, the customers are the customers: every team wants to sell its season tickets, seat licenses and parking for whatever the market will bear, but customers never "donate" to the team. If you walked up to the head coach of the Atlanta Falcons and said, "I'll donate one hundred thousand dollars if you let me travel on the team plane and stand on the sideline during the Dolphins game," the Falcons' coach would consider you a crackpot. But in the college sports milieu, this is a perfectly normal sort of transaction, if usually conducted in a more genteel way, via someone in the athletics development office.

The existence—indeed, respectability—of cash gifts from boosters has troubling implications for college football. One is that some boosters bet on games. College coaches may try to run up the score in order to cover the spread for high rollers who donate, resulting in blowout games with displays of poor sportsmanship. When Oklahoma State faced 67-point mega-underdog Savannah State in 2012, boosters who wagered on the contest would have been in an uproar if the Cowboys failed to win by at least 67. The fourth quarter began with Oklahoma State leading 70–0, just above the margin needed to exceed the spread; Coach Mike Gundy kept calling passes in the fourth quarter, since continuing to score meant taking no chance of not producing the number that satisfied boosters who had placed bets. Oklahoma State won 84–0—covering the spread while having a few laughs at the expense of sportsmanship.

NFL coaches are aware of the point spread, but since there are no cash-giving boosters at the professional level, an honest NFL coach has no incentive to care whether his team covers. There are also no polls at the NFL level, only the standings: to a professional, a 1-point victory has the same value as a 20-point win. College football coaches sometimes run up the score to impress pollsters—if the starters are still on the field when the team has an insurmountable lead, this does not necessarily mean the coach is concerned about the Vegas line. But the presence of boosters who can in effect hand money to college coaches is an unseemly influence not found at the professional level.

Boosters love blowout wins, and the result is a new secondary market in weak teams certain to lose games and make the home team look good. In 2011, Berkeley, suffering its fourth consecutive year of budget cuts, tuition hikes and classroom-size increases, nonetheless found $400,000 to pay the football team of Presbyterian College, a lower-division school, to fly out to California and be resoundingly defeated—the final was Cal 63, Presbyterian 12—before the host's boosters.

The next season, Presbyterian took a $400,000 paycheck from Georgia Tech to come to the Yellow Jackets' home field and lose, 59–3. The Georgia legislature had recently cut the educational budget for the

state public university system, to which Georgia Tech belongs. But
$400,000 was available to bring a football traveling show in for the
school's boosters. One week later, Presbyterian received another $400,000,
this time from Vanderbilt, to go to the Commodores' stadium and lose,
58–0. Nashville's *Tennessean* newspaper drily reported that $400,000 is
"the customary rate" for Presbyterian to agree to lose on the home field
of an SEC or ACC football team.

In 2012, Florida State opened its season by paying Division IAA
Murray State $450,000 to come to Tallahassee and be pounded 69–3,
then the following week paid Division IAA Savannah State, a perennial
doormat, $420,000 to visit Tallahassee and be pounded 55–0. That
the Seminoles' staged exhibitions over Murray State and Savannah State
mocked the sportsmanship collegiate athletics are said to teach was
beside the point. Florida State alums were happy because their school
was certain to win, allowing the boosters to party; the Florida State
athletic department came out ahead on ticket and concession sales.

Between the Oklahoma State and Florida State contests, Savannah
State received a total of $860,000 for allowing its players to be used as
tackling dummies by two football factories. For Savannah State, which
had $1.3 million in football revenue the previous year, the $860,000 in
game fees was significant. For the megabucks Florida State and Oklahoma State programs, the payments were pocket change.

Many colleges believe football is essential to keeping boosters active, which inspires alumni giving. In 2010, Rutgers had its first losing
football season in some time, and alumni donations for the following
year declined by about $1.5 million. In a 2012 paper Michael Ander-
son, an economist at the University of California at Berkeley, showed
that adding five wins to a college's football season would increase alumni
donations that year by roughly a third, while increasing student applications for the next year by roughly 5 percent.

Football encourages alumni giving—but often to athletics, not
academics. Pickens has given at least $400 million to his alma ma-
ter, Oklahoma State—about $300 million for sports, including the

construction of an "athletic village" on campus, versus about $100 million for academics. On New Year's Day 2013, Northwestern University beat Mississippi State in the Gator Bowl, Northwestern's first bowl victory in sixty-four years. Not long after, Northwestern, which has many wealthy alumni, announced $70 million in donations—to the athletic department, not the academic endowment. In 2006, the Princeton football team won the Ivy League title. That's pretty exciting. Princeton alum William Powers got excited and gave the school $10.5 million. The breakdown was $10 million for football, $500,000 for academics. For many colleges and universities, football may inspire donations that otherwise would not have occurred—or may cannibalize donations that would have gone to academic scholarships or the endowment.

THEN THERE'S THE WORD *DONATE*. When an NFL fan purchases season tickets, no one thinks that person is making a "donation." At the college level, money exchanges between boosters and schools are structured to appear to be donations—thus generating tax deductions.

Suite seats at Georgia Tech cost $225 per game. The school says, "A portion of your price is considered a tax deductible donation to the Tech Fund." Nearly 40 percent of the $108 million total athletic revenue at the University of Florida in 2010–11 was, on paper, donations—which would generate about $15 million in tax deductions, assuming most people who give to college athletics are in the top tax bracket. North Carolina State University will sell you the right to purchase, in perpetuity, one of the best seats in its football stadium—so long as you make an annual "donation" of $7,000 to the athletic department. For a top-bracket individual, that "donation" would cut federal and state tax bills by $2,000 to $2,500 each year. Gimmicks such as this transfer money from average people who cannot afford to attend major-college sports events to high rollers, since for every tax deduction claimed by a well-off person, either taxes must rise on the average, or services be cut, or government must go further into debt.

Donations can lead to amusing results, among them endowed

coaches. At Stanford, David Shaw is not the football coach: he is the Bradford M. Freeman Director of Football. At Cornell University, the women's volleyball coach is not just the women's volleyball coach, she is the Wendy Schaenen '79 Head Coach of Volleyball. At Yale, the football coach isn't just the football coach, he is the Joel E. Smilow '54 Head Coach of Yale Football; the offensive and defensive coordinators are the Joel E. Smilow '54 Associate Head Coaches. In 1988, Smilow gave $2 million to put his name above the doors of coaches' offices; considering top rates at the time, about $900,000 of that amount likely was tax deductions, passing the bill for Ivy League athletics along to average people. Of course academic and other kinds of donations to colleges are tax-deductible too. But money given to academics at a college might benefit society as a whole. Money given to sports does not serve a larger social purpose.

In 2012, several major football programs, including Duke and Michigan, were seeking $5 million donations to name their football coaches; such a donation would result in roughly $1.5 million of tax deductions, billed to average people. Some colleges even sell names to football positions, conferring tax deductions. The guy taking the snap in a North Carolina State game is the Marek and Mabel Alapin Quarterback; the guy launching the punt is the Longley Family Punter. Every time North Carolina State punts, taxpayers should wince.

The University of Oregon's football team made the national title game following the 2010 season, and the school was rewarded with $74 million in athletic donations in 2011. The donations likely generated about $20 million in federal and state tax deductions, passing the $20 million cost along to average people. That same year, 2011, was when Penn State sank into disgrace. The Nittany Lions Club, the booster fund, received $87 million in donations, which would have generated about $25 million in tax breaks—meaning Americans across the country were hit with a tab to support high living in the Penn State athletic department.

A study by Bloomberg News found that in 2010, all colleges and universities combined received $998 million in athletic donations. Much of the "donations" were for luxury boxes and insider privileges. Assuming most donors were high-income, this would have generated around $300 million in federal and state deductions—a sizable hidden subsidy to collegiate sports, which is already rolling in money.

IN THE EARLY 1950s, AROUND 20 million spectators per year went to a college football game. By 2012, attendance would reach 50 million, versus the 17 million who attended an NFL contest. NFL spectators spend more per capita than college football spectators, as many college games are informal Division III affairs. Still, college football has advanced to a nearly three-to-one margin over the NFL for paid attendance. That's serious business.

But in a five-hundred-channels era there always will be more customers who will watch at home than attend any type of sports event. Most of the big money generated by college football comes from television, just as most of the NFL's income is television money. NFL ratings are the pinnacle of the television business, but their rate of growth is flat; NCAA ratings keep climbing, enough so that combined viewer numbers for college football may pass professional football.

The 1984 Supreme Court decision that decentralized control over college football broadcasting meant a free-for-all on the airwaves. For the opening week of college football in 2012, forty-two games were shown on regular networks, cable and "sports tier" cable in the Washington, DC, area, with even more available via pay-per-view. The money generated is spectacular.

In 2010, ABC and ESPN agreed to pay the Atlantic Coast Conference, home to Virginia Tech, about $13 million per year per member school to televise ACC sporting events, mainly football. Just two years later, ESPN voluntarily ripped up the freshly signed deal and agreed to pay $18 million per season per member college to the ACC. The 38 percent rise in payments per school, merely from 2010 to

2012, reflected the accelerating popularity of football, and the attendant value of television rights.

The athletic balance sheet of a typical ACC member institution, Florida State, shows $8.1 million spent on NCAA scholarships and $11.7 million on coaching salaries, athletic facilities, travel and overhead. Summing the expenses, it costs Florida State about $20 million annually to field football and basketball teams, plus swimming, track, tennis, men's and women's golf, regular women's volleyball and bikini beach volleyball, which the NCAA demurely calls "sand volleyball." The outfits have nothing to do with it! These figures mean the ESPN TV-rights deal alone not only covers the entire cost of NCAA scholarships at Florida State, the ESPN payment covers just shy of all athletic expenses at the school.

Virginia Tech and other ACC member colleges show similar numbers. ESPN in effect pays for every ACC athletic scholarship, along with most other costs of ACC college athletics, in exchange for the fees ESPN receives from selling its signals to cable carriers, and the advertising revenue that ABC and ESPN receive from broadcasting football. After ESPN pays the basic cost of athletics at ACC universities, game-day revenue, TV-rights deals with other networks, logo fees from shoe and apparel companies—that's all gravy for the universities.

Television numbers for other conferences are similarly impressive. Each school of the Big 12—Texas, Oklahoma, Oklahoma State and other football powers—receives roughly $20 million annually from rights deals with ESPN and Fox. Colleges of the Pac-12—USC, UCLA, Oregon, others—receive nearly $21 million annually from ESPN and Fox. Members of the Southeastern Conference, which often produces the highest-rated college football broadcasts, receive about $17 million annually from CBS and ESPN, a figure expected to rise. The contracts contain escalator clauses that could push the payouts higher, if college football ratings continue their skyward course.

In 2011, a seemingly opéra-bouffe realignment of college football conferences occurred. Pitt and Syracuse jumped from the Big East to the ACC. Temple, Memphis, Houston and other colleges agreed to join the Big East over a series of years; Boise State, located in Idaho, also agreed to join the Big "East." Nebraska jumped from the Big 12 to the Big Ten, while Colorado left the Big 12 for the Pac-12, with Texas A&M and Missouri leaving the Big 12 to join the SEC TCU left the Mountain West, announcing it would join the Big East; then, before ever playing a game in that conference, departed the Big East to join the Big 12. Boise State also left the Big East without ever playing a game there.

This musical chairs was dictated by money: each time a conference realigned, altering membership, that created a justification for tearing up existing television contracts. In some cases, "exit fees" were involved. In 2011, West Virginia, a public university supported by West Virginia taxpayers, paid an $11 million exit fee to break its contract with the Big East and join the Big 12, while Nebraska, a public university supported by Nebraska taxpayers, paid a $9 million exit fee to break its contract with the Big 12 and join the Big Ten. Both colleges felt they would come out ahead by creating a pretext to redo their television-rights fees: in 2012, Big Ten member schools each received $24.6 million in television-rights payments, almost all derived from football. So is switching conferences smart economics? The trouble is that "coming out ahead" in this sense may mean using taxpayer subsidies from a university's general fund to increase television-rights payments specifically for the athletic department.

Along with voting to switch football conferences, the University of Nebraska regents also approved $56 million to expand the Cornhuskers' football stadium. This came a few days after the state legislature cut $50 million in funding for academics from the state university budget.

While college football conference television fees were climbing, a new form of broadcasting developed. The Big Ten formed its own Big Ten Network. Followers of Michigan, Illinois, Northwestern or other colleges can pay their cable carriers a fee to watch the football games that ABC, ESPN or CBS don't show. Contracts allow the primary buyer, in this case ESPN, to choose each week whatever are perceived as the most important Big Ten games. Whatever conference games are left air on the Big Ten Network. The Pac-12 followed by founding its own network with a similar second-helpings format. Soon all major college football conferences may have in-house networks, generating still more football income.

Why stop at conferences? The University of Texas formed Longhorn Network, with production and broadcast work done on contract by ESPN, which remits to the University of Texas $11 million annually, in exchange for ad revenue and cable fees. Since the University of Texas spends about $8.5 million per year on athletic scholarships, Longhorn Network alone pays for the tuition, room and board of all Longhorn athletes, with the gravy flowing thereafter.

What can you see on 24-7 Longhorn Network? Just one football game per year; all others are already sold to CBS, ESPN or Fox. Longhorn Network airs pretty much everything else in University of Texas athletics—baseball, softball, women's soccer, track, golf. If college kids do it wearing burnt orange, Longhorn Network shows it. If you'd like to tune in to University of Texas football players in shorts and helmets ("going bobblehead") when running cone and ladder drills, you can— the team's practices are shown on Longhorn Network. People watch.

YET FOR ALL THE TELEVISION income, booster largess and tax favors, many big-college athletic programs bleed money directly from academics—an inconvenient truth that often is not disclosed.

Federal figures show that despite fielding a football team that won the 2012 BCS title game, realizing the maximum in television and bowl revenues, the University of Alabama athletic department drew a $6 million subsidy from the university's general fund that year. The University of Florida transferred a $5 million subsidy from academics to athletics in the 2010–11 school year—meaning that $6 million "donation" to academics that the school's independent-business athletic department boasts about actually is a $1 million donation, and that a net of just 1 percent of University of Florida athletic income supports academics.

Virginia Tech's athletic department drew $8 million from general university funds in the most recent year; athletics at the universities of Iowa, Kentucky and Michigan received general-fund subsidies. The athletic department of the University of Maryland drew $16 million from main university funds, even as the university was raising tuition and cutting classes. The Rutgers athletic department drew $29 million from the school's general fund, even as Rutgers was raising tuition and cutting classes; Oregon State athletics drew $18 million from the school's general fund. Of major football programs, only LSU, Ohio State, Oklahoma, Nebraska, Texas and Texas A&M operate without subsidies from general university funds, federal figures show.

General-fund subsidies originate with regular students—on whom far less is being spent than on athletes to begin with. At most major universities, regular students paying up to $50,000 annually are forbidden to work out in the athletes' weight rooms, forbidden to jog on their training fields, forbidden to eat at their special training tables. It's great that Virginia Tech has a well-appointed lounge where football players can relax, and a special study area with forty workstations—but why should regular-tuition students be denied entry? Many regular students at large universities would like to dine on nutritionist-supervised athletic-training-table dinners; why are only the athletes offered this privilege? Bad enough that universities have facilities open only to NCAA athletes; worse, regular students pay for them. Often the subsidies come from mysterious "activity fees" tacked on to the invoices mailed to parents, without clarification that the regular students who are being billed are banned from the activities. Sometimes, sports subsidies are deducted straight from tuition payments—money parents thought they were spending on their children's education, and that the schools dressed up to look like educational costs, is instead subsidizing the athletic department.

Old Dominion University in Virginia, a Division IAA school that plans to join football's Division I in 2015, has been charging students a $549 annual athletic fee—not for intramural athletics in which they might participate, but for gridiron play. The University of Virginia charges students $657 a year to support its football program, a number folded into the tuition price to hide it from parents. The University of Maryland charges students $398 annually for football support. William Kirwan, chancellor of the Maryland state university system, notes, "There would be general outrage if the University of Maryland assessed all students a $398 annual fee to support the orchestra. Yet somehow sports fees are sacrosanct."

The $29 million Rutgers tuition subsidy for athletics worked out to nearly $1,000 per student. In-state tuition that year—Rutgers is a public university—was $12,754, meaning about 8 percent of "tuition" charges paid by parents actually were charges for NCAA athletics. Had Rutgers not spent $29 million to subsidize sports, it could have added about 150 full-time faculty.

Virginia Tech charges students $257 annually for NCAA athletics, less than most big colleges, in part because Frank Beamer is content with roughly half the salary demanded by other football coaches at his level. But this only means the Hokies' situation is less offensive than at other large institutions.

In 2012, Rutgers and the University of Maryland announced they would leave the Big East and ACC, respectively, for the Big Ten conference, because the Big Ten pays schools several million dollars more per year in football television revenue. At a news conference announcing the shift, UMD president Wallace Loh declared with a straight face the reason was not football money but that joining the Big Ten would improve UMD's academic standing. Yet leaving the ACC meant withdrawing from affiliation with Duke and the University of Virginia, two of the nation's foremost colleges.

Sports-conference affiliation has almost nothing to do with how students are taught in any case. When a college president issues public statements that are obvious lies, the school's faculty, alumni and chancellor ought to feel ashamed. But on the modern large-university scene, if football money is involved, all other considerations are waived.

The behind-the-scenes factor was that News Corporation, owner of the Fox networks, is the majority shareholder in Big Ten Network. Having Rutgers and UMD join the Big Ten adds the New York City and Washington, DC, television markets to Big Ten Network, allowing News Corporation to sell that product to cable carriers in two of the nation's largest regions.

So did the University of Maryland at least come out ahead? To realize several million more per year in football money, UMD had to pay a $52 million exit fee to the ACC. The college hoped to get the fee reduced, but failing that, planned to stiff Maryland taxpayers for the $52 million—in effect, removing $52 million from the state's budget for public education. When the University of Maryland regents voted to approve this swindle, they met in secret, in defiance of a Maryland state law requiring that regents' meetings be open. The regents declared they would not comply with the law because the situation was "an emergency." The emergency was that the regents did not want the public to know they were shifting taxpayers' money from education to football.

THE ROARING RIVERS OF SUBSIDIES flowing through big-college football—taxpayer funding, deductions for "donations" that are actually entertainment expenses, tuition charges to regular students, free labor from players—is the core reason high pay to college coaches is offensive.

If an NFL coach earns $5 million a year, that is the judgment of the marketplace, since while pro football stadia may be built with public money, otherwise the league functions along free-enterprise lines. Princely salaries for NCAA football coaches often are rationalized by their institutions as being free-market results. But the money used originates with taxpayer funds, public subsidies and hidden fees on students. This is so even if a college football coach's pay comes mainly from the school's athletic foundation, a booster club or apparel endorsement fees. Dollars are fungible, and every dollar that a big university's alumni pay to a coach, or that Nike pays to a coach, is a dollar the university's general fund does not receive.

• In 2012, Alabama head coach Nick Saban signed a contract that pays him $5.6 million annually, plus country-club memberships and use of a private jet, plus health insurance and pension benefits funded by taxpayers, because Alabama is a state university. Saban's haul works out to $66,000 per year per scholarship football player under his supervision. A month after the Saban deal was finalized, the Alabama legislature cut $150 million from the state's budget for public schools and universities.

At the news conference announcing his contract, Saban repeatedly used the royal plural, saying, "We wanted to stay at Alabama. We're staying at Alabama and we're not interested in going anyplace else." His deal includes about $700,000 in potential bonuses for victories and about $75,000 in potential bonuses for player GPAs, suggesting that at the University of Alabama, football is nine times more important than education.

• In 2012, Urban Meyer signed a contract that will pay him at least $4 million annually as head football coach at Ohio State. Meyer's deal includes potential bonuses of $550,000 for victories and $150,000 for improvement of the team's average GPA, suggesting that at Ohio State, football is 3.7 times more important than education. Meyer also receives a $25,000 annual car allowance, reported by the school as if this were somehow different from income; fully paid membership in two country clubs; thirty-five hours per year of personal use of Ohio State's private jet; and a $250,000 bonus for moving expenses, suggesting Meyer needed to move a paddle-wheel steamboat to Columbus.

- In 2011, Jimbo Fisher signed a contract as head coach of Florida State football. Fisher received $2.8 million in pay, plus potential bonuses worth up to $755,000 for victories and $50,000 for academics, suggesting that at Florida State, football is fifteen times more important than education. Fisher gets half his "academics" bonus if the team achieves an Academic Progress Rate of at least 925. Under the Academic Progress Rate, an NCAA disinformation system to be explained in detail later in this book, 925 is the equivalent of a D average. Florida State considers a D average to be a step forward for its football team!

- In 2011, Brady Hoke signed a contract that pays him $3.3 million annually as head football coach at Michigan. He can receive up to $500,000 in bonuses for victories, with the victory bonus rising in each year he remains on the job.

  Michigan had to cover a $1 million buyout to San Diego State University because it hired Hoke while he was still under contract to that school; for some reason, Michigan believed a coach who broke his promises to his previous employer will be honest with his new employer. In 2008, Michigan covered a $2.5 million buyout to West Virginia University when the Wolverines hired their previous head coach, Rich Rodriguez, while he was still under contract elsewhere. For some reason, Michigan believed that a coach who broke his promises to his previous employer would be honest with his new employer. Discovering this was not the case, in 2010 Michigan gave Rodriguez a $2.5 million severance to fire him. Michigan, a taxpayer-subsidized public university, wasted a total of $6 million in buyout and severance payments in a short time, in order to end up with the services of a second consecutive head coach who had walked out on his previous employer.

- In 2009, TCU imposed a 10 percent across-the-board spending reduction—excluding football coaching salaries.

- In 2011, Texas Tech froze salaries for faculty, then awarded a $500,000 raise to football coach Tommy Tuberville.

- In 2011, with the California state budget in meltdown—layoffs, education cuts, $14 billion in short-term debt and $600 billion in unfunded liabilities—Cal head coach Jeff Tedford was the state's highest-paid employee, with a $2.8 million salary. His salary dwarfed that of California's second-highest-paid employee, Ronald Busuttil, who was merely chief transplant surgeon at UCLA Medical Center.

- While head football coach at Penn State, Joe Paterno often said he declined raises because he was content with a modest income. This seeming humility became part of the Paterno mythology. Shortly after his death, Penn State paid Paterno's estate $5.5 million for his final year of coaching—that turned out to be his actual salary— the State of Pennsylvania paid Paterno's estate $13.4 million in deferred compensation. When Paterno said he was declining raises, what was really happening was that the value of the raises was being deferred—so he could bask in admiration for feigned humility.

SUBSIDIZED RICHES ARE ONLY ONE factor in the financial lives of many big-college football coaches. Professors Raquel Alexander of Washington and Lee University and James Gentry of the University of Kansas have found that many college football coaches utilize the tax subterfuge of having their salaries sent to corporations they control, allowing them to claim write-offs on everyday living expenses. In theory many people could employ this subterfuge, but tax-law details and legal fees make the maneuver most appealing to those with high incomes and an at-least-on-paper appearance of nonprofit activity.

Gentry and Alexander found that LSU coach Les Miles, who in 2011 received $4.4 million at a public university, and his wife have registered five corporations to receive his income; the only apparent reason to go to this trouble is to avoid taxes. Saban's income, they found, goes to a virtual corporation called Sideline Inc. Miles and Saban roll in money subsidized by the taxes of average people, while taking steps to avoid paying their own fair share of taxes.

As funding for education is cut, assistant football coaches also are doing well. In 2012, USC defensive coordinator Monte Kiffin was paid $1.5 million, while Alabama defensive coordinator Kirby Smart made $950,000. The president of the University of Alabama made $487,000 that year. In 2010, Erick Smith of *USA Today* found that twenty-six assistant college football coaches earned more than any faculty members at their universities.

The athletic directors of big colleges sign these coaching deals, and they are not fools—athletic directors know how exaggerated football salaries have become. From their point of view, it doesn't matter.

At many universities there is no fiscal discipline regarding football: No one on the board of trustees ever brings up such trivial matters as education versus sports. Hiring an expensive coach excites the alumni, implying success to come, and raises the program's recruiting power. If a $5-million-a-year coach arrives in a private jet to woo an impressionable teenager—former University of Maryland football coach Ralph Friedgen used a university-paid helicopter for recruiting—while a $1-million-a-year coach arrives in rental car, who will have the inside track?

Expensive coaches may fail. A study by William Tsitsos and Howard Nixon of Towson University found that when college teams hire a football coach who receives significantly more pay than the coach he replaces, 60 percent of the schools do no better than they did with the lower-price coach, and 20 percent do worse. But lavish pay for the football coach covers the athletic director's tracks: "It's not my fault, I hired the most expensive guy out there."

And if money rains on the football coach and his assistants, shouldn't the athletic director to whom they report be highly paid too? Alabama athletic director Mal Moore earned about $700,000 in

2010–11. Athletic director David Brandon of Michigan, the school that wasted $6 million on mistakes in coaching hires, was paid $705,000 that year. In 2011–12 Jeremy Foley, athletic director at the University of Florida, received $1.5 million. Considering the tuition subsidies from the general fund to University of Florida athletics, middle-class and average families sending their children to the University of Florida were compelled to make Jeremy Foley wealthy, so that in return he would do for them—absolutely nothing.

IF A MAJOR FOOTBALL PROGRAM has a good season, a bowl game awaits. Bowl games are viewed as the pinnacle of the college football profession. They are also the pinnacle of money shenanigans. Bowl games have no educational purpose: they are strictly revenue-seeking businesses. Yet Congress allows them to masquerade as nonprofits, paying no taxes as those with insider positions enrich themselves.

Most bowl games have a CEO and a "bowl committee"—people who receive cash, luxury travel or both throughout the year for the incredibly onerous task of staging one football game in a glamour locale. The Orange Bowl, held annually in Miami, has a CEO, a president, two "vice chairs," a secretary, a treasurer, sixteen bowl-committee members and twenty-two corporate members, all benefiting from the tax exemptions that attach to impersonating a civic philanthropy. In 2011, the Orange Bowl disclosed to the IRS that it had increased the salary of its CEO, Eric Poms, from $350,000 to $500,000, owing to increased responsibilities—he had shouldered the super-onerous task of supervising two football games in a single year!

In 2011, the Fiesta Bowl, held annually in Arizona, fired CEO John Junker—to call the manager of a single football game a CEO is absurd glorification—after it was revealed he was paying himself $600,000 a year plus using Fiesta Bowl funds to cover his country-club memberships, while charging a $33,000 birthday party for himself to his expense account. Junker also put on his expense account a $1,200 evening at a lap-dance club, calling this a "security site planning" meeting.

Worried about their bowl going out of business, Fiesta Bowl committee members hired a law firm to investigate Junker's actions. The firm's report showed Junker asked assistants to donate $47,000 to Arizona politicians, then used expense accounts to reimburse the assistants. The report showed the Fiesta Bowl spent at least $1.3 million on an annual "Fiesta Frolic," a junket of hotel rooms, golf, spa services and fancy dinners for cronies, politicians and their spouses. The Fiesta Frolic masqueraded as a business meeting. No one could possibly stage one single football game without a week at a resort!

In 2012, Junker pleaded guilty to a federal felony charge; six other Fiesta Bowl officials pled guilty to state or federal crimes. The Fiesta Bowl remains in business and still holds an annual junket, though it now carries the sedate name Valley of the Sun Experience. The new Fiesta Bowl CEO, Robert Shelton, is paid $455,000 annually, plus bonuses, for managing one single football game. The Fiesta Bowl remains tax-exempt.

In 1972, the Internal Revenue Service issued a brief letter calling the Fiesta Bowl a tax-exempt 501(c)(3) organization, the category for entities with "a charitable or educational purpose." At the time, many college bowl games yielded little revenue—there would not have been much to tax in any case. Four decades later, the Fiesta Bowl and its fellow BCS events have become licenses to print green sheets of paper bearing pictures of former presidents. The Fiesta Bowl received about $30 million in 2012 in broadcast-rights fees, plus millions more from ticket sales and concessions, and ended 2011 with $32 million in assets, according to its own reports.

Yet the IRS has never revisited its 1972 opinion, nor similar letters making other football bowls tax-exempt. Nor has Congress altered the tax exemption of football bowls. The IRS does not act on bowl-game tax exemptions because the corporate sponsors are politically connected. Congress and state legislatures do not act because bowl officials make political donations, and most politicians are more concerned with free seats in luxury boxes than with doing fiscal harm to typical voters.

The Fiesta Bowl is not by any stretch of the imagination an educational organization; it is used as a subterfuge for the personal enrichment of persons such as John Junker and Robert Shelton, and to confer insider status on the bowl committee's cronies. Most big-college football programs only peripherally aid education; some actively detract from it. Yet the coaches and athletic directors involved draw substantial sums, often at the expense of taxpayers and schools' general funds.

Why do they do this? Because they can. Until such time as public attitudes change, those at the top of the college football pyramid will keep getting away with whatever they can.

This is troubling not just because college coaches and athletic directors are paid too much while budgets for education are cut. It's troubling because universities are supposed to set a shining example for society. Instead, many of the nation's leading universities use football to broadcast a message of cynicism and low standards.

The next chapter: Does the outsize role of money in college football mean the players are being exploited?

5

ARE COLLEGE FOOTBALL PLAYERS EXPLOITED?

At age twenty, Akiem Hicks was, according to the NCAA, a very, very bad person. Hicks's high school GPA was unimpressive, which initially held him back from Division I football, redirecting him to Sacramento City College, a juco—scouts' slang for "junior college"—near his hometown of Elk Grove, California. But grades were not the reason for the NCAA's wrath.

Hicks was a very, very bad person because he crossed the NCAA by failing to abide by every line of its 426 pages of petty-tyrant rules. In 2009, after Hicks spent two years at the juco, an assistant coach at Louisiana State University, a Division I power, made "impermissible phone calls" to him, using a cell phone that was not on the list of phones that LSU annually submits to the NCAA. Hicks was such a bad person that when his phone rang, he answered!

Speaking on the phone was appalling enough—Virginia Tech records all phone calls from coaches to possible recruits and keeps the tapes five years, to refute any accusation of impermissible phone calls. There was more to Hicks's shocking transgressions. Offered a scholarship

to LSU, Hicks explained that he had little money, having made the
mistake of not being born to affluent parents. He accepted plane fare, then
lived for a few months in a vacant Baton Rouge apartment owned by an
LSU booster, not paying the full market rent. Prospective LSU students
from well-to-do families don't worry about paying their travel expenses
to college. So why didn't Hicks arrange to be born into a well-to-do
family? That worked for other kids!

Finally, after accepting help whose sum reached *several hundred dollars*, Hicks let an LSU student buy him a meal. The horror! The
NCAA's bylaw 16.5.2.h reads, "An institution may provide fruit, nuts
and bagels to a student-athlete at any time." But other meals, even sandwiches and cookies, are subject to elaborate regulations.

In 2010, Secretary of Education Arne Duncan publicly ridiculed
the bagel rule, saying the NCAA paid more attention to snacks than
to academics. Was the NCAA embarrassed to be called out by the
secretary of education? No, because the NCAA is beyond embarrassment. It has evolved an elaborate system to convert the free labor of
young men into luxury living for NCAA and college-conference officials. Petroleum-cartel officials fantasize about the kind of market
stranglehold enjoyed by the NCAA. Energy customers can buy from
a broad range of suppliers; the customers who want to televise major-college athletics buy NCAA-branded products exclusively. The games
must be of high quality. Whether education is of high quality is not
the NCAA's concern.

The Hicks case is not some isolated instance. In 2008, the Raleigh, North Carolina, *News & Observer* reported that University of
North Carolina football and men's basketball players were enrolled in
e-mail Swahili "courses" that had no instructors, never met and always led to A's. Eventually, an investigation conducted by a former
governor of North Carolina found the school had courses that required no work, which many football and basketball players enrolled
in so as not to cut into athletic time, and found many altered grades with
forged signatures. Some professors were fired or forced to retire, the

football coach was fired, and the University of North Carolina was, as it should have been, profoundly embarrassed.

The NCAA sanctioned the University of North Carolina football program for a second scandal, involving sports agents, that was a factor in the firing of the coach. The NCAA took no action against the school for its extremely low athletic educational standards, though did elaborately investigate, then permanently ban from NCAA sports, a football player named Michael McAdoo. He couldn't understand the "class," so asked a former tutor to help him with an assignment: the tutor ended up doing the bibliography, which would be an honor-code violation at any university. Fitting punishment might have been a letter of reprimand. Hilariously, an attorney for the NCAA declared that McAdoo had to be banished because "the NCAA takes academic fraud very seriously"—yet was silent on the university's systematic offerings of fake courses. McAdoo was a convenient fall guy, while the University of North Carolina is a moneyed institution whose cash flow had to be preserved.

There are no words strong enough to express how little the NCAA cares about whether the football or men's basketball players who generate economic returns also receive an education. To the NCAA, the barometric pressure on the planet Neptune matters more than whether football and men's basketball athletes receive educations.

LEARNING IN THE HICKS CASE OF THE DEEPLY SHOCKING phone calls and the free cheeseburger, the NCAA conducted an investigation that must have cost a hundred times as much as the benefits Hicks received. Acting without fear or favor, the supersleuths from NCAA headquarters in Indianapolis discovered the smoking Post-it note: several times Hicks called an LSU football office assistant who had been nice to him, to ask if she'd heard if his scholarship offer was going to go through. When she saw his messages, she returned the calls. The horror! NCAA rules say that potential enrollees may call colleges, but in most instances colleges can't return the calls. This rule dates from the time when long-distance service was expensive—the logic was, make the kids' families be the ones to pay for the call.

The NCAA got to the bottom of those returned phone calls and banished Hicks permanently from NCAA sports. Hicks spent a year working in a corporate call center, then enrolled at the University of Regina in Canada, beyond the reach of the NCAA. Completing school, Hicks was drafted, in 2012, by the New Orleans Saints. With luck, he will achieve the three-year average NFL career. The kicker: in 2013, the NCAA eliminated the phone-call restrictions it used to throw Hicks out of American collegiate football.

TRYING TO HUSTLE UP A scholarship is an extremely grave offense, according to the NCAA, if you are a penniless prospective college student. If you're a wealthy head football coach who's thinking of breaking his word, putting yourself first is fine. Around the time the NCAA investigated Hicks's shocking attempt to enroll at LSU, Les Miles, the head football coach there, while under contract to LSU, talked to the president of the University of Michigan about that school's vacant head-coaching position.

Miles was a hot commodity, as LSU was about to face Ohio State in football's national title game. For making a few phone calls, a poor kid named Akiem Hicks was banished from the NCAA. For making his phone calls, the millionaire Miles was rewarded with a contract extension, raising his pay to $3.7 million annually; Michigan's interest gave him leverage. Later his deal would be raised again, to $4.4 million annually, plus the promise of a stunning $19 million severance payment should he be fired. The big severance number essentially made Miles a tenured football coach.

When Hicks tried to shop for his best deal, the NCAA was outraged. When Miles shopped for his best deal, that behavior was totally fine with the NCAA—as was LSU's 44 percent graduation rate for African-American football players for the year in which the Tigers defeated Ohio State, winning the national title.

While the NCAA took no action regarding low educational standards at big-money, football-factory universities whose games regularly air on national television, woe unto the Occidental College women's volleyball team! In 2013, the NCAA dropped the hammer on Occidental women's volleyball—a Division III program that does not award athletic scholarships. Occidental, the NCAA declared in full gravitas, "arranged for a booster to provide travel, lodging and meals to student-athletes." Amusing enough is the notion that lurking in the shadows is a wealthy booster for Occidental women's volleyball, which annually squares off against the likes of Claremont-Mudd-Scripps and Cal State San Marcos. The NCAA's sanction announcement read like a *Saturday Night Live* sketch, pronouncing "public reprimand and censure" for Occidental, and declaring "the vacation of volleyball records," which makes it sound as if the records are on their way to Los Cabos.

The NCAA comes down like a ton on bricks on Occidental College, which has a strong academic reputation and almost no sports revenue, while averting its eyes from low graduation rates at the big-money football factories. Auburn has fake classes for football players, Occidental has a booster who pays hotel bills: Occidental is the one punished. But then to the NCAA, the price of sorghum in Tajikistan matters more than education.

THE NETWORKS THAT BROADCAST COLLEGE sports feel the same way. ABC, CBS, ESPN, Fox and NBC almost never speak the words *graduation rate* while airing college football. Mentioning this is bad for business! Though, the networks do sometimes run little sidebar snippets about what a great student some member of a team is, in order to generate a pleasing impression that all is well.

Richard Southall, a professor at the University of North Carolina, found that at the sixty-four colleges that sent men's teams to the 2012 March Madness tournament, black athletes were 33 percent less likely to graduate than black nonathletes attending the same schools. (This figure takes into account basketball players who leave college early for

the NBA.) Southall has also found that in 2010, the average graduation rate for Division I football players was 55 percent, compared to an
average male graduation rate of 68 percent at the same colleges. The
television audience wants to be entertained, not reminded that players
are being taken advantage of. For the NCAA and its broadcast-network
partners, and *partner* is the term both sides use, mentioning graduation
rates is bad for business.

LET'S NOT JUST BLAME THE NCAA. To many big universities and their
boards of regents, whether revenue-sport athletes receive educations is
less important than, say, tide tables for the Gulf of Bothnia. All that
matters is whether the money flows.

When the football program causes public controversy that threat-
ens the money flow, many schools just cut to the chase and fabricate.
In 2011, the Ohio State program was enmeshed in a football scandal
that led to a bowl-game ban. University president Gordon Gee, paid $2
million annually by a taxpayer-subsidized school, declared Buckeye
athletics should be viewed sympathetically because Ohio State football
"ranked first in academic performance among the nation's top twenty-
five teams."

Don't you feel better now? But the statement was a lie. Gee's office
told me he was citing a ranking of football programs by Academic
Progress Rate. Ohio State had indeed just received an NCAA commen-
dation for improving its APR. But the Academic Progress Rate does
not measure "academic performance," rather, measures change from
a previous score. What happened was that the prior Ohio State APR
was awful, while the new APR rose to okay. Gee was mischaracterizing
the content of a source document, an offense that would cause any college student to fail a course. In a spin-cycle world, all that mattered
was that Gee lied and got away with it.

Other colleges noticed! A few months later, a football scandal began at the University of Miami. Donna Shalala, president of the school,
tried to squirm her way out by declaring, "Nationally, the academic

achievements of our student-athletes are mentioned in the same breath and spirit as Notre Dame and Stanford." Allie Grasgreen, a reporter for the invaluable newsletter *Inside Higher Ed*, showed Shalala's claim simply was not true: that year, Notre Dame and Stanford graduated an impressive 91 percent of scholarship athletes, while the University of Miami graduated 67 percent. The only person who mentions University of Miami academic achievements "in the same breath" as Stanford and Notre Dame is Shalala herself.

Caught in football scandals, the presidents of Ohio State and the University of Miami, major national institutions, bluffed their way out by saying things that weren't true. Major universities ought to feel ashamed when their presidents lie in public. But if football money is involved, university integrity goes out the window.

DON'T GET THE IMPRESSION THE NCAA penalizes only poor African-Americans. Beginning in 2009, the NCAA conducted what the organization described as a "twenty-two-month investigation" of University of Tennessee men's basketball coach Bruce Pearl, a well-off white man, who would be fired in 2011.

Pearl lied to the NCAA during the absurdly long investigation, and just as college presidents should never lie, neither should coaches. But what triggered the investigation and led to the fib? Aaron Craft, a talented high school basketball player, was visiting the University of Tennessee with his family. It was an "unofficial visit," meaning at the family's expense. Craft and some relatives were invited to Pearl's house for a cookout. The barbecued chicken, coleslaw and corn bread consumed were, the NCAA ruled, an "improper benefit." High schoolers on campus visits cannot receive any item of value not offered to all students already enrolled. The rule is sensible as regardless envelopes of cash or Vegas weekends. In this case, the NCAA used a literalist reading to conclude that Pearl neglected to welcome the entire 21,250 University of Tennessee student body to the barbecue. Since any student may eat on campus but not all students were invited to Pearl's backyard, having the Craft family over for chicken was, the NCAA ruled, a major violation.

The lie Pearl told was that a blurry cell-phone photo of his shaking hands with Craft was taken on campus, not by his gas grill. The horror!

NCAA recruiting strictures don't distinguish between expensive, inappropriate gestures and routine hospitality such as providing dinner. Had Pearl offered no hospitality, then signed Craft and used him to win games, keeping Pearl's $3.1 million coaching salary flowing and sustaining the $7 million annual net profit the University of Tennessee enjoys from men's basketball, everything would have been fine. That, after all, is what the NCAA expects coaches to do—use kids to generate money, then keep the money. Paying for the Craft family's dinner violated the spirit of this enlightened arrangement.

Here's the kicker. In the course of the twenty-two-month investigation, culminating in a press conference with the chancellor of the University of Tennessee, the NCAA said nothing about the fact that Tennessee was graduating only 54 percent of its football players and 33 percent of its African-American men's basketball players.

THE NCAA IGNORES EDUCATION BUT comes down hard on violations of the exact wording of its petty rules because the petty rules are the NCAA's control structure. In 2012, the NCAA sanctioned the University of Nebraska for supplying professor-recommended books to football players—huffing that unless on a required reading list, books are an "impermissible benefit." In recent years, the NCAA has issued sanctions against Princeton and Cal Tech, colleges with excellent graduation rates and high academic standards, for trivial violations. Princeton's crime was that an alumnus paid part of the tuition for a tennis player who was a family friend. Shouldn't helping kids pay for college be lauded? To the NCAA, this was a "major violation." Something the NCAA frowns upon—getting an education—was involved.

While Princeton and Cal Tech were being sanctioned, the NCAA said nothing about the University of Arizona, a sports powerhouse, graduating 41 percent of its African-American football players and 25 percent of its African-American men's basketball players; said nothing about the University of Mississippi, school of Super Bowl MPV Eli Manning and of Michael Oher, hero of *The Blind Side*, graduating 52 percent of its African-American football players.

The NCAA was so mad at Bruce Pearl for not showing obeisance to its authority in petty matters that Pearl was effectively banned from college coaching. Yet the NCAA has never taken any action regarding University of Kentucky men's basketball coach John Calipari, whose prior wins at the University of Massachusetts were "vacated" owing to cash payments to a player, and whose prior wins at the University of Memphis were "vacated" because a star player faked his SAT scores.

William Kirwan, head of the Knight Commission, is a University of Kentucky graduate. "I bleed blue [Kentucky's color], but I could not make myself watch the 2012 March Madness championship game with Kentucky in it," he says. "Calipari is disgusting, Everywhere he goes, he makes a mockery of the whole concept of academics in college sports. And he gets away with it because the NCAA does nothing, the networks say nothing." Indeed, the CBS broadcast of the 2012 March Madness final game showed many adoring camera angles of Calipari pacing the courtside—great for his recruiting—but was nearly silent regarding his stained record. All that matters to the NCAA and to sports broadcasters is that Calipari assembles exciting teams that generate revenue.

In the rare cases when the NCAA takes substantive action, it first delays as long as possible. The NCAA sat for five years on information about serious violations at USC, before finally putting the school on probation and in effect revoking the Heisman Trophy awarded in 2005 to Reggie Bush. The NCAA took two years to act regarding medium-strength violations at Ohio State. The NCAA knows that the longer it drags its heels, the more money flows into the bank at big universities.

In 2012, the NCAA required just ten days to act after a report by former FBI director Louis Freeh detailed extensive corruption at the football program and administration of Penn State. Finally, rapid action by the NCAA! But it took the systematic rape of children, followed by a cover-up by Penn State's highest officials, to push the NCAA to quick action. Even then the Penn State penalties were calculated to ensure Penn State football would not be jeopardized. Systematic rape of children was, the NCAA thought, not good; but not enough for the NCAA to feel a college sports program had gone too far.

FUNDAMENTALLY, THE NCAA IS A business. Its business is converting the popularity of college athletics, and the good standing of higher education in American society, into luxury living for college coaches, presidents, athletic directors and NCAA officialdom. NCAA president Mark Emmert makes $1.6 million per year, money that wouldn't go into his pocket unless the NCAA power position were maintained. Libby Sander of the *Chronicle of Higher Education* reported in 2010 that below Emmert some fourteen NCAA officials averaged $429,000 annually in pay. Emmert and the other top NCAA executives realize their personal wealth partly by treating sports excitement as more important than education, including educations for low-income African-Americans. In many businesses, the CEO wallows in money as average workers suffer. That is also the NCAA arrangement.

The members of the board of directors of the NCAA, who approve Emmert's pay, all are presidents of universities or chancellors of state university systems: meaning it is in their interest for Emmert's salary to be high because the number will be used in the compensation surveys upon which their own incomes are based.

You've surmised of course that the NCAA is tax-exempt, enriching its executives while masquerading as a philanthropy. That $10.8 billion CBS and Turner Broadcasting have agreed to pay the NCAA? Mostly tax free. "The primary purpose of the NCAA is to maintain intercollegiate athletics as an integral part of the educational program," the organization's mission statement declares—in garbled grammar that suggests "the educational program" did not do NCAA officials much good. The actual primary purpose of the NCAA is to divert money from unpaid athletes to overpaid NCAA executives, college coaches and administrators.

YET IS THE NCAA to blame for all that ails collegiate sports? Some faint praise is due.

Gymnastics, fencing, soccer, tennis—in the many college sports that lose money, scandals are rare, graduation rates are strong. So the NCAA does regulate some sports well. Colleges don't have to join the NCAA: they could opt for its lower-cost rival, the NAIA, or simply not offer intercollegiate sports. Big universities join the NCAA to have access to its structured competition, while even high-end academic colleges without football join the NCAA—Swarthmore is a member—because its blue-dot logo is prestigious.

Overall at public universities, athletes have a higher graduation rate than students as a whole. Most athletes are disciplined, possess good work habits and budget their time, qualities that lend themselves to classroom success.

But high graduation rates in the nonrevenue sports mask low rates in the sports where the money comes from. The NCAA never tires of noting, often in television advertising during high-profile college sports events, that athletes graduate at a higher rate than students generally; the NCAA just doesn't add that "revenue sport" athletes, the football and men's basketball players who make money for colleges, graduate at a lower rate than students generally.

Playing college football or basketball is a major commitment, but does not involve so much time that good graduation rates cannot be expected. Women's basketball shows this. College women's basketball has nearly identical practice and performance schedules to men's basketball. At women's basketball power Baylor University, 90 percent of African-American female basketball players graduate, versus 50 percent for the men's team. At the University of Connecticut, another basketball power, the most recent year saw 83 percent of African-American women's players graduate, versus 14 percent for the men's team.

The NCAA has most control over basketball because the NCAA holds the rights to the annual March Madness tournament. A 2010 contract among the NCAA, CBS and Turner Broadcasting pays the NCAA an average of $770 million annually for the broadcast rights. The NCAA funds itself from this considerable treasure chest, then distributes the largest share to member conferences based on basketball victories. A small fraction is distributed for academic support, but there are no GPA or graduation requirements. A winning college with terrible educational statistics receives more than a losing college whose players graduate.

Take a wild guess what effect this incentive structure has on athletic directors. Secretary of Education Duncan said in 2011, "It is time the NCAA revenue distribution plan stopped handsomely rewarding success on the court with multimillion-dollar payouts to schools that fail to meet minimum academic standards." The NCAA ignored the secretary of education.

Yet without the NCAA or something like it—and the present NCAA is so sullied, "something like it" is needed—the college sports landscape would devolve into a Wild West, where payola was the norm rather than the exception, where even more football and men's basketball players laughed at the notion of going to class. The NCAA does fight a rearguard action against that outcome. For the 2012 football season, Central Florida, North Carolina, Ohio State and Penn State were banned from bowl appearances owing to scandals. Were it not for the NCAA, even such modest consequences would not loom, and scandals would be more frequent.

BUT IT'S ONLY SCANDALS, NOT lack of emphasis on education, that the NCAA opposes. Scandals cause bad publicity. Lack of emphasis on education is practically built into the NCAA system. For decades, the organization mandated that member schools offer only year-by-year athletic aid. That meant a football or men's basketball player admitted as a freshman was not assured of an athletic scholarship as sophomore; a sophomore granted a scholarship was not assured of one as a junior; and so on. In the NCAA-standard year-to-year scholarship, a coach can yank an athlete's financial support at any time, without so much as stating a reason.

As a practical matter, the year-by-year NCAA scholarship grants the football or men's basketball coach control over a player's life. The player must please the coach or lose his scholarship, which likely means leaving school. If a player needs to study for an exam but also is due in the weight room, he goes to the weight room. If a football or men's basketball player is not motivated to get an education, the fault is his. But a player who really wants an education may accede to a coach's insistence that sports come first, skipping class or taking a rocks-for-jocks course load. Washington Redskins star Alfred Morris majored in "exercise science" at Florida Atlantic. Even Stanford advises football players to enroll in "Social Dances of North America" and similar courses, according to the good-government organization California Watch.

For NCAA coaches, having players ignore the classroom helps them focus on football, generating victories that mean money for the coach, but nothing for the athlete. If football players fail to graduate, there are no ramifications for the college or the coach.

The year-by-year scholarship was required by the NCAA; member schools could not opt out. The arrangement was intended to keep football and men's basketball players powerless, unable ever to say to a coach, "I don't like the way you treat people," or, heaven forbid, "I need more time to study." A drama or history student on regular financial aid might lose that aid if he or she stopped turning in work. But if the student simply did not do as well in college as expected, the financial aid office would not toss him or her aside. NCAA football and men's basketball players have been sent packing by colleges simply for not looking good in games.

When Barack Obama was elected president, he asked the Justice Department to open an investigation of the NCAA's year-to-year rule, which seemed to constitute restraint of trade. The logic: Forbidding one school from offering a multiyear scholarship to an athlete restrains its ability to compete with other schools for the same student, which in turn harms the consumer, in this case the consumer of higher education. Faced with Justice Department action, in 2011 the NCAA announced it would allow members to offer multiyear scholarships.

This reform is hardly a panacea—colleges might offer a multiyear scholarship, then if a football player never starts, yank the scholarship by claiming violation of team rules. How would you know what rules were violated? You wouldn't.

THE FAMILY EDUCATIONAL RIGHTS AND Privacy Act, passed by Congress in 1974, is a godsend to hypocrisy in collegiate athletics. The law was intended to block public access to the school records of minors. Since reading its fine print, colleges have used FERPA to deny release of information about the classroom performance or behavior of football and basketball players, though all college athletes are adults. As recently as 2003, many universities cited FERPA as grounds to refuse to disclose even aggregate (anonymous) graduation rates for football and basketball athletes.

Since a 2004 agreement with the federal Department of Education, colleges have reported aggregate graduation data to the NCAA, which publishes the numbers without names attached. Disclosure had the desired impact. Embarrassed by low graduation rates, many colleges are putting more effort into educating football players. Since first disclosure in 2004, overall NCAA graduation averages have slowly but steadily risen.

FERPA has been useful to NCAA programs not wanting bad press about football players. In 2008, Cam Newton, who would in 2011 be the number-one selection of the NFL draft, was dismissed from the University of Florida. The school refused to comment on why it was sending away one of the nation's most sought-after football players. Florida said it could not explain without violating Newton's FERPA rights, an extremely convenient thing for Florida to say, especially about an adult. Later, court documents showed that Newton had been arrested for theft; charges were dropped after he completed a court-ordered program. FERPA gave the University of Florida a pretext for saying nothing about the theft allegation, which it knew of. Probably bad-behavior issues by NCAA football players often are hushed up using FERPA—though since nothing is disclosed, who knows? And FERPA makes it nearly impossible to determine whether an athlete who claims to have a college degree actually does.

THE MULTIYEAR SCHOLARSHIP, JUST BECOMING common as this book is written, may shift some leverage toward the athlete who truly wants an education. A better solution would be a six-year scholarship. Any young man signing a football commitment to a Division I university would receive a contract promising six years of tuition, room and board—essentially an extra year, after the NCAA-maximum five years in athletics concludes. There could be a neutral-arbitration clause to prevent holders of six-year scholarships from just hanging around college without doing schoolwork, or to sanction them for violating reasonable team or college rules.

Many college football players give their all to the game and discover, as their eligibility expires, that the NFL has no interest. By then they are down to at most one remaining semester of tuition, room and board—too late to repair a bad transcript. With a six-year scholarship, when a football player's on-field career ended and the NFL did not come calling, he would have three more semesters of tuition, room and board to be a full-time college student, not distracted by sports. That should be sufficient to finish his credits and graduate.

A six-year rule would not cause onerous costs to colleges—about $700,000 annually if all football players who completed their eligibility stayed for a sixth year. Not all football players would need or even want a sixth year, so the actual cost should be lower. Except perhaps at the lowest-tier programs—the University of Akron Zips, Division I's perennial doormat, had just $6 million in football revenue in 2010–11—an extra $700,000 could be found, for the progressive purpose of allowing football players to complete their degrees after their strenuous physical efforts to make money for the school.

A college could protect itself against sixth-year costs by placing serious academic requirements on football players, so they graduate with the class they entered with and don't require extra semesters after taping their ankles for the final time.

In 2011 THE NCAA, CONCERNED about its reputation, put in force a dramatic new rule—that Division I football and men's basketball teams must have a 50 percent graduation rate to appear in bowl games or the March Madness tournament. Take that, critics of the NCAA! Now there must be at least one player who achieves a diploma for each one who leaves college empty-handed.

Well, not "now." The rule does not take effect until 2015. The Knight Commission had been urging the NCAA since 2001 to mandate at least 50 percent graduation for the rewards of postseason play. That it took the NCAA a full decade to agree to this extremely modest reform—and then implementation was delayed—is NCAA politics in a nutshell.

A quick check of the database shows that had the 50 percent graduation minimum gone into effect as soon as approved by the NCAA, it would have barred powerhouse universities Ohio State, Syracuse, USC and Connecticut from recent men's basketball tournaments, the horn of the NCAA's plenty. So the NCAA enacted the rule but postponed implementation, giving big-money programs years in which either to improve or find ways to finesse the new minimum.

FINDING THE LOOPHOLE TURNED OUT not to take five years but five minutes. What the NCAA announced to the press as a strict new 50 percent graduation rate actually was a requirement of an Academic Progress Rate of at least 930.

In 2003, knowing the dreaded day was near in which graduation statistics would become public information, the NCAA devised the Academic Progress Rate. The plan was to change the discussion from diplomas and GPA, which are easily understood, to the APR, a metric lacking any commonsense meaning. In 2012, the NCAA announced that overall APR for intercollegiate sports increased from 967 to 973. Do you have the slightest idea what 973 means in educational terms? Good, because you're not supposed to.

Kirwan says the APR is "intended to be incomprehensible." The NCAA says for the record that an APR system is needed because graduation rates do not reflect athletes leaving college for the pros. But each year only about 1.5 percent of men's basketball players leave early for an NBA tryout, while far less than 1 percent of football players leave early hoping to reach the NFL. The claim about early-departure athletes is a smoke screen.

The APR scale is configured so that utter academic malfeasance registers about a 900, and perfection registers 1,000. It's as if an SAT test, with a maximum of 800, had a minimum of 750. The result is that every university's APR number is within shouting distance of the maximum, making it seem that every big-college sports program is closing in on educational perfection. "Hey, Mom, I got a 750 on my SAT!"

Maggie Severns is an educational analyst for the New America Foundation, who produces an annual Academic BCS showing which college football programs would make the top bowl games if graduation rates were a factor. She explains, "The APR is not rigorous. Half the score is awarded merely for having athletes enrolled in school, so everyone starts with 500 of the 1,000 points." That means the NCAA's claimed scale of 1,000 actually is a scale of 500—and the 2012 average, 973, is not 97 percent of ideal as the NCAA likes to say, but 95 percent, as the 973 equates to 473 on a scale on 500.

It's a small difference, but careful use of numbers is the sort of thing you're supposed to learn in college. The NCAA, which sets itself up as an arbiter of higher education, regularly issues studies or press releases containing grammatical errors, and often errs with numbers. A high school core-credit GPA of at least 2 is required to be approved by the NCAA's athletic clearinghouse center, for example. But the NCAA doesn't say a GPA of 2 or perhaps of 2.0—its documents say a GPA of "2.000" is required. NCAA officials themselves seem never to have passed a core course in numerical literacy.

Exaggerating the top end of the scale is the least of the APR's problems. Severns continues, "The other 500 points are awarded not for graduation rates or classroom performance, but for keeping athletes eligible to play. Eligibility is usually defined as passing eight credit hours in a semester, and eight credit hours is a part-time student. The APR goals are so amazingly low that exceeding the minimum is rolling-off-a-log easy. Amazingly low goals tell nothing about education."

According to the NCAA, an APR of 930 means a college is on track to graduate 50 percent of scholarship athletes. Why a proxy, rather than simply use graduation rates? Because everyone knows what "failing to graduate at least 50 percent of athletes" means. "Failing to achieve an APR of 930" is gibberish.

If colleges somehow are unable to roll off the APR log, little happens. When Auburn won the BCS title in 2011, it was ranked 85th of 120 Division I football programs for APR. There were no consequences. In 2012, the NCAA sanctioned fifteen colleges for low APR numbers—but none were football factory universities and only one was a big-money men's basketball school. The NCAA lowered the boom on Hampton University and North Carolina A&T but took no action on the University of South Carolina, a mega-money sports mecca that finished 2012 ranked eighth but graduates fewer than half its African American football players. The most serious APR penalty ever assigned to a BCS-level football program came in 2011, when the NCAA temporarily reduced the University of Maryland from eighty-five to eighty-two football scholarships. Take that!

•   •   •

APOLOGISTS FOR NCAA INACTION MAINTAIN that big sports victories can't happen along with strict academics. Yet the 2010 college football season ended with Stanford facing Virginia Tech in the Orange Bowl and TCU facing Wisconsin in the Rose Bowl: all four schools have strong athletic-graduation rates. That year TCU finished second ranked in college football, Stanford finished fourth—above colleges that have powerhouse football teams but lax academic standards, such as Alabama, Arkansas and Mississippi State.

Many colleges educate their athletes and also win big games. The 2010 March Madness tournament ended in a title contest of Duke versus Butler: both have strong athletic-graduation rates. In 2009 Villanova and William & Mary, both with outstanding academics, met in the Division IAA football semifinals; Villanova went on to win the Division IAA title. Four of the first forty-two players chosen in the 2012 NFL draft were from Stanford. At the end of the 2012 college football season, Stanford won the Rose Bowl, Northwestern won the Gator Bowl and Vanderbilt won the Music City Bowl. The latter two victories came over Mississippi State and North Carolina State, schools with low academic standards for athletes. Colleges where the football players go to class were also the ones that won high-pressure bowl games.

A happy milestone was reached in November 2012, when Notre Dame became the first college to be ranked number one in the football polls and number one in football graduation rates, proving a university can have high academic standards for athletes and still win. While one would have expected the NCAA to crow about Notre Dame's accomplishment, instead it said little. Keep that bar low!

COACHES AND BOOSTERS NEVER DECLARE that low standards are needed to win, but that is what they would like spectators and lawmakers to believe. And in the end, coaches and boosters have more say in the matter than the NCAA.

No one huffs and puffs more about the NCAA than the head

coaches, boosters and athletic directors of big-college programs, who want it to seem they live in terror of CIA-like compliance officers from Indianapolis. The coach and his recruiting coordinator may have a sleepless night waiting to hear whether a four-star commit had his transcript and SAT/ACT scores certified by the NCAA. Once that happens, the player belongs to the college, which makes almost all decisions regarding what he does and whether he remains eligible. In 2013, after Johnny Manziel of Texas A&M won the Heisman Trophy, *Sports Illustrated* reported that Manziel was "taking online courses [spring] semester to avoid the crush of autograph-seeking classmates." It is Texas A&M, not the NCAA, that determined that clicking pages online in your dorm room constitutes being a college student. Manziel may not receive an education, but Texas A&M will keep all revenues he generates.

Three conferences—the Ivy League, the Patriot League (schools such as Georgetown University, Bucknell and Lehigh) and the New England Small College Athletic Conference (institutions such as Williams, Bowdoin and Amherst)—impose higher GPA and SAT/ACT admission standards on entering athletes than do the rest of collegiate sports. Even in these academics-first conferences, once a football player has been admitted, it's up to the individual school whether he is eligible to play. Individual colleges are free to declare higher standards than the NCAA or conference minima, but few do.

When the money in college football began to skyrocket roughly around 1990, recruiting became a matter not just of pleasing the alumni with victories, but of attaining the premium athletes who would bring in the kind of big bucks now being bandied. The big bucks would ensure a cushy life for coaches, athletic directors and conference officials. By 2011, Larry Scott, commissioner of the Pac-12, would be paying himself $3.1 million annually, for administrating the logistics of college sports events. Other big-conference commissioners would enjoy similar paychecks, and as you have already guessed, big-college sports conferences are nonprofits, masquerading as public-service organizations while their executives roll in wealth.

When the money in college football began to rise, the conferences responded by lowering their internal standards for maintaining eligibility. A race-to-the-bottom developed. A recruiter from the SEC could say, "Don't commit to Notre Dame; at Notre Dame they make you attend class. Come here and it will be nothing but football and parties."

The three service academies, Boston College, BYU, Duke, Nebraska, Northwestern, Notre Dame, Stanford, Virginia Tech and a few others refused to lower their standards, and all save Stanford, with the lure of its dreamlike California campus environment, and Notre Dame, with its golden aura, have in recent years had trouble cracking football's Top 10 as a result.

No college football program with higher internal academic standards than its conference requires has ever won a BCS championship. The BCS victors are Alabama (thrice), Florida (twice), LSU (twice), Auburn, Florida State, the University of Miami, Ohio State, Oklahoma, Texas, Tennessee and USC (its victory nullified by NCAA violations). As the modern game has developed, winning the BCS title has become the same as announcing to the world that your school's standards are low. But the national television audience doesn't care, the NCAA doesn't care and its broadcast "partners" don't care.

That Virginia Tech is among the holdouts against the trend toward lowering academic and personal-behavior standards is a reason Frank Beamer has never won a national championship. Each year a pool of star-rated prep athletes with poor grades, or who have been in trouble with the law, are welcomed on a red carpet at most big programs but not accepted by the admissions departments at BYU, Northwestern, Notre Dame, Stanford or Virginia Tech. The small number of football-factory universities that cling to high internal academic and behavior standards for athletes have become long shots to finish number one.

The Virginia Tech football exhibit hall, with a glass wall looking out onto Lane Stadium, has a pedestal at the center. Adorned by nothing, the pedestal awaits a national championship trophy. Most likely Beamer will never place one there. For Virginia Tech, and for a few other admirable big football programs, what's needed to win the national championship is not to recruit the correct linebacker or tail-back, not to switch to the hottest new offensive tactics—rather, to lower standards.

Nothing is a surer path to college football success than lowering standards. Virginia Tech won't do that, which all but surely means Beamer won't ever win the national title. This truly may not matter to him, as Beamer is the rare individual who would rather have self-respect than a trophy, and he draws others like him to Blacksburg.

But at many big-college football programs, placing self-respect and high standards ahead of wins and money is viewed as a leftover from the Howdy Doody era.

WHATEVER ITS FAULTS, THE NCAA in the end is a convenient cover story for what former *Sports Center* anchor Brian Kenny calls "the athletic industrial complex." Here's how things really work at many big-college football programs:

• The athletic department is in effect an independent business enterprise leasing the college's logo and traditions.

• The head football and men's basketball coaches do not work for the university, they work for the boosters. Many are paid their salary by a booster fund, not the school. At public universities, this is presented as a way to prevent taxpayers' money from going directly to the football coach, which sounds good. But the boosters do not care about GPA, they want exciting games and big victory margins. Coaches strive to please their employers—the boosters—and so focus on wins and running up the score. In turn, players know they must please their coaches to retain their scholarships.

• College presidents don't like the situation, and not just because many earn significantly less than the head football coach. Any conscientious college president winces at the knowledge that the football coach is better known than all the university's professors combined.

The trouble is that a big-college president who tried to rein in the football program would not hold the job long. When football coach Jim Tressel got into trouble at Ohio State, president Gordon Gee was asked if he would fire Tressel. "No, but he might fire me," the president of Ohio State replied. The joke fell flat because Gee had inadvertently spoken the truth.

A big-college president who is raising funds and meeting alumni invariably is asked about the fortunes of the football team. If the answer were that football was being cut to channel resources to some superfluous concern like the history department, the boosters would be in a fury. Even alumni who majored in history would be in a fury, since while the majority long ago stopped following research or theory in their field, all know when their beloved alma mater will be on ESPN. With the student bodies of American higher education now 56 percent female, and the women's share continuing to rise, someday a big university's alumni bloc may back a college president who wants to deemphasize football. But not today.

• The college president who thinks football is too big, but also does not wish to take the heat for changing that, has a ready fall guy— blame NCAA inaction. If the NCAA vanished tomorrow, big-university presidents, who lead remunerative, plush lives, suddenly would be responsible for the state of their football programs. That's the last thing they want.

OF COURSE LOTS OF COLLEGE students cut classes and couldn't name the capital of Sweden or the author of *Great Expectations* if their lives depended on it. At least those undereducated football players go on to the NFL, right?

Hardly any do. About five thousand NCAA scholarship football players leave college annually. About three hundred land jobs in the NFL, and few of those jobs are anything like careers.

Players says the initials NFL mean Not For Long. Philadelphia Eagles star Troy Vincent, later head of the NFL players' union, noted in 2010 that the average NFL "career" is 3.7 years. Hardly any college football players ever receive an NFL paycheck, and of those who do, most are OOF—Out Of Football—by their midtwenties.

Not only is 3.7 years not enough time for the average player to make much money. In the fourth season an NFL player vests, qualifying for a long-term benefits package and a mandatory higher salary. The result is that large numbers of players are waived at the end of their third seasons and replaced with minimum-salary guys just out of college and desperate to please the coach.

Roll together the small number who reach the NFL, and the smaller number who stay more than a brief time, and find the odds of a scholarship NCAA football player having an NFL career are about one in fifty.

Those who reach big-college football discover that every player they encounter was the star of his high school team; those who reach the NFL discover that every player they encounter was the star of his college team. With the NFL having but 1,696 player jobs to begin with, and former college stars competing for each one, the situation is Darwinian. Frank Beamer and a few other ethical big-college coaches constantly remind players that their odds of performing in the NFL are not good, whereas those who leave college with a diploma are nearly certain to enjoy an above-median income throughout life.

But most Division I football coaches elaborately nourish a Grand Illusion that their players are headed to the NFL for money and celebrity. This makes players willing to go all out to win games for the coach—providing the coach job security and income, while not necessarily doing much for the player. The coach gets hefty bonuses for victories. Most players are used up and thrown away the moment their eligibility expires.

In 2009, Alabama head coach Nick Saban jovially told reporters that he got his Crimson Tide fired up for a game against 48-point underdog Chattanooga by warning players, "You would someday be an NFL player in a Mercedes-Benz and roll down your window to talk to a pretty girl and she'd say, 'You lost to Chattanooga when you played at Alabama.'"

Every football starter at Alabama is led by coaches to believe he will someday be a well-to-do NFL star who is swooned over by attractive women. Yet this is extremely unlikely, and Saban knows this. Encouraging the Grand Illusion improves Alabama football results, while distracting players from studying—which would mean more to the typical Crimson Tide player's future than football. Many other college football programs lead many other players on with the same illusion of future NFL wealth and recognition.

Forget the long overall odds. Let's look at the odds for players from the best college football teams—the ones that won BCS title games. Below are examples from relatively recent BCS winners, with enough time passed to determine what kind of NFL outcomes the teams produced.

The year 2000 football national champion, the University of Oklahoma, sent two players into the NFL for five or more years—a career in football terms—six players for two to four years, and one player for one year. Of the football scholarship holders at the University of Oklahoma in that championship season, 11 percent advanced to the NFL, while the rest went away empty-handed in football terms. Remember, this was the best team of 2000.

The year 2001 football champion, the University of Miami, was among the most talented collegiate squads ever, including future NFL stars Andre Johnson, Bryant McKinnie, Clinton Portis, Ed Reed, Jeremy Shockey, Sean Taylor, Jonathan Vilma and Vince Wilfork. That squad sent twenty players to the NFL for at least five years, twelve for two-to-four years, and four for one year. These numbers are good—but also mean that of one of the most talented college football teams ever assembled, 60 percent of the players never took a snap in the NFL.

Ohio State won the 2002 crown, and produced eleven players who were in the NFL for five years or more, sixteen who played two to four years and seven who played one season. Of the year's best college football team, two-thirds never took an NFL snap.

From 2002 to 2004, USC fielded exceptionally strong football teams, going 36-3 and winning the 2004 BCS title. Those three seasons produced twelve players who were in the NFL five years or more, fifteen who were in two to four years and thirteen who had single-season stints. About 120 individuals held football scholarships at USC in that period—two-thirds never took an NFL snap.

During the same period, LSU had a run of talented teams that went 30-9 and won the 2003 BCS title. From those LSU years, eleven players reached at least five seasons in the NFL, ten played two to four years and three played one year. Eighty percent of LSU football players from the glory years never took an NFL snap.

Nick Saban was coach at LSU during that period, then jumped to the Miami Dolphins, where for the first time in his coaching life he did not produce winning teams: he was 15-17 in the NFL, compared to 159-55-1 in college. Professional football coaching success is about game planning, making wise draft selections and getting along with players who have big paychecks and bigger egos. College football coaching success is largely recruiting. At Miami in the NFL, Saban learned that he is not particularly good at game planning, drafting or human psychology. So he walked less than halfway through his contract. The Alabama head-coaching job came open in November 2006, the Dolphins' season having many weeks remaining. Saban denied he would weasel out of his Miami commitment, saying, "I am not going to be the Alabama coach." Then he boarded a private jet and left for Tuscaloosa: When you hire a coach who's only in it for himself, you get a coach who's only in it for himself.

Returning to the college ranks, Saban brought with him a new way of thinking for what he is quite good at, recruiting. And recruiting's strongest tool is the Grand Illusion.

FOR DECADES, COLLEGE FOOTBALL RECRUITING has been oriented around selling the college: "Come here because we have tradition, a fine campus and a big stadium full of loyal fans." Sometimes money changes hands—in 1987, Southern Methodist University was banned from NCAA football for two years for cutting out the middleman and handing cash directly to players. But in the main, the recruiting pitch has been "Choose our wonderful college."

Saban realized that if landing rated players was the goal, a better recruiting pitch would be "My program will make you an NFL draft choice." Whether or not that was true, it sure sounded good to high school boys dreaming of bonus checks.

Saban had this realization about the same time the "Rivals effect" arrived in college sports. Internet rankings of high school players by Rivals.com, MaxPreps.com and ESPNU.com made it practical for seventeen-year-olds to know where other seventeen-year-olds were headed. If two or three highly rated seniors committed to Alabama, within hours other highly rated seniors knew that and gravitated toward what looked to be a monster program in the making. Monster programs win big games and draw the attention of NFL scouts.

Since arriving at the University of Alabama in 2007, Saban has specialized in the Grand Illusion—it is no coincidence he is the one who speaks openly of his athletes becoming NFL players in expensive cars. Some college coaches are uncomfortable with NFL scouts at their practices; Saban encourages them because it lends the impression that Alabama is the Triple-A league of the NFL. In his years at Alabama, the Crimson Tide has produced fourteen number-one draft choices, more than any other school. The sense is that Saban sends large numbers of players on to "the league."

The reality? Of the roughly 175 scholarship athletes Saban has had at Alabama, 23 have played at least one season in the NFL. Probably that total will rise: more years need to pass to enable the kind of evaluations made above with Oklahoma, Miami, Ohio State, USC and LSU. But so far, only 23 of 175—13 percent—of players in the nation's most NFL-focused college program actually advanced to the NFL. Most of the starry-eyed young men listening to Saban in the locker room will never take a snap in the NFL, much less become a celebrity athlete being chased by women.

But Saban's bonus money increases if his young men fall for that illusion. The harder Alabama players concentrate on football, believing they are headed to sports wealth, the more the Crimson Tide will win, and the more money Saban makes. But many of his players end up empty-handed—no NFL, no diploma. This happens across Division I football. Players give everything to football because they think it will take them to the NFL; victories enrich the coaches and the athletic department; by the time players snap out of the NFL dream and realize they should have studied in college, it's too late. The scholarship is exhausted.

GIVEN THE MANIFOLD WAYS IN which the collegiate athletic establishment takes advantage of big-program football players, many commentators conclude the solution is for them to be paid. The first and not inconsiderable problem with this remedy is that paying college players would make the system even more inequitable than it is today. The second problem is that reform must focus on sports' leading to graduation, because a college diploma is substantially *more valuable* than any pay a college athlete might receive.

Paying college athletes has an obvious appeal. But having read many articles, commentaries and books on what the historian Taylor Branch has called "the shame of college sports," and having attended debates on this topic, your writer has encountered few proposals on how paying college athletes would work.

Would there be some kind of free-market competition? That quickly would lead to a winner-take-all outcome in which a few stars received huge sums while most college athletes realized little or nothing.

Suppose there had been free-market bidding for college football players in 2010, the year Cam Newton led Auburn to the college football title. Newton's services might have gone for $5 million that season—booster clubs of a dozen big universities would have competed furiously to raise funds for an offer. But most players on the 2010 Auburn team would have been lucky to receive a few thousand dollars, if anything. In free-market bidding terms, most Division I college football players are worthless because they are easily replaced.

Philip Lutzenkirchen—what would he have been worth? Mike Berry? Byron Isom? Neil Caudle? All were starters with Newton on the 2010 Auburn title team, and in a free-market college situation, could easily have been replaced with someone willing to play for less or for nothing, simply to experience the glory of big-college football. Berry, a BCS-title-team starter in 2010, just two years later was OOF. Isom spent a few weeks on the practice squad of the Kansas City Chiefs, but was waived without ever drawing a game check. Caudle could stand at the center of Auburn's Jordan-Hare Stadium and no one would have a clue who he is.

In an open-bidding system, most starting college football players would have scant market value. Just imagine what would happen to backups and the scout-team performers.

Joe Nocera, a delightfully relentless critic of the NCAA, has proposed annual pay of $25,000 per Division I football player. That would cost a school $2.5 million per year, manageable for most of the universities that play football on television. Nocera also would allow colleges a maximum of $1 million annually in bonuses to attract star players, and would end all NCAA restrictions on college-to-college movement. So if, say, the University of Colorado needed a quarterback and knew UCLA had a good backup quarterback, the Buffaloes could call and offer a bonus for him to transfer immediately.

Paying Division I football and men's basketball players $25,000 per year would improve the situation in some ways but might backfire by driving yet another wedge between NCAA revenue athlete and classroom. A nineteen-year-old football player with no living expenses and a $25,000 check might feel as though he's already got it made—though college credits and a diploma mean more to his future than anything he could accomplish during a game.

In 2011, the NCAA voted to allow Division I schools to give scholarship athletes a $2,000 annual stipend, in addition to the per diem Division I players receive for away games. The stage crew at the college theater, staffers at the college newspaper—they get stipends because they perform work that contributes to the life of the college. Stipends for college football and men's basketball players, those in the revenue sports, make sense by the same reasoning.

So far most big colleges are not offering the stipend, but should. Two thousand dollars would prevent football and men's basketball players, who generate funds for their schools, from walking around without the cash to afford a cheesesteak and a milk shake. But players would continue to live the modest lifestyle that is the centuries-long norm for university students. The $2,000 stipend would grant Division I football and men's basketball players a small cut of the money they produce, while keeping them amateurs. Then the focus can move to fixing other parts of the system.

College football reform that shifts emphasis toward the diploma is needed far more than payments to players. The reform program:

- Six-year scholarships, so when a football player exhausts his eligibility and the NFL does not call, he has two to three paid semesters remaining to fix his credits and graduate.

- Factor graduation rates into football rankings. The Associated Press, *USA Today* and BCS organization publish elaborate computer and poll-based rankings of college teams. The rankings avidly are followed by fans and determine bowl invitations; rankings will be central to the expected Division I football playoff system. Colleges and college coaches desperately want high rankings because these please the boosters and increase revenue. If graduation rates were a factor in the rankings—say, a quarter of the weight—coaches and athletic directors instantly would care whether players were at the library and in class.

Human beings respond to incentives, and right now, Division I coaches and athletic directors have incentives only for victories. Give them an education-based incentive, and they will respond.

At the NFL level, where football is pure entertainment, power rankings need only reflect quality of teams. Colleges are expected to teach and to play a role in guiding society. It is amazingly superficial of the Associated Press and *USA Today* to rank college teams on victory margins only, as if colleges existed solely to provide entertainment for sports fans. Add graduation rates to the rankings and college football will have an internal incentive to clean itself up. Internal incentives for reform are better than those imposed from without.

- In most cases, Division I athletes who transfer must wait one year before accepting an NCAA scholarship at the new college. So levy the same before their contracts are up. In 2012, Pitt head coach Todd Graham, who had been at the school just eleven months, was offered more money by Arizona State and instantly bolted. If Graham wanted to leave Pitt for Arizona State before his contract expired, he should have been required to sit out a year. Imposing a waiting period on coaches would reduce the mercenary atmosphere of big-college football and cause more coaches to set good examples.

• Make penalties follow the coach. The NCAA sanctions individual athletes, but almost never individual coaches. This means coaches know that if a scandal looms, they can simply jump to another school. The character education movement says actions have consequences; for college football coaches, actions rarely have consequences.

Suppose a college receives, say, a two-year probation. The head coach for the period when the violations occurred should be required to spend the same amount of time away from collegiate sports, regardless of switching employers. If college football coaches knew they would suffer consequences for taking shortcuts, fewer shortcuts would be taken.

• For any year in which a college football team's graduation rate is below the rate of students as a whole at the same university (crediting for players who transfer and graduate elsewhere), the head coach is suspended for one year, and the penalty follows him to any NCAA member school. *That* would get coaches' attention.

Human beings respond to incentives. The incentives described above would cause college football coaches to care about education.

IN THE END IT IS not the lack of pay but the lack of diplomas that is the fatal flaw of American college football.

Of course many highly accomplished people never walked in a robe and mortarboard to "Pomp and Circumstance." Edward Elgar, who wrote the music that has become the commencement anthem, himself never graduated from college. But in contemporary American society, no step more closely links to achieving a materially secure life than earning a college degree.

College is "the gateway to the middle class," President Barack Obama said in 2012. That year the unemployment rate for those with a high school diploma was 9 percent; for those with a college diploma, was 3.5 percent. Researchers Anthony Carnevale, Stephen Rose and Ben Cheah of Georgetown University have found that compared to a high school degree, a bachelor's adds $1 million to the average person's lifetime earnings. The bachelor's is a perquisite for a master's, which adds $1.4 million to lifetime earnings. For the 99 percent of college athletes who will never spend a day in the pros, the diploma is worth far more, financially and sociologically, than any cash payment they might receive for NCAA participation.

That the college football establishment actively lures a mainly African-American group of young men away from studying and graduating, by nurturing an illusion they will receive instant wealth in the NFL, is what is rotten about the NCAA apple. That the money-rich athletic conferences and big-university boards of directors go along makes their apples rotten too.

Education is the agency of economic and of political power not just for the person who receives the degree but for his or her family line. Studies show that the best predictor of a child's educational success is not race, income, or school type, but the highest educational attainment of adults in the household. One person who graduates from college may found a line of others who do.

For those African-Americans who come into collegiate sports from disadvantaged backgrounds, a check for $25,000 would be nice, but will not change their family circumstances. A diploma could change their lives—and the lives of their children and children's children, allowing them to achieve independent economic power that belongs to them, not to someone else.

Rightly or wrongly, in contemporary American society college sorts out who rises and who falls, who acquires economic power and who is cast adrift. The college football establishment gathers the fruits of the physical labor of African-Americans, without ensuring they receive the diplomas that represent economic power—often, actively distracting them from the classroom work that would give them power. The system may not have been designed to keep blacks down. But it functions that way.

The next chapter: the concussion crisis is all too real.

Do Concussions Mean Football Should Not Be Played?

6

YOUR KNEE CAN BE FIXED, BUT YOUR BRAIN IS EXPENDABLE

On a Saturday night in 2009, Oklahoma State faced Texas Tech in one of college football's big games of the year. Sixty thousand spectators packed the seats at Boone Pickens Stadium in Stillwater, Oklahoma—newly renovated at a cost of $300 million, about $100 million ultimately supplied by taxpayers, considering the project was funded by deductible donations. A national television audience watched.

Star quarterback Zac Robinson led the home team. With less than two minutes remaining, Robinson rolled out and headed upfield. If he could lunge a few yards for a first down, the Oklahoma State Cowboys, holding the lead, would ice the contest. Texas Tech defenders knew that if Robinson reached the "line to gain," the game was over. Tech star safety Jamar Wall drew a bead on Robinson, who had dropped his shoulders to plow forward, thus exposing his head. Wall lowered his helmet and aimed at Robinson's helmet—some coaches teach defenders that hitting a ballcarrier really hard on the crown of the helmet can knock him woozy, causing a fumble. Robinson and Wall, both sprinting full speed, both with heads lowered, collided crown of helmet to crown of helmet. The ball came loose. Both players dropped to the turf, arms and legs twitching in violent spasms.

"What a shot!" announcer Mike Patrick gushed.

"What a great hit!" color man Craig James seconded.

"That's the play of the night!"

The announcers discussed the game situation—whether Texas Tech, now in possession after the fumble, had time to tie the contest—while continuing to rave about the hit. "He was really blown up, Jamar Wall just laid him out!" Patrick effused. James declared in an admiring tone, "That's what effort and character will do for you!" In this sports usage, causing injury while risking your own neck is "character."

Wall and Robinson were surrounded by doctors and trainers. Cameras showed Oklahoma State and Texas Tech players kneeling in prayer, some crying. Patrick and James seemed oblivious to how the scene on the field had transformed from exciting game into nightmare. An excruciating three minutes and fifteen seconds—a long time in live-broadcast terms—passed between the hit and when Patrick and James finally switched from bubbly to concerned. An additional thirty seconds passed before the word *concussion* was spoken.

In the aftermath Robinson, the quarterback, lost his stellar playing style. He would eventually spend time on the low-paid practice squads of three NFL teams, once being activated to a game roster by the Seattle Seahawks, only to be waived the following day. Still trying to catch on in 2013, Robinson had earned little more than travel and lodging expenses as he crisscrossed the country trying to find anything resembling a career in the sport he had been training for year-round since age ten. Wall, the defensive back, would lose his star status too. Eventually Wall spent a couple weeks on the rosters of three NFL teams, then played for the Georgia Force of the semipro Arena League, then landed on the injured-reserve list of the Calgary Stampeders. Wall was among the top phenoms in the annals of prep football, as a high school senior recording a hard-to-believe forty-two touchdowns, recognized and cheered wherever he went in his hometown of Plainview, Texas. He realized a few thousand dollars in pro football earnings.

Whether Robinson and Wall can expect a lifetime of neurological problems is anyone's guess. If they experience such problems, they're on their own.

The NFL offers former players health-care coverage for the first five years after they leave football; those who play at least one full season can purchase an NFL-sponsored plan beyond that. The league knows that most chronic conditions caused by sports do not manifest until early middle age; the five-year period is designed to end before coverage is likely to be needed. The league also knows that marginal NFL players never will complete a season, qualifying for nothing.

At the college level, most universities provide health care for athletes during their eligibility, but not after. The NCAA covers catastrophic expenses exceeding $90,000, but only if the health problem manifests while the athlete is enrolled. Once an injured athlete leaves college, the NCAA washes its hands. Both the NFL and the big-college conferences think profits from football should be theirs exclusively, while long-term health consequences should be someone else's problem.

THE ANNOUNCERS WHO SAID INFLICTING harm shows "character" were not heartless—rather, were trying to divert attention from the downside of football. Sports announcers fundamentally are part of the act. Their role is to smile and wave, smile and wave. Just a few examples:

"Tony Romo is a great quarterback who played a great, great game." Said by color man Phil Simms of CBS just after Romo threw three interceptions as his Cowboys lost at home.

"This Patriots' defense is outstanding!" Said by Ron Jaworski of ESPN at a time when the New England defense was ranked last in the league.

"That was a tremendous throw by Mark Sanchez!" Said by Simms of an interception Sanchez tossed directly into a defender's hands.

Comments by Mike Tirico, Jon Gruden and Jaworski during a broadcast of *Monday Night Football*:

"Phenomenal catch!. . . . That was a good play. . . . I love what their quarterback just did. . . . Excellent play, a heck of a throw. . . . He is one of the best in the league. . . . He did everything exactly right. . . . Free agents want to play for this coach because they know his system works. . . . That was a terrific play and even better catch, just perfect. . . . That's an awesome play, wow, that's one for the ages. . . . This team is a thing of beauty." All these comments were about the St. Louis Rams, who would finish the season 2-14, worst record in the league.

The smile-and-wave nature of broadcast announcing is endemic to professional sports, part of the culture in which announcers are trained. Some play-by-play voices incorporate more poise and independence than others: Tirico of ESPN and Al Michaels of NBC are tops in their profession. But no one in the football "booth" for any major network questions on-air the assumptions underlying marketing of the sport: that injuries magically heal, that education is no issue, that the football player's life is wine and roses. If a football announcer pointed out that the NFL sets an example to youth of reckless behavior; or noted the league lists the colleges of players to imply that they are graduates though a large percentage are not; or pointed out that NCAA coaches are fired for losing games but never disciplined in any way for ruining educations—such an announcer soon would lose his or her job. No announcer wants to see a player harmed. But if there is harm, announcers pretend it's exciting when players drop motionless to the ground. What a shot!

ONE SUNDAY IN OCTOBER 2010, several extreme helmet-to-helmet hits occurred in NFL contests. Josh Cribbs of the Cleveland Browns fell unconscious after being drilled helmet to helmet by James Harrison of the Steelers; Cribbs was reaching for a pass and could not see Harrison coming (was "defenseless" under the rule for this situation). Zack Follett of Detroit lay motionless on the field after a helmet-to-helmet hit; he would never play again. DeSean Jackson of the Philadelphia Eagles collapsed after a deliberate helmet-to-helmet hit; the player who hit him, Dunta Robinson, left the game with his own concussion. Other NFL players sustained concussions the same day.

Was this dismaying? No, entertaining! "Wow, what a hard-hitting rivalry the Steelers and Browns have," CBS announcer Kevin Harlan said as Cribbs lay unconscious. Later in the game, Harrison of the Steelers knocked a second Browns player out with another deliberate blow to the head. Harlan gushed, "Harrison was really laying the wood!" Harlan did not intend to sound callous: he was merely vocalizing the way in which football culture avoids dealing with the game's underside. Football is full of thrills and electric moments; announcers know how to talk about those. Announcers are not supposed to mention anything bad for business, so they lack a vocabulary in which to discuss moments of dread.

That night on NBC's NFL wrap-up, Dan Patrick showed the Cribbs injury *as a highlight*, chucking, "Cribbs gets a big hit from his former college teammate." Cribbs and Harrison both attended Kent State. It's not a concussion, it's nostalgia for bygone college idylls!

In 2009, Clinton Portis of the Washington Redskins was hit hard on the head, wobbled around for a moment, and collapsed. Previously a Pro Bowl participant, he sat out a year with a severe concussion, attempted a comeback, then left football. On the night he was hit, NFL Network, the league-owned channel, showed the injury *as a highlight*. While the tape rolled, announcer Deion Sanders chortled, "Night-night. He's going to sleep. He's dreaming." ESPN once had a regular feature called "Jacked Up"—canceled in 2006 after protests from neurologists—in which a panel would show head blows and rate them for viciousness. There was practically a laff track. High school and youth football players were sent the message that dangerous behavior is what they should imitate.

In 2010, with the Tennessee Titans on *Monday Night Football*, ESPN aired old clips of a Titans coach, Chuck Cecil, when he was a player in the 1980s. Cecil had a reputation as a headhunter, someone who tried to knock opponents out of games by bashing his helmet against theirs. Highlights presented by *Monday Night Football* under the rubric Cecil's Greatest Hits were shown: all were helmet to helmet. Jon Gruden narrated the Greatest Hits. "Chuck Cecil, he's my guy," Gruden said with enthusiasm. "He could knock you out! He could knock you sideways! And he's a quality guy, he loves football."

In a 2012 game between the Carolina Panthers and Tampa Bay Bucs, Tampa safety Mark Barron, the team's number-one draft choice, launched himself helmet-first into the helmet of Carolina receiver Steve Smith. "Ooooo, Smith gets rocked, that will look good on highlights," Fox announcer Ron Pitts said admiringly. "This is why they drafted [Barron], form tackles, form tackles will stop them dead in their tracks," color man Mike Martz said with enthusiasm.

Neither Fox announcer pointed out that leading with the head is the single most dangerous thing a football player can do. Neither explained that "see what you hit"—keep your head up—has for years been taught by progressive NFL, NCAA and high school coaches as the safe technique for tackling. If a player sees what he hits, then it's impossible to use the crown of the helmet as a weapon; this in turn avoids compression stress on the brain, neck and spine. Both Fox announcers held up to young players for admiration a dirty, dangerous move. Martz even called deliberate helmet-to-helmet contact a "form tackle," a bizarre comment coming from a past NFL head coach

After the game, Bucs coach Greg Schiano singled out Barron for praise. In 2010, when Schiano was head coach at Rutgers University, Scarlet Knights player Eric LeGrand was paralyzed while making an unsafe head-down tackle. Schiano has observed for himself the terrible harm that can occur when football players don't "see what you hit," yet he lauded a player for violent helmet-to-helmet, head-down contact. Then again, Schiano was never penalized in any way when a young man under his care became paralyzed. Reaching the pros, Schiano knew that if Mark Barron or anyone else on his team were severely harmed by making a vicious hit, he as a coach would never pay any price. But if Rutgers or the Tampa Bay Bucs didn't intimidate other teams and win, Schiano would be fired.

In its September 24, 2012, issue, *Sports Illustrated* ran a six-page double spread of dramatic pictures of big-college and NFL players making vicious hits to each other's heads. The accompanying text extolled leading with the head—one helmet-to-helmet hit was described as "a perfectly timed hit, jarring the ball loose"—while saying nothing about concussions or safe tackling form.

In a 2012 game between the Houston Texans and Baltimore Ravens, Brian Cushing of the Houston Texans drove his helmet into the helmet of Ed Dickson of Baltimore, a thuggish hit that caused Dickson to stagger. "Now that is how you deliver a shot!" burbled CBS announcer Dan Dierdorf. Neither he nor partner Greg Gumbel said anything about the dangerous nature of helmet-to-helmet hits or about proper, safe tackling form.

Because the NFL and NCAA have broadcast-partner or cable-carrier business relationships with ABC, CBS, Comcast, ESPN, Fox, NBC and Time Warner, most of the country's major communications corporations have a financial stake in football ratings. (Comcast owns NBC, which airs the NFL, and also carries NFL Network; Time Warner, publisher of *Sports Illustrated*, carries NFL Network; both cable giants carry nearly all NFL and NCAA broadcasting, plus extra-cost "sports tier" programming that is mainly football.) This can mean the very communications corporations best positioned to report on the harm done by football have an incentive to downplay health damage. Reporting about concussion harm has tended to come from newspapers with no financial stake in NFL broadcasting, such as *The New York Times*, much as reporting about NCAA corruption has tended to come from magazines with no financial stake in college sports, such as *The Atlantic*.

There are some positive indicators. During a 2012 game between the Washington Redskins and the New Orleans Saints—whose head coach, Sean Payton, was suspended for a season after he and his staff offered players money bounties for each "cart-off" of injured opponents— a helmet-to-helmet hit occurred. Fox announcer Daryl Johnston declared, "These kinds of vicious hits have to stop." CBS analyst Boomer Esiason, ESPN analysts Merrill Hoge and Mark Schlereth, Fox announcers Johnston and Troy Aikman, and NBC analysts Chris Collinsworth, Tony Dungy and Rodney Harrison, all accomplished former NFL players or coaches, have in recent years emphasized on-air that players should never lead with their heads.

But the attitude of sports broadcasting toward football safety still leaves much to be desired. Kids, want to show you are a quality guy who loves football? Lead with your head!

CONCUSSIONS HAVE LONG BEEN A concern in many activities, including diving and bicycling. If a boy told his mother that instead of trying out for the football team, he planned to play soccer, ride his bike and go sledding, mom would feel relieved. Yet according to a 2011 study by the federal Centers for Disease Control and Prevention, soccer, biking and sledding are about as likely to cause brain trauma, per hour of participation, as is football. From 2001 to 2009, the CDC found, there were 26,212 emergency-room visits for concussions from bicycle accidents, and 25,376 emergency-room visits for concussions from football. That bicycling can lead to concussions does not cause anyone to say young people should not ride bicycles. Nor should concussion risk, in itself, be an argument against playing football.

Concern about concussions and football has risen in recent years owing to better diagnosis, to advances in understanding of the brain and to the national obsession with football. At a time when NFL games draw higher ratings than presidential nominating conventions, if an NFL player drops to the turf unconscious, the entire country knows. If a high school girl drops to the gym floor unconscious from a concussion sustained in a volleyball game, no one except her family knows. Because football is the highest-profile sport in the United States, football concussions have become the highest-profile athletic concern. That, in itself, does not necessarily mean that concussion risk makes football bad.

Here are a few fundamental points to bear in mind:

• Football creates risks but also has benefits, including health benefits. Risks should not be considered in a vacuum, rather, weighed against benefits. Young people who play football are more active than most of their peers, and physical activity is good for overall health. Football helps teach self-discipline, a valuable life skill. College football can confer the benefits of an athletic scholarship or of an "athletic admit"—admission to a more selective college than a young person otherwise would qualify for. NFL football can offer the benefits of celebrity and wealth.

• A 2012 study published in the technical journal *Neurology* reported former NFL players are three times more likely to die of neurodegenerative conditions linked to concussions, such as Alzheimer's and Parkinson's, than other American males of the same ages. That scary finding received extensive media coverage. Unmentioned was that the same study found former NFL players had a 50 percent lower mortality rate than males of the same age. Football created a brain-trauma risk but overall was beneficial to players' health, increasing longevity.

• Head harm might be a factor in suicides of former football players, but this is speculative, in part because when a man takes his own life, often the reasons die with him.

The 2011 suicide of former Super Bowl star Dave Duerson, and the 2012 suicide of former Pro Bowl player Junior Seau, drew tremendous levels of media attention, with many commentators suggesting brain harm from football was the cause. A 2013 lawsuit filed by Seau's estate and children against the NFL cites a chilling

1993 NFL Films special glamorizing big hits—until 2010, the NFL sold highlight reels of vicious hits as VCR cassettes and DVDs, a perfect holiday gift!—in which Seau says he knows he's just made a terrific hit "if I can feel some dizziness."

Though Duerson and Seau sustained traumatic head hits playing football, shortly before their suicides both experienced personal problems unrelated to sports. Duerson was $15 million in debt, his wife had recently divorced him and filed a lawsuit against him, and he had just lost his home to foreclosure. Seau was divorced. Did concussions contribute to their suicides, or would those awful moments have come anyway? For an individual, society may never know. For former football players as a group, if concussions lead to suicides, this should manifest in data. A 2012 study by the Centers for Disease Control found that former pro football players commit suicide at about half the rate of other males their age.

• Reggie White, a Hall of Fame player, died in 2004 at age forty-three. Other well-known former NFL players have died young, and this is sometimes presented in commentary as proof that football inflicts lethal damage on the body. Pop star Whitney Houston died at age forty-eight. Jim Fixx, a health nut who helped popularize running, died at age fifty-two. Sally Ride died at age sixty-one, and as an astronaut, her health was closely monitored throughout her adult life. When well-known persons die before their time, this is noticed. Overall, former football players live longer than other men from their age group.

• Football players grow ever faster and stronger, but this may not be the reason for the rise in reported concussions. Both increased awareness of head trauma and players' coming forward about their problems—rather than pretending to be fine in order to get into games—are likely the primary reason concussion numbers have risen. A 2010 study in the journal *Neurosurgical Focus* found that reported ice-hockey concussions had risen to 3.3 times the rate for ice-hockey players of the previous generation, even though today's ice-hockey players are far more likely to wear helmets. Improved awareness and reporting, rather than increased occurrence, was the first reason more concussions were reported.

• A likely factor in concussion trends is changes in football tactics. Once, the sport was dominated by rushing plays: until 1983, every NFL season knew more rushing plays then passing plays. Today most football teams, even at the high school level, are pass-first. Since 1984, in every NFL season there have been more passing plays than rushes.

During many running plays, no one gets to full speed—when a running back and a linebacker collide, it's a crunching hit, but neither is at full sprint. Most passing plays involve wide receivers and defensive backs reaching maximum sprint. The more passing plays, the more chances that a receiver running full speed in one direction will collide with a defender running full speed in the opposite direction. This type of contact is rare on rushing plays.

The no-huddle, quick-snap fad also increases the total number of downs, and thus the total number of hits. In the first Super Bowl, between the Kansas City Chiefs and the Green Bay Packers in 1967, there were 115 offensive plays. The most recent Super Bowl, between the San Francisco 49ers and the Baltimore Ravens, had 130 offensive plays, 13 percent more chances for a concussion. The fashion for no-huddle, quick-snap offenses that increase the total number of downs has spread across pro, college and high school football. When the University of West Virginia defeated Baylor University in a 2012 college game, there were 180 offensive plays. That's half again as many chances for a concussion as occurred in the first Super Bowl.

• Some autopsies of the brains of deceased football players suggest they suffered from chronic traumatic encephalopathy, a degenerative condition. Seau's brain, dissected after his suicide, was found by Russell Lonser, a former neurologist at the National Institutes of Health, to show signs of CTE, which is associated with memory loss, exaggerated mood swings and other disruptions of brain function. CTE is a serious concern for all contact sports and also for the military, since infantry near explosions and artillery are at risk of brain trauma. The brain of Owen Thomas, a college football player who killed himself in 2010 at age twenty-one, was dissected and showed a significant level CTE. Degenerative conditions that manifest late in life are one thing; for a twenty-one-year-old to have a degenerative brain condition is alarming.

 Though existence of the condition has been known to researchers for decades, CTE is poorly understood, having become a medical-school concern only in recent years. Chronic traumatic encephalopathy may turn out to happen to many people, caused in part by the normal hazards of living and aging—but so far detected only in deceased pro athletes and soldiers because brain autopsies are so unusual. In 2011, Boston University's Center for the Study of Traumatic Encephalopathy reported that its bank of ninety-nine specimens contained "more brains diagnosed with CTE than have ever been reported in the world combined." If brains were routinely autopsied, CTE might prove ubiquitous.

• Generations of coaches told football players they were wimps if they did not go back into games after "getting their bell rung." Rising awareness, coupled to fear of litigation, finally is changing this coaches' mind-set. Today when a concussion is feared, smart coaches say, "Take his helmet away," so the player cannot attempt to reenter the game.

• The 2006 book *Head Games,* by former Harvard football player Chris Nowinski, laid out in spooky detail how the football establishment pressured players to stay mum about concussions. Playing with blurred vision and memory loss was seen as manly; telling others that your head hurt was seen as breaking football's omertà. Nowinski reported that when football players were surveyed about whether they'd experienced concussions, only 5 percent said yes. If the word *concussion* was removed from the survey but concussion symptoms were described, nearly 50 percent reported the symptoms. Nowinski's tireless crusade on this issue was a major factor in forcing the world of athletics to confront head trauma.

• As recently as 2007, the NFL handed players flyers that said, "Current research with professional athletes has not shown that having more than one or two concussions leads to permanent problems, if each injury is treated properly." This is the sort of statement that may be literally true, but deceptive. Many events cannot be proven conclusively to cause permanent problems, since a person might have health problems in later life regardless of being hit in the helmet during a football game or falling off a ladder or any other life event. The NFL undeniably tried for a long time to sweep the concussion issue under the rug. Players' biceps and knees were essential to selling the product; their brains were not.

• As recently as 2010, when Philadelphia Eagles linebacker Stewart Bradley dropped to the ground with "jelly limbs" after a hit to his head, came off for a few plays and then reentered the game, the NFL hid behind the extreme technicality that since Bradley had taken himself out rather than been signaled out by a trainer, he could continue playing. League policy then said only a player "removed" from a contest owing to concussion symptoms must receive treatment. Bradley had not been "removed."

Beginning with the 2013 season, each NFL team will have an independent neurologist—not a team employee—on the sideline to assess players with concussion symptoms. Obviously this is a step forward, one the NFL can afford, but that many colleges and most high schools cannot.

• Since concussion awareness began, former NFL stars including Lem Barney, Terry Bradshaw, Harry Carson, Jim McMahon and Kurt Warner have said that because of head-trauma concerns, they wish they'd never participated in pro football or think children should not play the sport.

It is hard to know whether these sentiments are genuine or an attempt to have it both ways: former players wanted the income and celebrity associated with performing in the NFL, yet with their days of living large in the past, wish they had been more cautious. This is like the older person who says, "Now I wish I saved when I was young, instead of spending freely."

Kansas City Chiefs tackle Eric Winston said in 2012, "I have come to the understanding that I may not live as long as if I hadn't played pro football, and that is the choice that I made." New York Giants star Osi Umenyiora said the same year, "Football is dangerous, but all NFL players know that. They play because of the benefits involved, including the lifestyle you get to lead." Smoking and drinking, Umenyiora noted, are known to be dangerous, but also provide the benefits of pleasure: if you choose to smoke and drink, don't complain later when the health consequences arrive. Former NFL players with cognitive problems deserve the best possible health care, but it's not clear they deserve public sympathy. No one compelled them to play in the NFL; they could have walked away.

• Trainers and neurologists increasingly emphasize "second-impact syndrome"—that anyone who has recently had a concussion is much more likely to have another, and the second will be worse than the first.

A sprained ankle swells, but there is room for the ankle to expand. A concussion causes the brain to swell, and because the skull is rigid, the swelling brain has nowhere to go, resulting in the blinding headaches and temporary memory loss associated with concussions. If the brain is already swollen from an initial concussion—such swelling cannot be seen, making concussions an invisible injury—the brain becomes vulnerable to impacts that under other conditions would not be harmful. If a second concussion occurs, a second phase of brain swelling may cause death.

The NCAA acknowledged the existence of second-impact syndrome in 2003, warning college doctors and athletic trainers. The NFL did not acknowledge the existence of second-impact syndrome until 2009.

• Though spectacular hits have long been assumed the primary cause of concussions, recent research suggests the accumulation of lots of little, routine hits does more harm to the brain than the occasional spectacular hit. Someone out sledding may take a hard hit to the head, but probably won't take lots of routine hits to the head over many years. Football players take lots of routine hits to the head over many years. The younger a person begins to play football, the more routine hits are experienced.

• Orthopedic care for athletes has improved substantially in recent decades. A generation ago, a torn anterior cruciate ligament of the knee meant the end of an athlete's career; now full recovery is common. Bobby Burnett, among the top college football players of the 1960s, started only one season in the NFL owing to orthopedic problems that today would be considered minor. Shoulder, elbow and wrist problems that once sidelined football players for months now may be resolved in weeks using arthroscopy.

But treatment for brain trauma has not improved, and it is unclear if it can be improved. At present the sole treatment for concussion is rest.

• In 2011, star quarterback Peyton Manning said players deliberately "tank" a baseline concussion test. The test measures time to solve visual problems. The theory is that if a player sustains a concussion, he should not be cleared to return until he can do the test as quickly as on his pre-injury baseline. "After a concussion, you take the same test and if you do worse than you did on the first test, you can't play," Manning told sportswriter Rick Reilly. "So I just do badly on the first test."

Later Manning claimed his statement was a joke. The joke was on the young, since as football's highest-paid player when endorsements are included, Manning's statement might inspire high school players to "tank" their tests.

• While the concussions suffered by NFL stars get the attention, the overwhelming majority of concussions occur to football players who are not in the pros.

Annually, about 3 million play youth football; about 1.1 million play high school football; around forty thousand play college football; fewer than two thousand play NFL football. Concussions from football mainly strike boys and young men who, unlike NFL stars, will never receive any tangible gain from football, but may be left with lifelong neurological problems.

The young are more likely to sustain concussions than NFL-aged players; the CDC notes, "Compared with adults, younger persons are at increased risk for traumatic brain injuries, with increased severity and prolonged recovery."

• Between a rising population and the explosion in football popularity, today far more young people play tackle football than a generation ago. They start younger, practice more hours and perform in more games. Today there are far more youth football players than a generation ago, more than twice as many college players as fifty years ago, two hundred thousand more high school players than in the 1980s. The cohort of American boys and young men exposed to brain trauma from football has been rising fast, while the number of desirable job openings in professional football has increased by only a tiny bit.

Accumulated brain harm from lots of minor hits is a greater danger than one spectacular hit; more football played year-round means ever more boys and young men endure more hits to the head. This simply cannot be good, especially as society becomes increasingly knowledge-based.

More head hits to the young, not the legal problems of the National Football League, is the concussion crisis.

FOOTBALL CONCUSSIONS HAVE PRODUCED HEARTRENDING stories. In 2004, Jake Snakenberg, a Colorado high school freshman football player, passed out in a huddle and died the following day. He had been hit hard the week before and reported tingling in his fingers: a concussion symptom. Whose fault was it that he went out to play despite this symptom—his coach's, his family's, his school's, his own? In 2012, Dana Payne, a Tennessee high school sophomore, passed out after being hit at a football practice and died in the ambulance en route to a hospital.

In 2011 Derek Sheely, a player at Frostburg State University, dropped unconscious at practice after a routine hit and died a few hours later from second-impact syndrome. Coaches called 911 immediately; Sheely was airlifted to a hospital; surgeons pumped him with drugs and cut into his skull, trying to relieve pressure from brain swelling; it was too late to save him. Sheely grew up in a town near mine; I saw him play in high school. His parents, Ken and Kristen, have established a small foundation in his honor and are doing what they can to warn others about the horror they suffered. The Derek Sheely Foundation is not the only memorial organization established by heartbroken parents for someone who died young because he played football.

Sorrowful though football deaths are, they are uncommon. Death rates from football have fallen steadily since the 1960s, principally because the advent of polycarbonate helmets has all but eliminated skull fractures. A player was fourteen times as likely to die as a result of football in the late 1960s as in 2011. But because polycarbonate helmets are so strong, they feel to players like strapping on a weapon, tempting defenders to launch themselves into helmet-to-helmet hits.

The National Center for Catastrophic Sport Injury Research reports that in the decade from 2001 to 2011, 163 boys and men died as the result of football games or practices, with the causes being head trauma, heatstroke, congenital enlarged heart and complications from sickle-cell trait. The majority of the deaths, 130, were of high school athletes.

Sixteen deaths annually from football, the last decade's average, is a horrible number. But during the same period an average of seven hundred people died annually from riding bicycles, with the main cause head injuries. There is roughly a one-in-a-million chance a teenager will die in any one hour of driving a car. Adjust for hours at practice and in games, and there is a roughly a one in 6 million chance a teen will die as the result of an hour of high school football. As regards mortality, a teenager is safer playing football than behind the wheel driving to school for class.

But normal driving does not cause blows to the head, as does normal football. That leads to the question of how many football concussions occur.

MOST SPORTS INJURIES ARE OBVIOUS: broken arm, swollen knee. But if an athlete does not report head pain, others have no way of knowing. Because it is impossible to know what another person feels, all concussion estimates are rough.

The NFL's injury-disclosure system is notoriously untrustworthy—some teams report every routine bruise, others hide information thinking this confers an advantage on the field. Neither college nor high school football has injury reporting. The result is a wide range of estimates regarding concussions.

The NFL Players Association hired Edgeworth Economics, a consulting firm, to review team medical records. The study found 266 NFL concussions in the 2011 season. There are 267 NFL games per season—a rate of one concussion per contest. (Many concussions actually occur in practice, but games provide a simple metric.) About two thousand players are on an NFL roster in a season. If 266 concussions happen in a group of two thousand in one year, the result is a roughly one in seven chance per season of an NFL player's sustaining a concussion.

No similar specific data exist for the high school level. Researchers led by Steven Broglio of the University of Illinois estimated in 2009 that each year there are 43,200 to 67,200 concussions in high school football, adding that "the true incidence is likely much higher" because many concussed boys either never are examined by a physician or say nothing about brain pain because they fear the bench. This suggests a high school football player has roughly one chance in twenty per season of a concussion.

The 67,200 concussions per year in high school football are being sustained not by wealthy NFL celebrities but by teens. NFL players receive significant benefits in return for the risks they take; college players receive scholarships or admission to elite universities. High school players receive a letter they can sew onto a varsity jacket they must pay for.

Big-college and NFL teams have medical staffs; high school players may lack regular access to physicians, let alone neurologists. Most public high schools do not have athletic trainers. At high school practices, there may be no one present who is certified to recognize and treat concussions. At youth football practices, there is almost never a trainer or physician present.

RESEARCHERS LED BY STEFAN DUMA of Virginia Tech have found the typical youth-league football player sustains about a hundred head impacts each season. The typical high school player sustains about five hundred head impacts annually, and the typical college player about a thousand. Most are routine impacts. But imagine what the accumulated effect of hundreds of "routine" hits to the head might be. The median football head hit, Duma found, is 15 g's—fifteen times the force of gravity. This is less dramatic than may sound; a 15 g hit should not harm a player wearing a properly fitted helmet. Impacts of around 40 g's, Duma thinks, are where concussion worries start, especially in youth players. College and professional football players have experienced hits of 100 g's.

In recent years, helmets worn by some college and NFL teams have had accelerometers embedded in the lining. At Virginia Tech, if the accelerometer registers a dangerous force level on a hit, a pager goes off on the team physician's belt, and he removes the player from practice or a game to be checked.

Most football players rarely are involved in the sorts of spectacular hits that set off physicians' pagers or make highlight reels. Almost all football players, though, experience regular head hits of varying intensity. Boxers who have kept going through roundhouse hits may suddenly drop to the canvas after a tap—the straw that breaks the camel's back. The same can happen with football players: no apparent harm from a hard hit, then a concussion from a routine play.

Researchers led by Philip Schatz of Saint Joseph's University in Philadelphia, Pennsylvania, concluded in 2011 that former football players who sustained two or more concussions during youth "showed significantly higher ratings of concussion-related symptoms," such as cognitive impairment, for many years after direct concussion symptoms, mainly headaches, had resolved. If 67,000 or more high school football concussions happen annually, and two concussions can lead to long-term neurological problems—the football-concussion crisis is all too real, and its focal point is not the NFL, rather, the local Pop Warner game and the local high school.

•   •   •

THE NFL IS THE "LEADER institution" on this issue, and its leadership has been dreadful, from the little to the big.

A little area where the NFL sets a poor example is helmet fit and mouthguards. Proper helmet fit reduces concussion risk. Helmets should be snug; it should be necessary to pull the flaps outward to get a helmet off. Yet many NFL players slip their helmets off as if they were baseball caps. Loose fit means players' helmets may come off during hits. "When a helmet goes flying off, that helmet was not properly fitted," says Grant Teaff, former head coach of Baylor University and now director of the American Football Coaches Association. In addition to proper fit, helmets should have four-point chinstraps—two buckles on each side—to ensure snugness. Yet the NFL does not require properly fitted helmets nor snapped chinstraps. The helmet flying off makes for a highlight video on *NFL Total Access*. Pro players know that if their helmet flies off, they will become a highlight, looking cool on TV. Young players see the pros letting their helmets fly off and imitate such dangerous behavior.

Double-sided or individually fitted (Type 3) mouthguards probably reduce concussion risk; the evidence on this point is not ironclad, but proper mouthguards are a simple, low-cost expedient. Some NFL teams offer players proper mouthguards; the New England Patriots dispense Type 3 mouthguards fitted to each player by a dentist. But the league does not require proper mouthguards—nor mandate any mouthguard at all. An NFL-NFLPA collective-bargaining rule says players make their own decisions about certain types of equipment, including knee pads and mouthguard.

Teens and young boys see NFL stars without mouthpieces and imitate that. Under rules of the NCAA and National Federation of High Schools, lacking a mouthguard is a penalty, but the rule is hard to enforce without checking each player pre-snap. Players need to be responsible for their own mouthguards, and many are not. They are following the NFL's terrible example.

A big area where the NFL sets a poor example is the helmet itself.

Until recently, the NFL made no assessment of the safety of helmets, requiring only that helmets be certified by the National Operating Committee on Standards for Athletic Equipment. NOCSAE is an industry-funded rubber stamp that sells its seal of approval to all helmets. Crumpled-up tin foil on your head would receive NOCSAE certification, so long as you paid the organization a fee.

No helmet can prevent concussions; changes in the culture of football are more important to safety than helmet design. But studies conducted at the University of Pittsburgh Medical Center suggest the best helmets lower concussion risk by roughly one-third.

By 2010, the NFL had data showing which helmet models were less likely to be associated with concussions. It sent teams a memo, but did not publicize the data nor instruct equipment managers to stock only those helmets that appear superior. Some teams, such as the New York Giants, did this on their own—protecting their own players, but offering no advice to young players or their parents. Systematic foot-dragging by the NFL on helmet safety may have been a factor in thousands of concussions sustained by pro, college and high school players who were wearing substandard helmets about which they had not been warned.

THE NFL BELIEVES THAT IF it mandates a helmet type, it becomes liable for head injuries sustained by anyone wearing that helmet; if it leaves the choice to individual players, then the player is responsible for whatever occurs. "Do you take a player who's worn a certain helmet for years without problems and tell him he must wear a different helmet?" Kevin Guskiewicz, a professor of sports science at the University of North Carolina and head of NFL concussion research, asked me. "He was fine in Helmet A. You tell him to wear Helmet B because you think that helmet is safer, then he gets hurt. Are you to blame?" In 2011, NFL commissioner Roger Goodell was asked why the league does not mandate the helmets that its own internal research shows are safest. His reply was remarkably similar: "The fact of the matter is that several players who have been playing with a specific helmet since college years or even high school years and have not had any issues may feel very comfortable in their helmet, and if we tell them they have to wear a different helmet, that creates liability."

Liability law is anchored in "asymmetrical information"—if one party knows of a risk and does not inform another party, the first party may be liable. If the NFL mandated the best-quality helmets while disclosing to players that they still might be injured, its liability exposure would seem slight, considering that football is known to all participants to be dangerous. The NFL has gotten some expensive bad legal advice in recent years, paying $4 million to $7 million per year to the white-shoe law firm of Covington & Burling, according to its disclosure forms, yet suffering a unanimous loss in a high-profile 2010 Supreme Court case, *American Needle versus NFL*, then in 2011 being completely outmaneuvered during an extended courtroom confrontation with the NFL Players Association. The NFL's belief that imposing safety standards on helmets exposes the league to added liability may be just another case of expensive bad legal advice.

That aside, think about what the NFL is saying when declaring that to avoid liability, it will not mandate safer helmets. The league is saying its profits matter more than the health of players; that profit for the league's super-rich owners matter more than setting a good example for a million high school football players.

In 2006, NFL spokesperson Greg Aiello told me the NFL was waiting for NOCSAE to make a recommendation on helmet safety. Seven years later, the NFL was still waiting. Since 2006, NOCSAE has issued a nine-page set of guidelines on how to stitch football gloves, but said next to nothing about football helmets and concussions, the most important equipment issue in athletics. "NOCSAE urges parents of athletes and athletes to get all the facts about football helmets and concussion protection," the organization announced. How? From "the hang tags that come with all new football helmets that address the helmet's abilities and limitations." That is to say: NOCSAE's advice is to read the disclaimer.

The league won't mandate safer helmets, and individual teams whose players have found safer helmets won't say what they are. In 2011, the Super Bowl pitted Green Bay versus Pittsburgh, a thrilling contest that went down to the final snap. Packers starting quarterback Aaron Rodgers sustained two concussions early in the regular season and was playing with fire—his later-life mental prowess—by risking a third. Rumor said Rodgers switched to one of the helmets league data showed was safer. I asked the Packers what helmet model Rodgers switched to. Green Bay spokesperson Jeff Blumb told me, "That is not information we are comfortable sharing outside our building."

Sports teams have a proprietary interest in keeping game plans to themselves; to refuse to disclose safety information is not just odd, it is irresponsible. But no NFL rule required the Packers, or any other team, to say what was on players' heads. After all, setting a positive example is not an NFL concern.

What Rodgers switched to was a Schutt AiR XP. Ben Roethlisberger, the other starting quarterback in that Super Bowl, had also sustained previous concussions and had switched to a Riddell Revolution Speed. Both Super Bowl quarterbacks previously wore the Riddell VSR4.

In 2004, the head football coach at my local public high school, James Collins of Winston Churchill High in Potomac, Maryland, forbid players to wear the VSR4 because of concerns it was unsafe. He staged a fund-raising campaign to replace the model with the Riddell Revo, then the most advanced helmet. Yet in 2010, star NFL quarterbacks were wearing a helmet that a high school football coach had banned from teen boys' heads years before. This happened because there was almost no public information on which helmet types reduced concussion risk. Into the breach stepped Stefan Duma.

•   •   •

A MEMBER OF THE VIRGINIA Tech engineering faculty, Duma began his career by working on auto safety, then on crash-survival systems for the Army's Blackhawk helicopter. He'd always attended Hokies games and yelled himself hoarse, but became interested in the engineering aspect of athletics when he realized there were no comparison studies of football-helmet safety. Duma proposed studies that would lead to an easy-to-grasp star-rating system, an idea that sports-equipment manufacturers strenuously opposed.

"A generation ago, automobile manufacturers said star-ranking systems for crash safety would never work," Duma says. "This turned out completely wrong. Star ratings communicate to buyers in a clear, simple way. The ratings caused automakers to rethink engineering, with the goal of getting five-star safety they could advertise. Since star ratings began, highway fatalities have declined steadily, even though the population is growing. The result is that driving today is less dangerous than it used to be."

Star-rating systems for automotive safety began in 1994, when there were 40,716 road traffic fatalities in the United States. By 2011, there were 32,310 fatalities, a decline of 38 percent relative to population growth. Star rankings are hardly the only reason for fewer traffic deaths, but they pressured manufacturers to engineer for safety. Once a hush-hush topic, safety is now widely touted in automobile advertising.

Duma wanted to do the same for helmets. Avoiding the inherent conflict of industry funding, as with NOCSAE, Duma put together financial support from the National Institutes of Health, Toyota and the Army, the last hoping he would discover something that improved the safety of infantry helmets. In 2011, Duma released his first star ratings. He found the Riddell VSR4—the most common helmet in football, including in the NFL—had poor safety performance, as did the Adams A2000. Riddell soon withdrew the VSR4 from the market. The Adams A2000 can still be found on sale; parents, do not let your children place one of these hunks of junk on their heads.

The initial Virginia Tech study gave five stars to the Riddell

Revolution Speed worn by Roethlisberger, four to the Schutt AiR XP worn by Rodgers. In a 2012 update, Duma's highest-rated helmets were the Riddell Revo Speed, Riddell 360 and Rawlings Quantum Plus; his best-value helmet was the Schutt DNA Pro, nearly as good as the top-rated model while costing $200 less. Annual rankings are at http://www.sbes.vt.edu/nid.php. In the dark for years, players, parent and equipment buyers now have a helmet-safety guide.

JUST BEFORE DUMA RELEASED HIS first helmet rankings, equipment manufacturers, football coaches and concussion researchers attended a helmet-safety meeting at the University of North Carolina. Mike Oliver, director of NOCSAE, rose to disparage independent research such as Duma's, then justified his organization's inaction by saying it would be "unethical" for NOCSAE to initiate safety reforms in the absence of "scientific certainty" regarding concussions. Scientific certainty is elusive, to say the least: physicians began urging patients not to smoke long before the link between cigarettes and lung cancer was airtight scientifically. Waiting for "certainty" can be a handy excuse for inaction. Oliver added, "All our income is from manufacturers, as licensing fees for putting our logo on their equipment."

Duma told the North Carolina meeting his studies found that the Riddell VSR4 provided significantly less concussion protection than other helmets. Thad Ide, Riddell's vice president of research and development, said, "We in the company have known about this for a number of years," adding that the Virginia Tech ranking of "marginal" for the VSR4 came as no surprise to Riddell since it "just reinforces what we have known for years." Essentially, Riddell was confessing asymmetrical information—that it was aware the VSR4 was substandard, yet withheld that information and kept selling the product. How many avoidable concussions resulted?

The Virginia Tech helmet-rating project had an immediate positive impact on athletics. I attend way too many football games, and in 2012 observed only a few VSR4s on NFL or NCAA players—the superior Revo Speed, Schutt ION and Rawlings Quantum are now on more heads than the VSR4. Duma's work was the catalyzing element in this change.

But two years after Duma's initial findings and three years after the league memo to teams about helmet safety, the NFL had still taken no position on what young football players should or shouldn't wear. The league continues to defer to NOCSAE—the organization that makes it living by licensing its seal of approval to every helmet, regardless of quality.

By EARLY 2013, ABOUT FOUR thousand former NFL players had joined concussion lawsuits against the NFL. Some former players may have been misled regarding concussion risks. Some may have reported concussion symptoms and been mistreated. Former Dallas Cowboys star Tony Dorsett alleged, for example, that after a hard hit to his head in a 1984 contest, he told Cowboys sideline officials he could "hardly see," yet the trainer sent him back into the game. Some former NFL players who report onset of dementia may be experiencing the decline that would have occurred regardless of sports, since many aging people lose mental prowess. And some former players in the lawsuits may be looking for a final payday from the league, whose ever-rising revenues are for the most part not shared with them.

Though a former football player with brain harm from concussions might have acquired the harm at any level of the sport, the NFL is the preferred litigation target owing to its deep pockets. Whether NFL doctors and trainers knew or should have known the dangers of concussions, and withheld that information from players, is the key issue. A joint investigation by the PBS show *Frontline* and the ESPN show *Outside the Lines* found that in the 1990s, an NFL retirement board quietly awarded at least $2 million to former players who the board found had suffered brain damage from football, including Mike Webster of the Steelers. This suggests the National Football League was aware of the extent of head-trauma risk years before disclosing its knowledge to players.

A prescient 2006 article by Peter Keating in *ESPN the Magazine* asserted that a physician named Elliot Pellman, head of the NFL's brain-trauma panel from 1994 to 2007, told coaches that because some players had sustained concussions and then reentered games without additional injury, therefore concussed players need not be withheld from games. This is like arguing that if you drive drunk and don't crash, therefore it is okay to drive drunk.

Motives of plaintiffs' counsel are clear. ARE YOU A RETIRED NFL PLAYER WITH LONG-TERM HEALTH ISSUES? YOU MAY BE ENTITLED TO COMPENSATION, advertising for one law firm announces. Practically everyone has "long-term health issues." The ad refers to an NFL Head Injury Lawsuits National Claims Center, as if this were some federal agency or court-established clearinghouse. The "National Claims Center" is an invention of William Kyros, an attorney with past wins in asbestos and Vioxx litigation.

Whatever the motives of the various factions, the litigation shows awareness of concussions is no longer a sports health taboo. Player career decisions are beginning to change as a result. In 2011, San Diego Chargers Pro Bowl lineman Kris Dielman was hit hard on the head during a game and suffered a seizure on the team plane a few hours later; he retired from football. In 2011, Pro Bowl safety Nick Collins of the Green Bay Packers sustained a neck injury that caused severe headaches—some trainers advocate strengthening the neck to reduce brain-trauma risk—and left the NFL. Mike Wright, a Super Bowl starter for the New England Patriots, suffered three concussions in about a year and in 2012 was thanked by being waived; he left the sport that year. Jacob Bell, a lineman for the St. Louis Rams, retired after sustaining a third concussion.

Players walking away from football, rather than trying their luck with second-impact syndrome, is a good sign. But much more reform is needed for concussion management during games, and for the penalizing of helmet-to-helmet hits. Colt McCoy, in 2011 the starting quarterback for the Cleveland Browns, sustained a concussion that left him with slurred speech; he says Browns coaches ordered him back into the game. McCoy's father, a high school football coach, was so furious he denounced the Browns in public. The Browns responded by drafting another quarterback and showing McCoy the bench.

The January 2012 NFC title game between the New York Giants and San Francisco 49ers was decided when 49ers' kick returner Kyle Williams fumbled a punt in overtime. Williams had suffered a concussion a month before. Giants special-teams player Devin Thomas told the *Newark Star-Ledger* that New York players knew about Williams's concussion history and "We were just like, 'We gotta put a hit on that guy,'" meaning hit his head to make him fumble. Earlier in the contest, New York players delivered vicious shots to Williams's head; later he fumbled, and the Giants advanced to the Super Bowl. No penalties were called. The league front office did nothing, despite Giants players openly boasting to the sports press about going for the head. The NFL's message to young players? Aim for the head.

NEW RULES AND STRICTER OFFICIATING should mean at least as much to improving football safety as advanced equipment. Recently the NFL and the NCAA moved the kickoff spot forward, so that many kickoffs sail into the end zone for touchbacks. Kickoff returns produce more concussions per play than any other action in football; touchbacks preclude the return.

"It would be fine with me if they eliminated the kickoff entirely," says Bob Milloy, head coach of Our Lady of Good Counsel in Olney, Maryland. He is Maryland's all-time winningest high school coach and runs one of the top prep football programs in the country. Good Counsel is always nationally ranked; its campus a veritable way station for big-college recruiters.

"We never do kickoffs when we scrimmage because they cause excessive risk, and we don't practice kickoffs much for the same reason," Milloy says. "Plus the special-teams players tend to be backups who have been standing around, not loose, then on kickoffs try to impress the coaches with recklessness. If the kickoff was eliminated and teams just started at their thirty, this would reduce injuries but not diminish the game."

Other changes may be coming. The three-point stance for linemen could be eliminated. In the conventional three-point stance, the lineman's head is down and play begins with contact to his helmet. In a two-point stance, the lineman's head is up at the snap. Because of the increasing emphasis on the passing game, many coaches want the offensive linemen's hands on hips at the snap anyway, as this position is superior for pass blocking.

In 2010, the NFL made the unnecessary-roughness rule more strict, saying players would be penalized for helmet-to-helmet hits on opponents who cannot see them coming, and penalized for "launching" into an opponent's helmet as opposed to contact in the course of a routine hit. In this the NFL was behind the NCAA, which in 2008 amended its rulebook to increase penalties for helmet-to-helmet hits, and behind the National Federation of High Schools, which in 2007 made head protection an officiating "point of emphasis."

Some on-field behavior has changed because of the new NFL rules, but not enough, because players know the new officiating emphasis is not strict. In 2012, a total of 257 unnecessary-roughness penalties were called, across 267 NFL contests—a little less than one unnecessary-roughness call per game. The NFL has begun handing out fines for helmet-to-helmet hits, but a $10,000 fine does not zing a player who earns millions. The NFL has also threatened to suspend players for vicious hits to the head. Rodney Harrison, a former Pro Bowl player and now NBC Sports analyst, has said that while NFL players do not care about fines they strongly fear suspension, since any player who loses his starting job may not get it back. By the end of the 2012 season, only Eric Smith of the Jets (2008) and Joe Mays of the Broncos (2012) had been suspended for using the helmet as a weapon.

The NFL says it cares about player safety, but does the league only care that concussions bring bad publicity and congressional hearings?

One Sunday in November 2012, star starting quarterbacks Jay Cutler, Michael Vick and Alex Smith of the Bears, Eagles and 49ers left games because of concussions suffered on deliberate helmet-to-helmet hits. No player involved was suspended by the NFL.

The same week these concussions occurred, the league was running a TV commercial in which stars Tom Brady and Ray Lewis, plus Lewis's mother, talked to a medical researcher about how the NFL was devoted to football safety. The commercial ended with Lewis's mother declaring, "Wow, now I feel a lot better about him playing."

Except it was not Lewis's mother, the woman was an actress; this was not disclosed to viewers. The "medical researcher," the centerpiece of the commercial, was an actor, his "laboratory" a stage set; this was not disclosed. Everything about the commercial was intended to mislead the public—which pretty much sums up the NFL's attitude toward head injuries.

BECAUSE MORE CONCUSSIONS HAPPEN IN practice than in games—there are more practice hours than game hours—reforming practice is essential. The 2011 collective bargaining agreement between the NFL and its players reduced the number of practice hours in which contact is allowed and stipulated that during summer two-a-days, only one session can be in pads. Some college conferences, notably the Pac-12, have placed limits on contact hours in football practice; in 2010, the Ivy league limited contact to twice a week. Many individual schools have cut back—at Good Counsel, Milloy does not allow live tackling in practice once the season begins.

In 2012, the Pop Warner organization imposed stringent limits on practice contact and banned the infamous Oklahoma and Nutcracker drills. In the former, two players battle in a tight space until one yields; in the latter, two players bash helmets till one yields. The day after the Pop Warner announcement, its competitor youth organization, USA Football, sponsored by the NFL, matched the new strictures. Nutcracker drills—all but designed to cause concussions—have been part of football practice for generations. When, in 2010, players of the San Francisco 49ers complained about sustaining concussions in Nutcracker drills required by coach Mike Singletary, he responded by publicly questioning their manhood.

For pro, college and even high school coaches to instruct players—children, in the case of high school players—to bash each other's heads until one screams in pain is at the least sadism, and perhaps criminal behavior. A high school teacher who told students to bash each other's heads would go to jail. Why is this okay when a high school coach gives the order? Such drills reflect the long-standing coaches' view of football players: that making them suffer is the coach's role, but if they are harmed, that's somebody else's problem.

As recently as a few years ago, most states had no laws regarding high school football practice or coaching standards. Not until 2007, for example, did Texas, with the country's most intense youth-football culture, require high school football coaches to know concussion and heatstroke symptoms. When, in 2006, I became a high school assistant coach in Maryland, I was amazed to learn that I had to give fingerprints and submit to an FBI background check to show I was not a convicted sex offender, yet was not required to know first aid, concussion symptoms or heatstroke management. The thousand-to-one chance a coach would be a sex offender was taken more seriously than the strong chance a high school boy would be in health danger and his coach wouldn't know what to do.

This is no abstract point. In July 2009, a sixteen-year-old boy collapsed during football conditioning at Northwest High School in Germantown, Maryland, a well-off community thirty miles from the White House, then died from heat stroke. Years later, litigation had not resolved exactly what occurred. But the adults present either acted irresponsibly or were ignorant of heatstroke symptoms and treatment.

During two-a-days at my kids' high school the following month, August 2009—the Washington, DC, area is hot and humid in the summer—the biggest player began to feel faint. The hefty are more prone to heatstroke than the skinny, as their bodies have relatively less surface area, compared to mass, to radiate heat. One of the coaches moved the boy into the shade and gave him water. I looked into the boy's eyes—his pupils were dilated. His skin felt strangely dry, though he should have been sweating. His hands were shaking, and he could not feel his fingers. These are symptoms of heatstroke. I called 911, the other coach and I poured on him everything cold we could find. Soon he was in an ambulance and on IV; he was released from the hospital that evening. I wasn't born knowing how to recognize and treat heatstroke, nor born knowing that rapid response is essential to save a victim. I knew these things because when I began my modest experience at coaching, I took a sports first-aid course on my own.

In part owing to the efforts of the parents and friends of Jake Snakenberg, most states now require high school coaches to pass a course in concussion awareness and heat management. By the time you read this, all states may have such laws. States gradually are signing on to the recommendations of the National Athletic Trainers' Association, which include slow heat acclimatization when August practice begins and only one session per day in pads during two-a-days. Georgia, where two high school players died of heatstroke during summer 2011, now observes NATA rules.

USA FOOTBALL, THE NFL-FUNDED youth league umbrella group, in 2012 became active in promoting "see what you hit" tackling form. The NFL does not want to lose the concussion lawsuits filed by former players, but knows it will stay in business should this happen. What the NFL fears is litigation against public school systems. The NFL can throw cash at any problem. Public school systems in many localities are strapped and, if they lose football concussion lawsuits, may have no choice but to stop sponsoring the sport.

A decline in high school football is the NFL's doomsday scenario. If concussion lawsuits cause public school systems to stop sponsoring football—and it cannot be repeated too often that nearly all high school football players are, legally, children—then football's training system will implode.

Today the NFL takes the best athletes produced by thousands of high school programs around the country, profits, and gives back nothing in return. It is a pretty sweet setup for the National Football League. Without public high school football, the NFL would have to fund its own club-level sports system, similar to those that support professional soccer and basketball in Europe. The NFL is much better off if high schools continue to bear the cost and risk. In 2012, the San Marcos Unified School District in California paid a $4.4 million settlement over a severe neurological injury that left a high school football player confined to a wheelchair. Concussion liability has the potential to undo football, but the time bomb is ticking at the high school level, not the NFL level.

AFTER HE WAS DRILLED HELMET to helmet by James Harrison of the Steelers, Josh Cribbs of the Browns said, "It's his job to try to knock me out." Acting indifferent about your own body's being harmed is part of the machismo of football. Some former players now in broadcasting have made small of concussion concerns because this is a way of saying, *I am such an incredible macho man that I went through that awful pounding and I'm still here.* After Harrison was fined for vicious hits on Cribbs and others, he called Commissioner Goodell "the devil." Many NFL players have expressed anger at Goodell for trying to make the game less violent, not only because they don't want to be fined, because they like to stride off after brutal contact. But then, only the survivors speak well of war.

It decidedly is not any football player's job to try to knock other players out. In prizefighting, the purpose is to inflict harm. In football, the purpose is to score more than the other team. Injuries happen, but they are accidents or unintended side effects. Modern dancers may ruin their knees; ballerinas who perform en pointe are inviting back problems. But harm is an unintended side effect of producing great dance. Harm should also be no more than an unintended side effect of producing great athletics.

Defending his hits, Harrison has said, "I want to play football the way I was brought up to play." So let him start his own Neanderthal Football League, with unrestricted helmet-to-helmet contact, and see how many parents bring their children to games. An orthopedic surgeon who claimed, "I was brought up to make huge gashes in people's joints, I don't like these new, tiny arthroscopic devices," wouldn't have patients long. Times change. Few Americans today perform their professions exactly as they were performed in generations past. Athletes aren't exempt from the forces of change.

Playing in the NFL, the NCAA or high school football is a privilege, not a right. This privilege requires obeying rules. Once a field goal counted for five points, now it counts for three. Once grabbing the face mask was legal, now it's not. Once the head slap was legal, now it's not. None of these rule changes ruined the game—arguably, all made the sport better.

Once deliberate helmet-to-helmet hits were legal—and now they are not. But while that change is welcome, football has not changed nearly enough to reduce brain-trauma risk to the lowest possible level. New unnecessary-roughness rules must be much more strictly enforced. Helmet-to-helmet contact in practice must be reduced. The three-point stance should be eliminated.

Ferocious as football is today, when players are told that until 1956 any player could grab any other player's face mask, they view that as barbaric. The helmet-to-helmet hit must become seen as barbaric if football is to continue to be played.

The next chapter: in a nation with epidemics of childhood obesity and prescription-drug abuse, the most popular sport celebrates weight gain and allows even healthy players to be injected with painkillers.

When Football Sends the Wrong Messages
About Weight, Drugs and Cheating

7

HOW 307 POUNDS BECAME UNDERSIZED

The NFL draft of April 2011 was in progress. Some 42 million Americans watched, more than twice as many as tuned in to that year's highest-rated episode of *Hawaii Five-0*. Tens of millions of Americans observed names called, followed by muscular young athletes walking across a stage to give crushing man-hugs to the NFL commissioner. Football was not being played, merely talked about. Watching football merely being talked about would prove the highest-rated US television event of the month.

When in 1981 the fledgling ESPN first broadcast the NFL draft, even sports nuts thought this was crazy—who would sit around staring at the tube as men in team Windbreakers spoke the names of unknown linebackers? By the mid-1980s, large employers such as the Detroit automakers began to puzzle over workers calling in sick on the same weekday in April, eventually realizing they were staying home for the NFL draft, then held during regular business hours. The league would shift the draft to Saturdays to increase viewership, then to prime time.

Perhaps the lure of the draft has to do with collective memories of choosing up sides in gym class. Practically everyone has a humiliating memory of being the last one chosen, or being laughed at when made a captain by some clueless gym teacher. By watching the draft, viewers can experience schadenfreude as others suffer through a high-tech version of gym-class choosing-ups: every year some famous college player is expected to be taken high and must sweat for hours on camera as others are selected instead. Or perhaps Americans are simply so enamored of professional football, they will tune in anything that begins with the NFL shield and chiming bells.

In April 2011, the San Francisco 49ers chose Aldon Smith of Missouri, and the Tennessee Titans picked Jake Locker of the University of Washington. Next the Dallas Cowboys were on the clock. The 'Boys needed an offensive tackle and were expected to select Tyron Smith of USC, which has produced many of the NFL's best offensive linemen. ESPN host Chris Berman furrowed his brow. Smith, he said, might be undersized. On NFL Network, analyst Mike Mayock worried that Smith was not big enough for the NFL. Dozens of websites fixate on the draft: by consensus, their verdict about Smith was "undersized."

On draft day, Tyron Smith was six foot five inches tall and weighed 307 pounds. A generation ago, a 307-pound football player was a giant. By Smith's draft day he was spoken of as if he were a lissome ballerino.

Once, football players were not notably different in physique from their peers. Ben Schwartzwalder, who would coach the great players Jim Brown and Ernie Davis at Syracuse, in the 1930s lined up at center for West Virginia University at 146 pounds. In 1941, the heaviest player in the *Life* magazine football all-American issue weighed 210 pounds. Guard Endicott Peabody II of Harvard, later to be governor of Massachusetts, was known as Chubby, *Life* reported, because he tipped the scales at 180 pounds.

The postwar era has seen an increase in the American waistline across all demographics, but the change in football is especially pronounced. My high school, Kenmore West of Kenmore, New York, had a

1969 team with 140-pound Mark Leous starting at nose tackle. Today a 140-pound boy would be hard-pressed to make a high school team as a punter, let alone play the line. Consider some comparisons:

- The Green Bay Packers played in the first Super Bowl, in 1967, fielding a defensive line that averaged 254 pounds. When the Packers played in the forty-fifth Super Bowl, in 2011, their defensive line averaged 320 pounds.

- The offensive line of the 1972 Miami Dolphins, pro football's only perfect team, averaged 262 pounds. No one on the team weighed more than 300 pounds. By the 2013 Super Bowl, Baltimore Ravens versus San Francisco 49ers, thirteen of the twenty-two starters weighed at least 300 pounds.

- In 2011, offensive linemen of the *Washington Post* All-Met team of top high school players in the nation's capital area averaged 310 pounds.

- Extreme heft is not limited to the sort of high school football players who earn All-Met distinction. In 2010 at Euless Trinity, a Texas public high school that is a football power, the offensive line averaged 262—same as the 1972 Miami Dolphins. Saint Ignatius of Cleveland, a private school power, had ten football players who weighed at least 250 pounds. Jenks High of Tulsa, Oklahoma, a public powerhouse, had an incredible thirteen boys of at least 250 pounds.

- In the 1991 Super Bowl, the defensive tackles were Jeff Wright of the Buffalo Bills and Erik Howard of the New York Giants, each listed at 270 pounds. By the 2012 Super Bowl, defensive tackles included Vince Wilfork of the New England Patriots, listed at 335 pounds, and Linval Joseph of the New York Giants, listed at 325 pounds.

- When the University of Wisconsin faced USC in the 1962 Rose Bowl, the heaviest Badger weighed 247 pounds. In 2012, Wisconsin listed eighteen players weighing more than 300 pounds. Nearby at the University of Wisconsin–Whitewater, which competes in Division III, the average lineman weighed 270 pounds. At the Division III level, there are no athletic scholarships. Division III often draws players judged not big enough for higher divisions.

- The actual weight of many professional athletes is believed to exceed listed weights. Women's sports delicately avoid the pounds question by listing female athletes by height, no mention of weight. Male athletes traditionally are listed by height and weight. But unless the athlete steps on a scale before witnesses, as wrestlers do, it is hard to know if his weight claim is accurate.

  Wilfork, listed at 335 pounds, may be as much as 400 pounds. When he stands next to other NFL linemen, themselves heavyset, his waist and rear end are visibly larger. Former New England defensive tackle Albert Haynesworth, listed by the team at 335 pounds, is believed to have weighed at least 375 pounds. It is likely, but impossible to prove, that many major-college and NFL players understate their weight—not out of concern for their girlish figures, but because the true numbers would be a source of embarrassment.

ARE THE EXAMPLES IN THIS section anecdotal evidence or a trend? The answer comes from Mel Kiper Jr., both a commentator upon and a product of American football fever.

As a young man, Kiper obsessed about draft prospects in the same way young men of a prior generation obsessed about tables of baseball statistics. It was the 1970s—no YouTube, no highlight videos, just smudgy mimeographed newsletters sent to NFL clubs by local scouts. Then, some teams made their first-round draft choices based on whose names they had seen in out-of-town newspapers. Gil Brandt, then general manager of the Cowboys, sent letters to the editors of college newspapers asking if he should know about anyone on their school's team. Brandt offered gifts to those who proposed drafting any collegian who made the Dallas roster.

In that 1970s milieu, Kiper filled a spare room with handwritten sheets of information on college seniors. Someday that room should be on the National Register of Historic Places because Kiper would land a job with ESPN obsessing on air about the NFL "selection meeting." Kiper helped make the draft the national event it has become and in the process earned a living by talking about draft choices. Only in America!

At my request, Kiper went through his files from 1979 forward, to assess the size, dash speed and strength—measured by football's "rep test" of how many times a person can bench-press 225 pounds—of players at the NFL's annual predraft Combine event in Indianapolis. His report: "Speed hasn't changed that much. Deion Sanders and Barry Sanders [no relation] were among the fastest football players ever, and they came out of college more than two decades ago. The skill-position players"—those who handle the ball—"are a little bigger today on average than a generation ago, and a little stronger, but only a little in both cases. The change is in the trenches. Lineman have gotten much bigger and much stronger."

Kiper analyzed his records for top NFL prospects at each of the three offensive line positions, at five-year intervals from 1979 to the present. First the reps tests. How many times an athlete can press 225 pounds gauges "functional strength," muscle power available after fatigue sets in. Some who post amazing power-lift results are too stiff or easily winded for team sports. The reps test is widely viewed as measuring of the kind of strength an athlete can use on the field. Kiper found that offensive tackles have increased from an average of 22 reps to 26; guards from an average of 22 reps to 29; centers from an average of 21 reps to 30.

Linemen's weight and height, Kiper found, have risen markedly.

From 1979 to 2011, highly rated offensive-tackle candidates enlarged from an average of 6-4, 264 pounds, to 6-6, 314 pounds. NFL-bound centers enlarged from an average 6-3, 242 pounds, to 6-4, 304 pounds. Guards supersized from an average 6-3, 250 pounds, to 6-4, 317 pounds. Today's offensive linemen are on average 24 percent heavier and 31 percent stronger than their counterparts of a generation ago. Kiper's assistant Chris Sprow used another set of records to determine that defensive linemen are today an average of twenty-five pounds heavier than a generation ago.

Improved nutrition and supervised lifting are factors in rising football tonnage. In the 1970s, the Nautilus system was devised; resistance training, which builds muscle mass, became more efficient. Next came widespread use of free weights—requiring extensive weight rooms with spotters, indulgences added as money began to flow to football. Today every major-college program has a weight room and aerobics area the size of, and nicer than, a high-end commercial health club. Jenks High School has a $6 million, thirty-six-thousand-square-foot football training and locker facility with hydrotherapy pools, plus ten thousand square feet devoted to free weights. A public high school!

The size and strength increase is one reason why today's football is performed at such a high level. The game has never been better. Most NFL contests are well played; spectacularly good NFL games have become almost routine. Each weekend in autumn has dozens of terrific college matchups, many resulting in games you wish you'd been at. Small-college football is competitive and well played, in addition to being rich in tradition; the Amherst-Williams game, played since 1884, draws huge crowds to the campuses of these small colleges. High school football games are better than ever, with an increasing number of prep programs that look like little colleges with modern weight facilities, turf fields, press boxes and high-fashion uniforms. Quality of play in high school games, especially in the hotbed states of California, Florida, Georgia, Ohio and Texas, is terrific. If you have not attended a high school football game recently, try one. You are likely to be impressed.

But it simply cannot be good that in a nation with a childhood-obesity epidemic, the most popular sport celebrates weight gain.

OBESITY IS "THE NUMBER-ONE health problem facing young Americans," says Tom Peterson, a pediatrician at the Helen DeVos Children's Hospital of Grand Rapids, Michigan, and chair of a youth-weight study conducted by the American Academy of Pediatrics. "Obesity can cause diabetes," he continues. "Eight to nine percent of today's adults are diabetic, but thirty-three percent of American children on track for diabetes, based on childhood obesity. Can you imagine what will happen to health-care costs if one-third of the nation is diabetic? It's worst for minorities—at least forty percent of African-American and Hispanic children are in the risk group for diabetes, owing to their weight. And who are American children taught by television to idolize? Football players who weigh too much."

Peterson started on a winning Michigan State football team of the 1970s, with Kirk Gibson, later a baseball star. He says, "When I played, 250 pounds was big. Now coaches tell 250-pound players they have to get bigger, even in high school. Evolution did not prepare us to weigh 325 pounds; this places tremendous stress on the heart and joints. If you bulk up to play football, then lose back to your natural weight after your career ends, you are likely to be fine. If you keep the weight, you are on track for diabetes and a host of other problems.

"The worst danger is the millions of kids who eat too much and are sedentary see huge NFL linemen with their bellies hanging over their belts and think that means obesity is okay. A 2010 study of Ohio State players found many had early indicators of diabetes and heart disease despite leading very active lives. If this is what's happening to the bodies of athletes, imagine what is happening to the bodies of sedentary children."

Studies of the national waistline are uniformly alarming. A 2007 study published in the *Journal of the American Medical Association* found that 45 percent of high school football players were overweight, even when accounting for active lifestyles; 9 percent were classified as "severely obese," a condition almost unknown in children in previous generations.

Those on track for cardiovascular disease are said by physicians to have metabolic syndrome, meaning abnormal readings in several categories—blood pressure, weight, glucose and triglyceride levels, "bad" cholesterol. Any one of these should be manageable, but in combination, they spell trouble. A 2011 study conducted under the auspices of the American College of Sports Medicine found that one-third of linemen playing big-college football had metabolic syndrome. And these are *athletes.* The journal *Pediatrics* reported in 2012 that 20 percent of young Americans overall have metabolic syndrome, double the rate of the previous generation.

Researchers led by the Harvard School of Public Health have studied American Indian children, who began to exhibit significant weight gain a generation before the effect spread broadly to all social classes. They reported in 2010 that childhood obesity roughly doubles the risk of death before age fifty-five. In 2012, researchers led by Phil Zeitler of the University of Colorado reported that type 2 diabetes, all but unknown in children of previous generations, not only was being detected among the young, but was resistant to treatment. Kids were getting so heavy so young that standard therapies did not help.

American kids are sitting on couches munching junk food while watching football games in which being heavy is presented as a desirable quality that seems to have no consequences. Or kids are holding the controllers of football video games where the same obtains. Of course, American kids are also sitting on couches watching a range of shows in which perfect-10 bodies are held up as ideals. The ubiquitous proliferation of low-cost sugary and fried foods has done more to cause childhood obesity than anything from the worlds of either athletics or entertainment. But with a childhood obesity epidemic in progress, it simply cannot be good that the nation's most popular sport celebrates weight gain.

WITHIN FOOTBALL CULTURE THERE IS tremendous pressure to "get big." High school players know they may not see the field unless they are big. Though it is possible to gain safe weight in a supervised program of diet and exercise, at age sixteen the shortcut may simply be eating too much. The result often is what scouts call a Fat Albert: high schoolers who are mammoth from pizza and french fries rather than from lifting and who will never be fast enough to play at the next level. For them, high school football ends, and they're overweight and on their own. No one is going to help them lose back to a healthy weight.

"When you are playing football, it's normal to get together with the other guys and eat three plates of dinner," Will Funderberg, who played football at Davidson College, says. "If you don't stop and switch to one plate once football ends, you could have lifelong problems with your heart and knees." Funderberg played at 255 pounds; within two years after graduating college he was down to 205 pounds, his natural weight. Jacob Bell, the player who retired from the Rams in 2012, in just six months dropped from his NFL weight of 305 pounds to his natural weight of 250 pounds. Philadelphia Eagles offensive tackle Antone Davis, who ballooned to 476 pounds after leaving the NFL, ended up a contestant on the reality show *Biggest Loser,* where he dropped back to his natural weight of 245. But many former football players either don't or can't take such care of themselves. Chris Mims, a former San Diego Chargers star, died in 2008 of enlarged heart at age thirty-eight, weighing 465 pounds on death.

At the top levels of football there is keen awareness that lean muscle provides a competitive advantage over fat. Virginia Tech athletic meals offer no fried foods or sugared soda, little cheese. Typical dinner is salads, fresh fruits, grilled vegetables, grilled chicken, wheat pasta with meat sauce, Gatorade, water, juice, skim milk and ice cream sundaes.

Friday night dinners before games add sirloin steaks, but never *frites*—any player who wants french fries will have to sneak out for those. Some big-college programs and all NFL teams go further, with chefs who prepare fresh fish, frittatas and restaurant-style dishes screened by nutritionists.

The NCAA's elaborate rules restrict how often athletes can receive meals that differ from those served to regular students on a university's board plan and, on paper, appear to restrict late dinners. If football practice concludes at 6:00 p.m., players at a large university won't make it to a school cafeteria for an hour, as they must put away gear, shower, then catch a bus. Typically college cafeterias end dinner at 7:00 p.m., about when the football team could arrive, and serve only snacks after that. In response, many big-college athletic programs have separate training-table areas for athletes only, offering special meals and open to late hours. The University of Florida, for instance, has two full-time sports nutritionists and an athletes-only dining facility where "product choices exceed those used for regular dining hall meals," according to the guide the school distributes to scholarship athletes. Parents of most University of Florida students pay $4,130 annually for board, only to find their children may not enter the athletes' dining area where higher quality food is served free—what they may think of the arrangement is anyone's guess.

That healthful eating has taken over collegiate sports surely is good. But if the biological markers for metabolic syndrome are rising even among college football players who eat healthful nutritionist-supervised diets, imagine what's happening with the million-plus high school players whose food pyramid is based on bacon burgers, double-cheese pizza and wings.

PETERSON BELIEVES THAT AT THE least the football players who generate significant sums of money for the college establishment should receive, as part of NCAA agreements, a year of follow-up nutritionist's care and supervised weight loss, so the moment football ends, they begin returning to their natural weights. This is much easier if done sooner than if put off till later.

The proposed six-year NCAA scholarship for Division I football players would sync well with this idea. In the sixth year, with football concluded, the former player would concentrate on finishing his coursework and on stepping back his body from pumped-up status. Every university has students majoring in nutrition; as a practicum, they could assist former NCAA athletes in a life-after-football transition. During many college football games young women mingle with the players on the sidelines. Many are majoring in sports medicine, or studying to become certified athletic trainers. Colleges consider it fine to offer them credits for helping the football team win. They should also receive credits for helping former football players reset the clocks on their bodies.

Systematic assistance with weight loss for former college players would not be difficult to arrange, given their relatively small numbers and the ocean of money in collegiate sports. For high schools, post-football help is harder to conceptualize.

Physicians often warn that the real worry about obesity is not where you are now but where you will be in twenty years. Unless habits change, weight gain tends to slowly continue. Suppose NFL players keep gaining heft at the same rate shown by Kiper for the most recent generation. By 2035, the four-hundred-pound lineman will be a norm. The field will need to be enlarged since rushing plays would become impossible if the center of the turf is clogged with linemen who resemble human bridge abutments.

Could weight in football be regulated? Suppose, say, the NFL gave each team an average body-mass-index target and penalized those over the target with fines or loss of draft choices. Maybe that would work. It doesn't sound promising.

Among the top coaches in football annals was Bill Walsh—tactical innovator, Super Bowl winner, leader and a sophisticated man who read *The New York Times* and literary novels. In 1963, when Cal lost the annual Big Game to Stanford, Cal's athletic director stormed into the locker room and fired the school's top two coaches—Walsh and Marv Levy, both eventually members of the Pro Football Hall of Fame.

Walsh told me in 2005 that football would never be able to discipline itself regarding weight gain; the pressure to win, and the temptation to take shortcuts, were too great. "Nothing will change about weight until medical studies demonstrate a clear, tobacco-like link between obesity and reduced mortality, and then public schools, universities or the NFL lose lawsuits on this point," Walsh said. "Nobody likes lawyers, so it's tough to root for litigation as a solution. But for football to lose a few lawsuits over player health—it would be good for players and good for the game."

FAST FOOD IS HARDLY THE only substance football players are putting in their bodies. Unlike Major League Baseball, the NFL and the NCAA have long banned nonmedical use of steroids, and enforcement is strict. Painkillers are another matter. Football players are major consumers of three kinds: Narcotic painkiller pills such as Vicodin, injected local anesthesia and Toradol, an all-purpose pain reliever that a disturbing number of NFL players have injected even when they are feeling fine.

Ryan Leaf is renowned for being a draft bust. Chosen second overall in 1998, immediately after Peyton Manning, Leaf's NFL stay was brief. Considering Manning's estimated annual sports income from salary and endorsements, the gap between Manning and Leaf is today about $50 million per year. Struggling as an NFL quarterback, Leaf tried to play for the San Diego Chargers with a broken wrist, making the injury worse; to get through this he took lots of painkillers and became an addict. Since leaving athletics in 2002, twice Leaf has pleaded guilty to felonies involving theft or illegal possession of narcotic painkillers. In 2013, he began serving a nine-month prison sentence in Montana.

Leaf is hardly alone among former football players in having problems with prescription narcotics. Just as head trauma is coming into the light of day as a football problem, so is painkiller abuse. Tom McHale, a player for the Tampa Bay Buccaneers and Philadelphia Eagles, died in 2008 of an accidental overdose of painkillers. Craig Newsome, a former Green Bay Packers star, told the *Milwaukee Journal Sentinel* in 2012 that he became a painkiller addict. Newsome played in fifty-three NFL games and left the sport with scars on both knees plus across his chest from surgeries; Percocet was his response. Former Houston Oilers star Earl Campbell, who began walking with a cane in his forties, left athletics habituated to painkillers; his scoliosis, which occurred naturally, was made worse by football contact, leaving him with chronic severe back pain. Walt Sweeney, a Pro Bowl offensive tackle for San Diego in the 1960s, in 1994 sued the NFL alleging his painkiller addiction was "directly related" to football injuries and to narcotics freely distributed by the Chargers. (Sweeney's claim won at the trial level; the NFL won on appeal.) In 2012, Ray Lucas, a former New York Jets and Miami Dolphins quarterback, told Toni Monkovic of *The New York Times* that after back and neck injuries, he became addicted to prescription painkillers, taking as many as twenty-five a day. (Three or four daily is a normal dose.) Lucas urges men or women with pill-dependence problems to contact www.TurnToHelp.com, an anti-addiction program designed for those who cannot afford rehab or fear its stigma.

Football players are hardly the only athletes to use opioids to alleviate pain. Tennis star Jennifer Capriati ruined a shoulder with high-velocity serves, became dependent on painkillers, and in 2010 was hospitalized after overdosing on prescription drugs. But incidence of narcotic use and dependence among present and former football players is believed to be higher than among other athletes, given the nature of football contact. In 2010, a study led by Linda Cottler of the University of Florida found that about a third of former NFL players reported misusing opioid painkillers during their playing days, and about

15 percent reported ongoing misuse. The rate of narcotic-painkiller abuse by football players, she found, was about three times that for men of similar ages.

High school players seeking to obtain narcotic painkillers legally must get prescriptions at physician appointments that are not easy for minors to arrange, then go to pharmacies, most of which exact scrutiny on minors seeking controlled substances. Generally, NCAA team doctors prescribe narcotics grudgingly. These factors are thought to limit legal use of opioid painkillers among high school and college athletes.

BUT IN THE PROS, THE pills are right in the locker room. All NFL teams retain physicians who examine players at team facilities, not at medical offices, and who may dispense pain pills legally from what is essentially a team's private stash. The former security director for the New Orleans Saints has alleged in a lawsuit that the team kept a large inventory of opioid painkillers in a trainer's closet, and though the pills were intended for distribution by the Saints' physician, players and coaches knew where the key was and when the closet was unattended. The allegation of unregulated access to painkillers in the Saints locker room had not been resolved as this book went to press. But the basic arrangement described—a small pharmacy within an NFL team facility—is not unusual.

Lawrence Brown, a Brooklyn specialist in addiction therapy, has since 1990 been the physician supervising NFL use of prescription drugs. Teams report to him—with names removed—the total amount of painkillers and other prescription compounds dispensed. Because incidence and types of injuries vary, and because doctors have different philosophies of pain management, some clubs may use narcotics liberally, others sparingly. But the NFL has no rules on narcotics consumption, other than that it must occur legally, by prescription.

"Physicians work for the individual teams; the NFL as a league is not in the business of practicing medicine," Brown says. "Each team physician makes an individual decision about what is appropriate based on the condition of each patient. Their best-practices guidelines come from their medical societies, not from the league. There are no NFL standards for prescription drug use and no NFL best-practices rules about narcotics."

Brown would not say what amount of narcotics the typical NFL team distributes in a year, other than to note, "Football players are more likely to experience pain than the population as a whole, so you would expect them to need prescription drugs." Asked if he had received any NFL team data that reflected a disturbing level of narcotics use, Brown gave this roundabout answer: "I have seen some data that needs improvement, but I have never seen anything that required reporting to the Drug Enforcement Administration."

Across health care, including in debate regarding the Affordable Care Act of 2010 ("ObamaCare"), there is controversy regarding whether there should be fixed standards of medical practice or if physicians should make decisions independently. Fair arguments can be offered for either position. Care standards allow for comparisons of therapeutic results, but medicine is as much art as science, so independent judgment is needed. In this context, the practical effect of pro football leadership saying the NFL "is not in the business of practicing medicine" is that a team physician is freed to dispense painkillers to get a player on the field, regardless of risk to long-term health.

Here, the difference between medical practice and workplace rules is central. The NFL should not mandate standards for how doctors set a broken limb, but could (and does) say, "Players are not allowed on the field with hard casts." By the same token, the NFL should not mandate how a physician interprets a player's pain, or what the best medication and dose may be. But the NFL could say, "Players are not allowed on the field less than twenty-four hours after taking prescription pain medication." Such a rule would meet the test of a workplace safety requirement.

By instead imposing no workplace rules regarding narcotics, the NFL both endangers the long-term health of its players and allows them to perform on national television as though fearlessly immune to pain. Youth and high school players see an example that appears to be of men so tough, they laugh at pain. The message sent is that young players should use their own bodies recklessly.

ACCORDING TO CENTERS FOR DISEASE Control data, in 2000 there were more fatalities from illegal drug use than from painkiller abuse. By 2010, the positions had reversed: nearly seventeen thousand Americans died after overdosing on opioid painkillers, compared to seven thousand deaths from cocaine and heroin. By 2011, five times as many Americans died of painkiller overdoses as died in fires.

Distribution of narcotic painkillers has risen at a remarkable pace. A 2012 White House study found that in 1991, some 79 million prescriptions were written for opioid painkillers; by 2011, the number was 219 million. Some physicians' and patients'-rights groups contend that in the past, pain has been undermedicated. Even if that is so, a 175 percent increase in narcotic painkiller distribution in twenty years sounds out of control. Declaring "rampant" painkiller overconsumption, in 2013 the Food and Drug Administration issued rules making opioids harder to obtain by prescription.

Most painkiller-abuse problems stem from people's own bad choices, or from Big Pharma marketing: aggressive promotion of Oxy-Contin roughly coincides with the surge in painkiller deaths. But having the nation's number-one sport being a major consumer of painkillers—athletes who gulp narcotics celebrated on television—could not have helped.

OTHER KINDS OF PRESCRIPTION-DRUG use is rising among the young—the ones most likely to be influenced by football players and Hollywood stars. A 2012 study in the journal *Pediatrics* found that 14 million outpatient prescriptions were written for minors in 2010, with the fastest rate of increase being in medications related to ADHD treatment. Whether it is wise to medicate large numbers of children with psychostimulants remains to be seen. The troublesome conjunction with sports is that use of Adderall, a popular drug for ADHD, is also rising among football players.

Compounds such as Adderall and Vyvanse can improve concentration and focus, regardless of whether the user has an attention-deficit disorder. Brightly packaged, covered with impressive trademark stamps and tiny-type disclaimers, chemically they are a high-tech formulation of amphetamines. Once, many football and baseball players took amphetamines, typically calling them greenies; before his 2013 death, former Chargers offensive tackle Sweeney wrote that greenies were "normal for gameday preparation" in the NFL. Amphetamine use was banned in baseball in 2006 and is thought to have declined in football in the previous decade. The repackaging of amphetamines from street drugs sold in Baggies into a respectable, corporate-marketed palliative for a polysyllabic syndrome has given the chemicals new legs.

In 2012, Aqib Talib, then with the Tampa Bay Buccaneers, was one of several players disciplined by the NFL for taking Adderall, without a prescription, to improve his play. All were defensive backs—a position where it is crucial not to have a lapse in attention. Had a physician prescribed Adderall to Talib, or to the other players disciplined, this would have been fine with the NFL. The league allows players to ingest Adderall and other ADHD drugs if legally obtained. The prescription can come from the team physician; there is no requirement that the player be diagnosed with ADHD. After all, the NFL does not practice medicine.

Most children, and most parents, don't know that NFL players are popping ADHD pills to improve performance. Supposing this becomes well understood, what message will football be sending? Take drugs to do better in school or at the office.

AUSTIN KING SPENT FOUR SEASONS in the NFL as a backup for Tampa Bay and Atlanta, leaving football, as many do, a little before the four-year mark, when he would have become eligible for significant benefits.

Unless a player is a blue-chip starter, he is waived before he can vest, easily replaced by another eager fellow who'll be let go just before *he* vests.

"There is a pervasive culture in football that you must do whatever it takes to get on the field," King said. "This is especially bad for the marginal players who know they can be replaced tomorrow. So you perform like a wild man on special teams, in order to impress the coaches. I hated the wedge"—the center of a kick-return formation, where players collide at maximum sprint—"and everyone in football does. If you don't show the coaches you will play with pain and take crazy risks like throwing yourself into the wedge, they will replace you with somebody who will, and your career is over. Teams also pressure their injured marginal players to take a few snaps in practice. If you know they'll get rid of you unless you practice, you ask for painkillers."

King's problem was chronic shoulder pain. Before games, often he was injected with Marcaine or lidocaine to numb his shoulders. Steve Tasker, a star of the Buffalo Bills' Super Bowl run of the 1990s and perhaps the best-ever special-teams performer, told a sport forum in 2007, "There were occasions in my career where I had to get assistance, chemically, to play the game. An injection into some body part, so I could cope with the pain in order to play. There were occasions where I actually went to the training staff and said, 'Can you get me ready?' and they offered me the option [of local anesthesia]." Tasker said teams did not twist a player's arm to take injections; rather, usually it was the players who asked to be injected. He concluded, "Those are the kind of things that happen behind the scenes in the National Football League, that players would really rather not have made public."

Injected anesthesia was common in football of the early postwar era: players would have their knees injected so they could perform fearlessly. Since pain is the body's signal that harm is occurring, numbing a joint masks damage that can lead to later-life problems, including early-onset arthritis. "Some of the guys I know who are in their fifties and sixties who played and now have orthopedic problems, getting injections before games must be part of the reason," says Tony Dungy, who won the Super Bowl as head coach of the Indianapolis Colts in 2007.

Rising awareness of the drawbacks of numbing joints before a game is believed to have led to a declining occurrence of injected local anesthesia, though neither the NFL nor the NCAA collect data on injected-anesthesia use. Mike Goforth, Virginia Tech's director of sports medicine, says the Hokies use injected anesthesia "maybe once per year," owing to fear that playing with local anesthesia can cause further injury. Goforth adds that across football, "It probably goes on more than people would care to admit." Andrew Tucker, team physician of the Baltimore Ravens, told me he sometimes performs game-day injections to numb hip pointers, a condition that is painful but not especially serious. Tucker said he considers it unethical to inject anesthesia into a player's knees or ankles. But the NFL imposes no restrictions: other NFL team physicians are free to conclude that such injections are ethical.

King reports that numbing shots into the shoulder "really hurt. The other guys, even NFL players, they make a face when somebody gets a large needle into a joint in the locker room. But lots of them line up for Toradol with B_{12}. That's an easy shot, into the butt, you hardly feel a thing. The guys waiting in line for Toradol would look away when they saw me about to get the big needle into a joint."

And there are lots of guys in line for Toradol.

TORADOL IS THE TRADE NAME FOR ketorolac, an anti-inflammatory that relieves pain but does not contain steroids. The drug is an amped-up version of the nonsteroidal anti-inflammatory found in Aleve, an over-the-counter painkiller. It is more potent, usually injected rather than swallowed, and available only by prescription.

The NFL receives data on the total number of players being injected with Toradol, but will not release the numbers. A 2002 study found that all but two NFL teams inject players with Toradol on game days. And here's the thing—Toradol in the NFL typically is not used to treat injuries. Rather, NFL players get shot up with the drug when they are feeling fine, in order to reduce sensitivity to pain. This allows them to perform with abandon, producing fantastic plays but also causing avoidable long-term health harm to themselves—while sending young people the wrong message, that violent activity does not hurt.

Football will always be a risky sport with ferocious collisions. But audiences don't know the extent to which NFL players use Toradol to numb themselves before going on the field. In 2012 the National Football League Physician's Society issued a recommendation that Toradol be administered solely to treat existing injuries, not as a prophylactic against game-day pain; that Toradol be given only to players whose names are disclosed on the team's weekly injury list; and that Toradol be administered orally rather than injected. But important as "the National Football League Physician's Society" may sound, the panel has no authority. Anthony Yates, a past NFLPS president and team doctor for the Pittsburgh Steelers, told me the Toradol memorandum is strictly advisory: nothing happens if teams ignore it. "Each NFL team physician is free to practice medicine as he or she sees fits," Yates said, adding that he'd heard BCS-caliber colleges were beginning to inject players with Toradol.

Since any responsible physician makes notes or a dictation before giving an injection or prescribing drugs, and members of the National Athletic Trainers' Association are told to keep therapy notes, total use of narcotic painkillers, Toradol and pain-numbing anesthesia shots could be tallied by the NFL and disclosed to the public, without jeopardizing the privacy of players. Publication of anonymized data is the essence of modern medical research. There is no reason the NFL could not publish anonymized data about painkillers—no reason, other than that the league would look terrible.

The NFL does publish an elaborate weekly list of the likely-to-play status of players who are nursing injuries, classifying them, by name, as doubtful, questionable or probable. Vegas casinos and offshore betting parlors are avid consumers of this information. So the league ensures the broad dissemination of football medical information that can be used to make money. But the league discloses nothing about narcotic painkillers or injected anesthesia. Bad for business.

FOOTBALL DOES NOT INTEND TO send young people the wrong messages about overeating and popping pills. But wrong messages result. As Emerson observed, "What you do speaks so loudly I cannot hear what you say."

Other wrong messages are sent by NFL veneration of criminality. Fathers, and more than a few mothers, take sons, and more than a few daughters, to visit the Pro Football Hall of Fame in Canton, Ohio. Each year former players are "enshrined" there, the league's grandiose term for having a bust installed. It is a pleasant tradition—in 2005, I took one of my sons to Canton to watch his favorite player, Dan Marino, inducted.

Wander through the Pro Football Hall of Fame and you'll find exhibits lauding O. J. Simpson and Lawrence Taylor. Simpson was acquitted of criminal charges in the savage murders of his former wife Nicole Brown and her friend Ronald Goldman; in a California civil trial, he was found guilty for the wrongful death of Goldman and for battery against Brown. In 2008, Simpson was sentenced to a maximum of thirty-nine years for armed robbery and kidnapping. In 2011, Taylor pleaded guilty to hiring a sixteen-year-old girl as a prostitute, and agreed to register as a sex offender.

The National Football League has done nothing about the presence of shrines at the Hall of Fame to a killer and a sex offender. The sports media committee that chooses Canton members has done nothing. The message the NFL sends—and that the Canton selectors endorse—is that it doesn't matter if a player commits crimes against women, so long as that player made money for football and gave the sports media something to laud.

The NFL and the NCAA further send the wrong message by rewarding, or lightly punishing, cheating. Many US institutions reflect this fault: the collapses of Enron, Lehman Brothers, WorldCom and other firms whose books were frauds showed that cheating is common at the pinnacle of corporate America.

But white-collar misdeeds are remote from the daily experiences of young people. What did Tyco manufacture? What were its management's crimes? Many could not answer. Football, on the other hand, is followed intently by much of the American population. Sports are readily understood in commonsense terms: Practically everyone has encounters with those who cheat at games. When cheaters at the top level of athletics get away with this, the message sent is "Cheat to win."

In the last decade alone, the football programs of Alabama, Auburn, Ohio State, Penn State and USC have been caught engaging in significant cheating, lawbreaking or defiance of the standards that ought to govern universities. Some trophies have come out of trophy cases, and some banners have been removed from walls. But the schools and coaches got to keep the money they realized from unethical behavior. Even Penn State's $60 million fine—to be paid over many years—allows the school to keep the far larger sums taken in during the period when Penn State actively was covering up child rape. The message is that cheating will be overlooked, winning is what matters.

Cheating in college sports hurts society more than cheating in professional sports since higher education should set a good example, while pro sports exist solely to entertain. Still, the worst football cheating scandal of recent decades, Spygate, led only to slaps on the wrist.

In 2007 the New England Patriots were caught videotaping the sidelines of opponents during games, in order to steal signals. NFL rules unambiguously forbid sideline videotaping. The Patriots had been taping opponents' sidelines for years and had gone to great lengths to conceal this activity. When caught, Coach Bill Belichick claimed he mistakenly believed sideline taping was permitted. If so, why did the Patriots elaborately conceal their actions?

Belichick is a talented coach, his Patriots a fine team that would have posted many victories whether they cheated or not. But the Patriots must have benefited from taping opponents' sidelines or they would not have done so for years. During the period when the illegal taping system was in place, Belichick's Patriots won three Super Bowls. Since the system was exposed, the Patriots have not won the Super Bowl.

In response to Spygate, the NFL fined Belichick about 10 percent of his income for one season; fined the Patriots about a tenth of 1 percent of their revenue for one season; and stripped New England of a first-round draft choice. Draft selections are important, but are so often wasted that the loss of any one pick means little. The year before Spygate, Belichick used the Patriots' first-round draft choice on Laurence Maroney, who started only a few games for New England before being waived out of football. The money and draft-choice fines were so trivial that other than through opprobrium, the Patriots and Belichick paid no price for Spygate.

After the Patriots' taping system was revealed, Roger Goodell ordered Belichick to turn over all illegal tapes—giving New England three days to comply, thereby plenty of time to erase anything the team did not wish the league to see. When the tapes were turned over to the NFL, Goodell had them immediately destroyed. Later it turned out a former Patriots employee kept a copy of the tapes, and a second level of the controversy began. The essential point is that the league's first reaction was to destroy all evidence of cheating by a Super Bowl winner.

The message that was sent by the front office of America's most popular sport? Hey kids, cheat to win!

The next chapter: at the youth and high school levels, year-round football is ruining childhood, while "showcases" mainly serve the adults who profit.

THE 5-STAR INVITATION-ONLY ELITE SHOWCASE

The February 2010 segment on ABC's *Good Morning America* was irresistibly charming. A thirteen-year-old boy with a Huck Finn grin, clutching a football, was interviewed with his proud father. Viewers were told the boy had just been offered a "groundbreaking" college football scholarship at his tender age. David Sills V, flanked by his dad, David Sills IV, had been discovered on YouTube, viewers were told. He was discovered as a pass-throwing prodigy by Steve Clarkson, a California mentor of quarterbacks, who recommended him to Lane Kiffin, head coach at USC. One glance at the YouTube clip and Kiffin "immediately" called to offer a scholarship. "It's always been my dream to play at USC," the boy said. Then he went out on a closed-off Manhattan street and demonstrated his arm by zinging the ball to *Good Morning America* staffers.

The scene was charming if you didn't know the backstory. Clarkson had not "discovered" the boy, rather been hired to promote him by Sills IV, who is wealthy. The verbal commitment to USC was meaningless—the NCAA does not recognize verbal commitments, which are unenforceable in any case. Kiffin's phone call may have been a violation of NCAA standards, which forbid football coaches to contact high school players until spring of their junior year, which for Sills V would not come till 2014. The boy cannot agree to a scholarship until February of his senior year, which will be 2015.

Clarkson is the best known of an expanding economy of middlemen who act as private coaches and work to match up teens with college football programs, for a fee. The connection that resulted in the *Good Morning America* segment began in 2004 when the elder Sills took his son, then in elementary school, to California and paid Clarkson to put the boy through some drills. By 2010, after the elder Sills had paid Clarkson a substanial sum for private coaching, Clarkson told Kiffin the younger Sills had promise.

Kiffin went along with the "discovered on YouTube" charade because Clarkson encouraged Matt Barkley, then USC's star, to attend that college. Kiffin owed Clarkson a favor and knew that because the verbal offer was unenforceable, he could always rescind it later. Clarkson got priceless publicity for his private coaching business, in which he charges parents as much as $1,000 an hour to tell boys things any quarterbacks coach would say, such as square your feet and hold the ball high. Clarkson urges parents to grayshirt their boys—have them repeat a grade, regardless of classroom situation. That way they will be a year older than their sports peers and have an advantage. Jimmy Clauson, a star for Notre Dame and a high NFL draft choice, repeated sixth grade at Clarkson's urging.

If Sills V does actually enroll at USC, his father may donate more to the university than an NCAA scholarship costs. In 2012, UCLA offered a basketball scholarship to Justin Combs, son of rapper Sean Combs. Bloggers wondered why the son of a wealthy man should receive an NCAA free ride. But football and men's basketball scholarships are not financial aid, which is intended for deserving students of modest means. NCAA scholarships are business deals. For UCLA, involvement with Sean Combs, who has become a Hollywood presence, could be good business—he might bring the school publicity and make donations. Similarly, USC's offer to the younger Sills yielded business dividends immediately. Paid advertising on *Good Morning America* would cost considerably more than the favorable publicity USC received for an unenforceable promise of a sports scholarship.

The elder Sills created not one but two high school football teams to showcase his son. First he donated liberally to football at Red Lion Academy in Delaware, near the Sills family home, only to be asked to leave when Red Lion officials felt football had become the tail that was wagging their school. Then Sills would donate freely to establish Eastern Christian Academy, across the state border in Maryland, which he called a school though it had no classrooms or teachers—just recruited football players, plus computer terminals where the "students" were said to take online courses. In 2012, Eastern Christian only played three games; most opponents canceled when they learned Eastern Christian was not accredited. On the rare occasions he could take the field, the younger Sills performed well. Whether he would have been better off as an athlete, to say nothing of as a child, simply attending a regular school is anyone's guess.

THE DISQUIETING ASPECT OF WHAT happened to the younger Sills at a tender age was not that a wealthy father tried to rig the world for his son. Many wealthy parents have tried to rig things for their children. Nor was it disquieting for a father to live a fantasy life through a child. Millions of parents have dreamed their offspring are prodigies in athletics or the arts. The most common pattern is that a child grows into an adult who achieves a fruitful life by middle age. But that does not happen until the parents are themselves old and facing their mortality, while the child is no longer a luminous youth. On the other hand if a child does well at sports, music, acting, dance or modeling at an early age, parents can revel in that success while they themselves are young enough that the future still seems unlimited. A child viewed as amazingly talented implies the parents must be amazing too; the slow nurturing of qualities that will make a child a success by middle age draws little notice to parents.

Some parents immerse their children in youth sports in hope that a few thousand dollars invested in baseball or soccer leagues will lead to an NCAA scholarship, saving them $200,000. That seems like good economics until children reach senior year of high school and parents discover that except for the revenue sports of football and men's basketball, most NCAA scholarships are "fractional"—a girls' soccer player will be offered a quarter or even an eighth of a scholarship. Suddenly those 4:00 a.m. Saturday departures to distant youth-league competitions don't seem like time well spent.

Companies with names such as Athletic Baby and Baby Goes Pro have begun marketing sports training for toddlers, appealing to parents' dreams of having an athletic prodigy, in the same way dance studios market moms the dream their three-year-olds will become danseuses, or musical-instrument stores market the purchase of pianos or organs for young beginners.

The sense of having a sports phenom in the family can be deceptive, owing to puberty timing. A boy who hits puberty early may be a stellar football player at age twelve; by the time the boy is a senior and his peers have caught up physically, he may not even start for the high school team. But parents don't want to believe that luck with hormones made their child a youth sports star. They want to believe their child is a prodigy—setting an expectation the child may fail to meet, bringing the word *failure* into his vocabulary before adulthood even begins.

So THE SILLS FAMILY SITUATION, if extreme, is not out of step with the experiences of many American families with children who are good at sports or music. What is disquieting about the Sills example is the sense that football has become a cult. Doing well is not enough; a child must be utterly immersed, to the exclusion of all else, from a young age.

Football has been popular in the United States for more than one hundred years, but now expands beyond popular into a mania. High school teams fly coast-to-coast for televised games. College coaches use private jets and helicopters to woo seventeen-year-olds. Three national high school all-star games air on ESPN, NBC and NFL Network, sponsored by the Army, the Marines and Under Armour. Dozens of local and regional prep all-star games have been established, with even youth leagues staging "all-star" games.

The 2012 NCAA report on Penn State decried "a culture in which the football program was held in higher esteem [than] the values of human decency," while concluding the entire university had been in thrall "to the omnipotent football program." Football omnipotence is expanding.

Privately run showcases, combines and football camps now take in millions of dollars annually in fees from parents, supposedly to introduce boys to college recruiters but most of the time just for a few days of football drills. Some of these events are run by promoters, some by coaches, some by hustlers. They are moneymakers for adults, but have little relationship to athletic admission to college. A fifteen-year-old who receives a letter or e-mail saying he has been "invited" to an "all-star camp" may not understand that: nor may his parents or guardian, who pay the fee because they think the letter means their boy is headed to sports glory.

"Prospect camps" have become a revenue stream for college coaches and their assistants. Large numbers of boys come to a campus in June or July to work out with college assistants, their parents paying for fees and travel because they believe being at the camp will translate into a scholarship. Every college athletic department website has a "for recruits" tab where teen football players are asked to fill out a questionnaire. A few weeks later a letter will arrive, urging the boy to attend a football camp at the college. Many boys react to such letters by mistakenly thinking they are being recruited. It's a joyful moment likely to be followed by keen disappointment—after parents have spent hundreds or thousands of dollars on camp fees and travel.

In 2011, Donovan Hill, a thirteen-year-old Pop Warner player in Los Angeles, was paralyzed when he made a head-down tackle—the most dangerous move in football—during a youth league game. Each year a small number of awful things happen to kids who are swimming, biking, going to summer camp, crossing the street: Life cannot be lived without risk. But Hill was hurt during the Midget Orange Bowl, a Pop Warner championship staged on a turf field before spectators with officials, cheerleaders and screaming coaches on the sidelines. A generation ago, Hill would have been playing sandlot football with friends. Instead he was in a highly organized league with pads, spring and summer practices, corporate sponsors, and coaches encouraging hard hits—a miniature NFL game.

Youth is the fastest-growing segment of the American football market. Pop Warner has been around for decades; in 2002, the National Football League founded USA Football, a tax-exempt (perhaps you guessed that) entity whose corporate sponsors include Gatorade, Sports Authority and Riddell. By 2012, an estimated 3 million boys as young as ten, plus a few girls, were playing tackle in USA Football and similar leagues.

Having coached youth football, I can attest that some coaches are conscientious men who patiently help young people have the kind of positive athletic experiences that teach self-discipline and teamwork. Others are little-bully types who scream at quaking twelve-year-olds. Some know safe tackling form and are aware of concussion symptoms. Others are ill-informed on football basics and make themselves feel manly by telling children to pummel each other.

There have always been problem adults in coaching, but as organized youth leagues expand, more children are exposed to them. In October 2012, the Pop Warner organization of central Massachusetts suspended two coaches, three game officials and two youth-league staff members after five boys suffered concussions from extremely rough play, including numerous late hits. The suspended coaches were deemed to have encouraged attempts to injure, while the officials and league staffers did not intervene.

Youth football is heavy on marketing. USA Football sponsors Player Academies in which boys as young as seven wear pads and engage in what the organization calls "modified contact," at a cost to parents of $500 or more. Maryland Youth Football stages $350 camps for boys as young as seven, in pads, plus "combines" in which eighth-graders are tested with cone drills as if they were at the actual NFL Combine. Grassroots Youth Football of Maryland and Virginia offers "combines" from age seven, posting the results online, and charges admission to spectators. Grassroots Youth Football plays its games in the spring and summer, so middle-school-aged boys can participate in games for their high school affiliates in the fall. A boy doing Grassroots or a similar spring-summer youth league, then a USA Football or high school affiliate league in autumn, might perform in twenty full-contact football games in a year—more than an NFL player.

Youth leagues that have high standards, such as Pop Warner and Five-Star Football of Washington State, restrict players by weight classes, to prevent large twelve-year-olds from smashing into slender ten-year-olds. But that reduces violence! Worried about lack of violence, Steve Clarkson helped found the Throwback Football League, open to sixth- through eighth-graders, which plays in the spring and has no weight-classification rules. Big, early-maturity kids can beat up on skinny, late-maturity kids to the heart's content of coaches screaming at them to hit harder.

WINTER WORKOUTS FOLLOWED BY SPRING play converts youth football into a year-round activity. When, in 2011, Deion Sanders was chosen for the Pro Football Hall of Fame, he received the news while coaching a practice session of the youth-football team he sponsors. Hall of Fame decisions are announced the day before the Super Bowl—which means his youth team was practicing in February.

Once athletes aspired to be "three-sport," which for boys meant football in the fall, basketball in the winter, baseball or track in the spring; for girls soccer, then basketball, then softball or track. With football becoming year-round, the boy three-sport athlete has all but vanished, and year-round soccer is causing three-sport girls to fade too. Increasingly, the year-round nature of football renders it hard for a boy also to do band, theater, debate, religious events, scouting or other traditional youth-years activities. It's football and nothing else, to the detriment of a well-rounded education.

Youth league football generally is crummy football, producing a high proportion of blowouts. The size and strength of twelve-year-olds varies much more than size and strength vary in college or the pros, and many youth leagues allow open recruiting, which results in the best players flooding to the hot team. Scores from the 2012 Grassroots League: 53–0, 44–0, 43–0, 42–0, 40–0, 38–0. When a youth game ends 53–0, no one on either side of the ball learned anything. But, the winning coach can boast.

Some well-run youth organizations, such as Maryland's Rockville Football League, monitor practices and enforce antirecruiting rules to ensure balanced competition. But close games and delimited coaches are the exception in youth football. Too many games are over in the first quarter, and too many coaches are working through their own personality problems by screaming at children and running up the score.

ROBERT CANTU, A BOSTON UNIVERSITY concussion researcher, believes full-pads football should not be played until age fourteen. Before then the braincase has not finished hardening; the mature skull resists impact better than a youth's skull. The necks of young people are underdeveloped compared to the necks of adults, resulting in more energy transferred to the head during some kinds of contact. Robert Cantu has written "a child cannot brace for a hit in the way that an adult does" because "a child's brain and head are disproportionately large for the rest of the body." All told, Cantu thinks, "a mild hit can do more neurological damage to a child than a severe hit to an adult."

Many assume that because youth players are lighter and slower than adult players, contact is not severe. This turns out to be a false assumption. On the Auburn Eagles youth league team that Stefan Duma, the Virginia Tech helmet-safety researcher, studied—well coached and safety conscious—accelerometers recorded six helmet-to-helmet impacts of at least eighty times the force of gravity. Eighty g's is the ninety-fifth percentile of NCAA football contact.

Nearly all the youth-league hard head hits in Duma's study occurred not in games but at practice. Game situations are chaotic. In a game, many players are stumbling, off-balance or going half speed when contact occurs; two players sprinting toward each other in a straight line doesn't happen often. During drills at practice, contact often is straight-ahead full power. The result, as Cantu and others have noted, is that practice reform is more important to protecting young football players than game-rules reform.

Young boys like to pretend to be NFL players—enthusiasm for youth football is high. Ten-year-olds wearing the same gear as the pros! But then young boys like to pretend to be generals, cowboys and secret agents too. Are ten-year-olds really better off in organized, full-equipment tackle leagues than they would be playing informal neighborhood games of touch?

Many football youth leagues are more about adults than kids—about middle-aged men pursuing a fantasy of being Don Shula, while draining away precious hours of carefree youth that boys might be enjoying in spontaneous play. *Pediatrics*, the journal of the American Academy of Pediatrics, has observed, "The shift from child-oriented goals to adult-oriented goals can negate the positive aspects of organized youth sports."

Joel Brenner, a pediatrician in Norfolk, Virginia, heads the American Academy of Pediatrics committee on sports medicine. He says,

"The number-one concern with youth football is the same one as in other youth sports—overuse. Too much practice, practices that are too long, leagues that run all year, leagues where organized events are more about the parents' egos than the children. Children younger than high school age should not participate in football, or any sport, year-round. Youth sports should be confined to one season, with three seasons either off or at some other activity. In season, children should not have four or five practices per week. They shouldn't be at practice two or three hours at a time. Like the all-new year-round leagues, year-round football is making it hard for young people to try a variety of sports and hard for athletes to participate in a range of extracurriculars. It is causing repetitive-motion injuries in children who haven't even gone through puberty yet."

Spontaneous childhood play—capture the flag, exploring the woods—may be romanticized. Often children left to find things to do on their own are lonely. But the pendulum has swung too far in the other direction. Today at football fields, baseball diamonds and soccerplexes across the nation are a never-ending progression of youth leagues in which adults scream at children to get hits or goals or touchdowns, and the children look as if they wish they were out exploring the woods.

WITH ORGANIZED YOUTH TACKLE FOOTBALL expanding, the big question for many parents is whether they should allow their children to participate.

Brenner does not see youth football as exceptionally risky, noting concussion rates are higher per hour in girls' soccer, and girls are more likely than boys to tear their ACLs, yet parents and educators enthusiastically encourage girls to play sports. "It's not that youth football is something parents should fear per se," he says. "But they need to know about the specific program—the quality of the coaching, whether safety and heat-exposure rules are enforced, whether there is excessive practice time with too much contact, whether the head coach is a screamer type, whether the coach will tell the child he is being disloyal if he has extracurriculars or if he needs to skip a practice for homework." Youth football, Brenner notes, keeps young people active physically, and, if the coach isn't a screamer, can be fun. "Right now the problem in most youth sports is that they are overdone—too many practices and games, overuse of young bodies, the self-image of the adults running things being more important than fun and learning for young people."

Tackle at a young age certainly does not translate to future football success; Pro Bowl performers Antonio Gates and Osi Umenyiora are among many NFL stars who never played youth tackle football.

As recently as a decade ago, youth flag football leagues were seen as the ideal compromise—flag teaches young players how to be in the right place at the right time, without the intensity and risk of tackle. Flag leagues have withered away as the fad for youth tackle has grown, especially as USA Football, with its sheen of NFL affiliation, has expanded. A decade ago Montgomery County, Maryland, just outside Washington, DC, had thirty-six middle-school-aged teams in its civic flag league, and a track record of flag players advancing to high school rosters. By 2010, the county flag league was reduced to ankle-biter teams from elementary schools—the tween boys all were in pads, playing tackle.

USA Football began in 2002 with $3 million in seed funding from the NFL and, according spokesman Steve Alic, has received at least $6 million in NFL funding since. Five of its board members are from the NFL; another is the president of the Sports & Fitness Industry Association (until recently called the Sporting Goods Manufacturers Association), which wants parents to buy more pads, helmets and cleats. USA Football has a well-deserved reputation for teaching safety. But the organization works to expand the year-round, cultlike obsession with football, which benefits the NFL and manufacturers of sporting goods, and no one else.

• • •

To KICK OFF THE 2012 high school football season, teens and coaches of Pulaski Academy, an Arkansas prep power, boarded a jet and flew seventeen hundred miles to Los Angeles to face Chaminade High, always a strong California competitor. Fifty-one players, seventeen coaches and staffers from Good Counsel High, Maryland's top prep power, accompanied by two off-duty police officers and four chaperones, flew twenty-four hundred miles to Las Vegas to face Bishop Gorman High, which has been investing heavily in football. Players and coaches of Gilman High of Baltimore headed to the runway to fly to Cincinnati for a game against Archbishop Moeller High School. And it was not just private schools in the air; two Florida public high schools flew their football teams to Texas to face public high schools.

In 2004, when a well-off booster covered all expenses for De La Salle High School of Concord, California, then riding the country's longest winning streak, to fly to Seattle and face Belleview High, this was considered extraordinary. Just eight years later, long-distant travel for high school football teams—paid for by boosters or by marketing firms such as Paragon and Inter Sport, which package high school football events—have become humdrum. Most Division III colleges do not send their teams to away dates beyond bus range. Whether big-money universities should fly teams to the opposite coast—in 2012, Syracuse played USC in Los Angeles—is controversial; inevitably, class time is missed. Yet long-distance away games are the new normal for high schools. And camera crews await. Over the course of 2012 opening weekend, ESPN2 and ESPNU aired fourteen high school football games.

Every high school has an athletic oversight organization, usually a small state agency for public schools and a local or regional association for private schools. Athletic oversight organizations could instruct members to face only in-state or nearby opponents. This is what would happen if high schools had sports in perspective.

The players headed to Las Vegas from Good Counsel were accustomed to college-quality athletic facilities. Good Counsel has a turf stadium that is the state's best prep football field, expansive weight-lifting facilities, two full-time athletic trainers and a dozen coaches. Arriving at Bishop Gorman, Good Counsel players began texting and tweeting friends that the sports facilities of the Nevada school were even more impressive. With alums now owning Vegas casinos, Gorman has fund-raised effectively. The school has a six-thousand-seat football stadium with a video scoreboard, a brand-new forty-one-thousand-square-foot athletic training facility with indoor track, carpeted and wood-paneled football locker room, ice baths, lots of "racks" (centerpoints of football weight lifting), and a ninety-seat theater for game film.

For the 2012 season, Gorman deployed no less than nineteen football coaches. The school recruits throughout the Southwest and offers financial aid to top players. The result has been four straight state titles, including a 63–10 state championship victory in 2012. The irony that Gorman is a Catholic school, yet football is what is worshipped there, is barely worth mentioning.

Gorman has such a lopsided edge in talent and resources that the school essentially purchases victories. In 2012, Gorman's average margin of victory was 40 points, with wins of 70–0 and 78–13. When the average victory is by 40 points, that means Gorman is lining up opponents that have absolutely no chance: what happens are not games, rather stunts. During blowout wins, players, parents and school officials get plenty to boast about, but no life lessons regarding teamwork or character are learned.

Deep-pocketed private prep programs don't have to function this way. Like Gorman, Good Counsel has significant funds at its disposal. But Good Counsel schedules its region's strongest opponents, rather than seeking easy wins as does Gorman. In 2012, Good Counsel's average victory margin was 13 points.

The life lessons football can teach can only be learned in fair competition. Close games help boys learn teamwork and sportsmanship. Good Counsel's desire to test itself against equal opponents, and thus teach through sports, is practically quaint at a time when boosters want what Bishop Gorman delivers—rigged runaway wins, followed by players strutting and pointing at themselves as NFL players do. The life lessons from those kinds of games are if anything negative.

COST-NO-OBJECT HIGH SCHOOL football increasingly is found across the nation. Dragon Stadium at Southlake Carroll High School in Texas seats 12,600, with all admission sold on a season-ticket basis. Voters in Allen, Texas, agreed in 2011 to issue a $60 million bond to build a state-of-the-art, eighteen-thousand-seat football stadium at Allen High. Jenks High of Tulsa has a ten-thousand-seat football stadium. Prep football has become such a big deal that in 2011, when the head coach's job opened at Florida's Leesburg High, a football power, seventy-one people applied for the vacancy.

Many high schools excuse in the football coach behavior that would not be tolerated from teachers. Something about the physicality of football seems to bring out negative instincts and spread them from the locker room into the high school proper.

To cite one of many examples, in 2012, Refugio High School of Refugio, Texas, a Gulf Coast town, was assigned a schedule that included a number of lower-division schools. Refugio won those games 84–0, 80–0, 77–0, 76–0, 70–0, and 56–0. The coach, Jason Herring, kept his starters on the field through the fourth quarter to humiliate opponents. Herring acted like the sort of low-level street thug who runs from a strong man but beats up on those who have absolutely no chance of striking a blow in return; the 84–0 victory came against a school that had a 1-6 record. When the *Austin American-Statesman* ran an article about complaints that Refugio High's football team was unsportsmanlike, the school's principal, Todd Deaver, told the newspaper other schools deserved to be humiliated because his boys were physically superior. When football turns even a high school principal into a little bully, something has gone badly wrong.

• • •

A GENERATION AGO, MANY STATES did not stage high school football playoffs. When my New York State high school finished undefeated in the 1969 regular season, that was that: no playoffs to attend. In 1982, *USA Today* began to rank high school football teams. Then the Internet spun up and Rivals.com, MaxPreps.com, ESPNU.com and ESPN Rise joined the rankings frenzy, making high school football rankings instantly accessible. Once teams were ranked, playoffs were the next step. Today, New York State awards ten prep football championships in different classifications, and that's just for public schools. In 2012, a total of 224 New York high schools made football playoffs.

Boosters, players, coaches and parents agitate for more high school football games. The traditional eight-game season became ten games, plus extended playoffs. Today in Texas, a high school state football champion must play sixteen games—the same as an NFL season. In the crazed Texas system, an amazing 608 high schools reach the play-offs, including many with losing records, such as Taft High in the postseason at 3-7 in 2011. Texas names twenty-two high school football champions in ten classifications, each with at least two divisions. Virginia's football playoffs in 2012 admitted 150 teams—nearly half of the 339 high schools in the state. Twenty of the schools reaching the 2012 Virginia high school playoffs had losing records; one matchup was 5-5 Cave Spring versus 4-6 Abingdon, a playoff pairing in which neither team had a winning record. California's high school football playoff system has taken grade inflation to a new low: in 2012, Rancho Bernardo High made the postseason at 1-9.

Mania for high school football is such that boosters and coaches just don't want the play to stop—though extending a high school season to as many as sixteen games means significant distraction from classwork. That English essay? Put it off till January. Longer seasons increase pounding on young bodies and add to the concussion toll. But the adults running the football establishment don't seem to care if more games means more injuries for children.

By 2011, the nation's fifty states were naming 326 high school football champions, in many different divisions and categories created to maximize the number of football trophies. That year Massachusetts named fourteen state high school football champions; Alabama named eleven; New Jersey had 397 high schools and crowned twenty of them state football champions.

As title games were expanding, so were all-star games. High-school-level basketball or soccer all-star games are common, as such events are relatively easy to put together. A football all-star game is quite a project, requiring significant expense and a week away from the classroom. A generation ago, there were no football high school all-star events. Today there are three national games: the Army All-American Bowl, broadcast on NBC; the Under Armour All-Star Game, broadcast on ESPN; and the Marines' Semper Fidelis Bowl, broadcast on NFL Network. Add to them many local or regional all-star games.

When the Army All-American Bowl began, in 2001, players were chosen at Thanksgiving of their senior year. The announcements kept creeping further up, until May 2012, when the game roster was announced before anyone's senior year even started—when it was unknown how players would perform, or if they would make their GPA minima. The United States Army didn't seem to care whether the All-American Bowl created an impression of leadership or good citizenship. The event was about football hype, and the sponsors wanted to start the hype rolling months in advance.

BOB MILLOY, HEAD COACH OF Good Counsel, is romanced annually by the head coaches of the nation's BCS programs. Paid twenty-five times what Milloy makes, they are dependent on him to send star-rated recruits their way. The spreading of the Grand Illusion into high school football worries Milloy. Though he has coached football for forty-three years and helped scores of young men attain NCAA football scholarships—in 2011, seventeen of Milloy's charges signed Division I offers—he has had only two players, Shawn Springs and Bob Raba, who became NFL starters. Two others made NFL practice squads but did not see the field. "That's it, that's all," Milloy says. "Yet I have an entire locker room full of teenagers who are convinced they are going to the NFL."

Milloy shows players a chart of their odds. The chart depicts the odds of a typical high school football player getting an NCAA scholarship or an athletic admission to college at one in fifty. The odds of an NCAA football player later putting on pads in the NFL are one in thirty-five. Together, the odds of a high school player reaching the NFL are nearly one in two thousand." Stated another way, there are at least twenty high school football teams where no one will make the NFL for each team where someone will. "My guys don't want to believe this," Milloy says. "They think high school football is about the next step in their journey to the NFL, not about having a sports experience while they attend school, learn and get ready for college."

At least Good Counsel is strict regarding academics—pass your courses or you don't play. Friendship Collegiate Academy, a magnet school in one of the worst parts of the District of Columbia, has the district's best football program; produces many NCAA athletes; and likewise is strict. Friendship will not allow upperclassmen to play unless they are passing at least one Advanced Placement course. The school is across the street from a rail line that shakes the building when freight trains pass. Boarded-up storefronts and signs like BIG D LIQOUR line the street. An armed guard is at the door. The physical facility, with peeling wallpaper, is the reverse of Good Counsel's. The coaches' offices are a converted storage closet. There is no locker room; the players change in an old storage container tipped on its side.

"Here you are in what is said to be one of the worst inner-city areas in the country," says head coach Aazaar Abdul-Rahim, "yet inside, the school is quiet and disciplined. Everyone is on time and acts in a respectful manner. All players understand that unless their schoolwork is complete, they do not practice."

But far too many high schools aren't like Friendship Collegiate or Good Counsel: academic standards for varsity athletes are quietly waived or grades changed. Everyone assumes football players will be okay because they will make a glorious living in the NFL. They won't.

I TRACKED DOWN ALL MEMBERS of the 2004 *Washington Post* All-Met football squad, fifty young men of sparkling ability and promise. NaVorro Bowman at the 49ers and Cody Grimm at the Tampa Bay Buccaneers became NFL starters. Two became anonymous journeymen. That was it—four of the fifty most promising football players from the Washington, DC, region reached the NFL.

One of the journeymen, Derrick Williams, was the Rivals number-one-rated high school senior in 2004, receiving fifty-two Division I football-scholarship offers. He spent time on the practice squads of the Detroit Lions and Pittsburgh Steelers. By 2012, his stat sheet on NFL .com said, in foreboding capital letters, CUT.

Of other notable 2004 All-Met players, Carl Ehrlich became captain of the Harvard football team, then went into the business world. Anthony Perkins played at Syracuse, was not drafted by the NFL, and joined the Colorado Ice of the semipro Indoor Football League. Steve Weedon signed with the University of West Virginia, but his grades were below the NCAA's lenient standard. Weedon played at junior college and in Division IAA; by the time his GPA was repaired, he had too little eligibility remaining to interest the big-money programs. Ike Whitaker, the *Washington Post*'s 2004 All-Met Player of the Year, is profiled in the next chapter.

One example doesn't prove anything, so I tracked down all players from the Army All-American game of 2004, the premiere prep all-star event. The eighty-six young men on the roster were the crème de la crème of high school football. Two became NFL stars, Adrian Peterson of the Minnesota Vikings and Chris Long of the St. Louis Rams. Seven became NFL starters, and six became NFL journeymen. That leaves seventy-one of the eighty-six top high school football players across the nation that year who never received a paycheck from the NFL.

• • •

DESPITE THE GREAT ODDS AGAINST a prep football player someday reaching the professional level, high schools and youth leagues keep putting more emphasis on football, playing more games, expanding playoffs and all-star contests, sinking more resources into a sport that's a lot of fun but spirals further out of perspective with each passing year. Especially cynical is the proliferation of year-round mandatory practice, coupled to seven-on-seven leagues—a kind of football that high school teams play in shorts and cleats year-round.

Seven-on-seven leagues began in Texas in roughly 2000. In this variant of the sport, a quarterback and receivers face off against defenders for passing only—no rushing, no blocking or tackling. Because no pads or hitting are involved, seven-on-seven can be played at any time of year. As a form of year-round high school football, seven-on-seven rose in popularity quickly, by 2003 or 2004 being played four to six days per week at many Texas high schools, every month.

The continuous passing drills of seven-on-seven caused Texas prep football to transition from its traditional I-backfield power-rushing format to "spread" offenses with four wide receivers and lots of yards gained. By 2012, Texas high school football scores would look like this: McAllen Rowe 63, Pharr San Juan 60. Texas-raised quarterbacks such as Andrew Luck, Robert Griffin III and Ryan Tannehill would be making their marks in the NFL, aided by endless hours of seven-on-seven passing when young.

But the pace of high school football life would change dramatically. A generation ago, athletic oversight organizations forbid prep football practice before summer, often with August 1 as the start date. Boys got together for "captains' practices," which were conditioning drills run by upperclassmen, with no coaches present—I sweated through them in July as a high schooler. As recently as 2010 in Virginia, high school football teams were forbidden to meet before May, even for conditioning, while in Maryland, high school football coaches were not supposed to have contact with players, beyond a hello in the halls, till the school year ended.

Today many states, notably Texas, allow public high schools to hold football practices during the winter, followed by spring scrimmages with crowds in the stands and officials, similar to the spring games at colleges. Louisiana allows public high schools, to hold full-pads contact practice throughout the winter. In 2009, the state sanctioning body for Pennsylvania voted to allow football practice in forty-nine of the fifty-two weeks of the year. In 2010, year-round football became allowable for Maryland public schools. As of 2011, Virginia high school coaches can hold "football specific events" at any time of the year except Christmas and spring break.

In all states, off-season football must be voluntary. This is like saying that wearing clothes is optional. Every boy knows that if he hopes to start, he'd best be present at every "voluntary" session.

Year-round football is terrific training for the tiny number who, like Andrew Luck, are bound for professional stardom. Year-round football is seductive for large numbers of boys who want to dwell as long as possible in an NFL dream—*Mom, I'd like to go to the library but coach says I need to be at practice*—rather than confront their GPAs.

Considering one prep player in fifty receives a recruiting offer, making high school football a year-round pursuit helps only that slim minority with a shot at college athletics—while shafting everyone else. The many, many boys who will never get any recruiting boost to college must surrender a significant amount of their high school years, plus any chance of participating in extracurriculars. Many boys delight in life as a high school football player—you're a BMOC, you wear the varsity jersey to school on Fridays, you spend a few pleasant years in a fantasy of reaching the NFL. But for nearly all high school football players, this distracts them from the schoolwork needed for regular admission to college.

Who is being served by year-round high school football? Coaches are made to feel more important; recruiting services get customers; equipment sales rise. Education takes a hit, but to the extent football has become a self-enclosed cult, not even high school principals seem to care about that.

"Exclusive MD High Five-Star Showcase," read the flyer for a gathering at a soccer complex in Landover, Maryland, in spring 2012. "This event is a must for any prospect who is serious about playing football at the next level," the flyer continued, promising those who attended would score "all-star game invites and potential scholarships" while meeting "top college coaches and former NFL players" plus hearing a "big-name keynote speaker." Boys as young as eighth grade could register. Anyone who paid the $75 fee was welcome.

Perhaps six hundred teens plus parents crowded into the packed indoor soccerplex. Almost all were African-American. By appearances, most were low income—chasing a vision of athletic glory, or of an NCAA scholarship. Boys dream of scoring touchdowns; parents dream of affording college.

Many boys at the showcase were impressively ripped. Barbells and squat racks, once found only in pro sports facilities, are now in high schools. Nautilus and Cybex machines, once exotic, are everywhere, as are devotees of Cross Fit, P90X and other conditioning regimes. Once only those training for the Olympics ran gassers and ladder drills; now middle-school football teams do. Now high school freshmen have scientific lifting routines with "legs days" or "pecs days" timed for maximum muscle-mass increase. Because of this, a reality of modern athletics is that well-built young men have become a dime a dozen. A generation ago, a seventeen-year-old Adonis with steely calves and defined triceps would have excited college scouts. Now, all promising high school players are ripped. If your muscles don't bulge through your T-shirt, you will be written off by scouts as JAG, or Just Another Guy.

As the soccerplex became warm and sweaty, attendees were separated into groups by position, then put through standard drills as at any football practice. The drills lasted two hours. Parents milled around looking for the important college coaches they expected to meet. None were present, nor was there a keynote speaker: though, meals and apparel were sold. Two reporters from Rivals.com, a recruiting website, snapped pictures. Then the event was over.

It dawned on parents they'd been taken for a ride. Six hundred kids at $75 a head is $45,000 for a morning that would be unlikely to help more than a handful be recruited to college, if anyone at all was helped. Everyone received a T-shirt, to show he'd been at a "five-star" event. Showcase T-shirts are high status among today's boys. But the T-shirt is all most ever get.

Rivals is owned by Yahoo! A company that carries itself as progressive, in 2012 appointing Marissa Mayer, a hip, thirty-seven-year-old woman, as CEO, had just reached into the pockets of low-income African-Americans for $45,000.

THE RECRUITING WORLD IS WHERE football's cultlike qualities, excessive high school football and the college establishment interact. Recruiting has become a small industry, third parties seeking fees for generating illusions that boys are bound for football greatness, and college coaches seeking the free labor that will ensure their personal financial success.

"National Underclassmen Ultimate 100 Showcase," read the come-on for an event staged in 2012 by David Schuman, one of football recruiting's entrepreneurs. The price was $90, and add another $69.95 to access an "insider website." Schuman's company held nineteen "ultimate 100 showcases" across the country that year, totaling thousands of boys attending something marketed as only for the "ultimate 100."

Those who went to the first round of camps, typically held at a park or public field, soon received a come-on for a regional showcase at another $90. The regional showcases were marketed as "invitation only," though invitations went to anyone willing to pay the fee. At the regional events, a man pretending to be a sports journalist did a brief video interview with each boy, later posted on YouTube. Boys could brag that they had been interviewed on YouTube about their football prowess!

Those who attended the first two rounds of showcases received invitations to an "Ultimate 100 Top Prospect Elite Camp," held at Oklahoma State University in July 2012. "You are among the very elite chosen for the NUC Ultimate 100 Top Prospect Elite Camp Presented by National Underclassmen," that come-on declared. Included was an activation code with the banner THESE INVITES ARE TOP SECRET TO AVOID PEOPLE CONTACTING US TO NOMINATE ATHLETES.

Top secret! As the holidays approached, Schuman sent yet another come-on, inviting five hundred boys to an All-American Performance Week, culminating in an NUC All American Game. The marketing made it sound like an invitation to one of high school football's three prestige events: the Army, Under Armour and Marine Corps all-star games. The price was $400 per boy, plus travel to Myrtle Beach, South Carolina, plus a week of hotel and meal expenses for the boy and perhaps a parent or guardian. If all five hundred spots sold, that's $200,000 for Schuman, and a much larger cost for parents, to create an illusion of all-star status for boys whose college recruiting odds will be precisely the same whether they attend an event like this or not.

FOOTBALL SHOWCASE MARKETING LEANS HEAVILY on terms such as *elite*, *five-star*, and *invitation only*. Schuman's Myrtle Beach all-star game was "invitation only" in the sense that a boy had to receive an invitation. Filling out a form on a company website resulted in an invitation.

Prices in the showcase world vary from $75 for a day event to hundreds of dollars, plus travel cost. In 2012, Baltimore Ravens star Ray Lewis put his name on an event called Football Academy, which charges $500 for a two-day showcase. The Army All-American Bowl markets a Football University, run by a company called Sports Link, at $600. Promotional materials imply that attendance will translate into an invitation to play in the Army All-American Bowl, though the camp is held after selections to that event have been made. Football University calls itself invitation only, though anyone who fills out a form at the company's website receives an invitation. *Mom, Mom, I got invited to a showcase at Football University!*

"Showcases are a waste of time and money," says the recruiting coordinator of a BCS football program. "Some kids who appear at showcases do get offers, but they get offers because they were going to get offers anyway, not because they were at a showcase. Once in a while if a coach knows a hot prospect will be at a particular private combine event, and it's a time of year when the NCAA forbids meetings, you might go to the showcase in order to 'accidentally' bump into the boy. Mostly, private showcases take advantage of people's lack of sophistication, and of boys and their parents wanting to believe that if they receive a letter about football, that means they are going to be recruited to play in college."

The Internet has been a boon to showcase marketing. Fifteen years ago, few knew who was being courted by which college or what high school players were considered good. Now Rivals, MaxPreps and ESPN's Recruiting Nation websites allow young athletes to know the names, watch the film and follow the offers and commits for hundreds of high school players across the country.

Being ranked or mentioned on any of these websites is hugely important to Web-era boys—their friends see!—though may do no good, since Internet ratings are often wrong. Rachel Bachman of *The Wall Street Journal* examined the list of all high school players who in 2004 were ranked five-star by Rivals. More than half were never drafted by the NFL. Many became college busts, dropping out or kicked out of school.

George Whitfield of San Diego, who is Steve Clarkson's competitor as a high-end private football coach—he boasts "100 percent college placement," which could mean almost anything—each June operates what he calls a Rock Tour, a sort of rolling showcase. He charges $2,500 a head, plus airfare to and from San Diego, to put boys on a bus and take them on a tour of major-college football facilities. Supposedly this gives them the inside track on "being offered." Anyone who seriously thinks a college coach will extend a scholarship to a rising senior because his parents paid $2,500 to have him arrive at campus on a tour bus has another think coming.

COLLEGE COACHES RECOMMEND THAT TEENS avoid private showcases and instead attend college tryout camps. Among the NCAA's least enforced rules is a prohibition against tryout camps. Many universities hold them, just don't call them that—they are "skills camps" or a "summer skills academy." Like private showcases, college camps are designed to separate parents from their money.

I tutor underprivileged boys from a Maryland housing project and, in the spring of 2012, had two class of 2013 boys with football promise whom I took to attend tryout camps at Georgetown University, Penn State (scandal aside, still a fine college destination), the University of Maryland, Villanova and Yale.

At Penn State, at least 150 boys were present, plus parents and family members who had come in the night before. I met parents who had flown from Montreal or driven from Minnesota for the event, which they—and their eager boys—believed was a final screening before a scholarship offer. To kick off the camp, Penn State assistant coach Craig Fitzgerald addressed the boys, saying, "This is an elite camp, you are the best of the best."

Yet anyone could attend by paying the $60 fee. That year Penn State held three camps for rising seniors. If each drew 150, the fees would be nearly $30,000; travel expenses would bring the families' total cost to much more. Penn State coaches got to look over some potential players, at no trouble or expense to themselves. Of hundreds of boys attending, if a handful got NCAA scholarships, they were fortunate. The rest got T-shirts.

The University of Maryland held two tryout camps in 2012, each with about a hundred boys at $65 a head. Tables blocked the entrance to guarantee no one got in without paying. On the morning of the first camp, if Internet services are to be believed, UMD already had accepted thirteen "commits" for its next recruiting class, meaning the Terrapins were staging tryouts for hundreds of boys yet held a maximum of twelve additional scholarships to offer. Boys flexed, sprinted and preened, believing they were about to be recruited—but were unlikely to get more than a T-shirt.

Penn State and the University of Maryland are football-factory schools. Even at Yale, perhaps two hundred boys were present at a pricey $145 a head. Chatting with parents, I learned many had come long distances—from Atlanta, Denver, Los Angeles—believing a football-camp invitation meant their sons were going to be offered athletic admission to Yale. Quickly I learned not to mention that at most three or four of the two hundred present would receive the magic letter. Better to let the parents have one more day of dreaming.

Not only did Penn State and UMD film their tryout camps—so did Villanova, an academics-oriented Division IAA school where the classroom has always come before sports. Even there, the football-cult mind-set has led to cameras high on scissor hoists filming seventeen-year-olds in shorts.

At Georgetown, a wonderful choice for the true student-athlete, before the $65-a-head tryouts, 150 or so teens were introduced to the school's football coaches—all fourteen of them, including a coach for inside linebackers and a coach for outside linebackers. Many excited parents were present, not seeming to grasp that few of their boys would receive the magic letter. None of the colleges whose tryouts I visited warned parents they were probably wasting their money—or even mentioned this complication.

MANY COLLEGES ALSO HOST JUNIOR Days, in which rising seniors meet coaches and tour facilities. Typically there is no cost for a Junior Day, though the NCAA primly refuses to let schools pay for lunch.

At the Maryland's Junior Day, I was pleasantly surprised to hear head coach Randy Edsall spend fifteen minutes talking about class-work, GPA and the long odds of making the NFL, before making his first mention of the football field.

Beamer had explained at Virginia Tech that expectations are essential to relationships with athletes—and expectations must be established at the outset. If the expectation is that a college player can cut classes and sleep late so long as he scores touchdowns, what do you think will happen? College programs that from the outset talk nothing but the victory column set the expectations low, and water always finds the lowest level. If on the other hand the expectation is that an athlete who doesn't graduate is letting his team down, then players will work hard to graduate. Bucknell University has both a successful men's basketball program and decades of admirable graduation rates in men's basketball, because expectations are set high: each freshman player, on arriving, is told that if he doesn't graduate, he will let down the many who came before him. Beamer takes a similar approach with his football players. Having potential recruits who visit Blacksburg first meet with academic counselors, before meeting any coach or seeing the football facilities, is not just for show. It is an exercise in setting expectations high. In sports everybody wants to start, and not everybody can. But everybody can graduate, which means more in the long run. It's a lot easier to make this clear up front.

SO IT WAS REFRESHING TO observe Maryland's Edsall setting expectations high. Another pleasant surprise—let me rephrase, a major disappointment—at Maryland's Junior Day was the absence of attractive young women.

Traditionally, football coaches hosting teen boys on recruiting visits ensure that good-looking women are present. Arizona State head football coach Todd Graham has bragged to the sports press that when boys visit, he has "girls out there in bikinis, sitting by the swimming pool." In 2006, I attended a recruiting day for the Williams College football program. Step one was the introduction to testosterone-pumped teen boys of four attractive athletes from the Williams women's teams, who served as campus guides. This wasn't Arizona State—it was Williams, an elite intellectual school.

The pretty-girl recruiting tradition changed in 2009 because the University of Tennessee football program caused a mini-scandal when it signed up good-looking female students to be "hostesses" for teens who might get football offers—to take them around campus and to flirt with them on Facebook. Being a "hostess" sounded more sexual than it likely was, but went too far when hostesses began to attend high school games in miniskirts and tank tops, blowing kisses toward star-rated players. The Tennessee situation raised the question: Why would a college coed want to travel to a high school football game and blow kisses at a younger boy? Sounds like the kind of thing you do to pass initiation into a cult. Until the mini-scandal, being a football hostess was prestigious at the University of Tennessee.

AT EVERY TRYOUT CAMP AND Junior Day that I visited, introduction of coaches included delineation of their recruiting territory. College football has become about speed, and its folk wisdom is that the best concentration of speed players is in Florida. The University of Maryland had assistant coaches who recruited Florida by county—one responsible for Broward County, one for Miami-Dade County and so on. Even Georgetown University, an elite academic institution that is not football crazed, had a coach responsible for recruiting Florida.

Until about half a century ago, much of college athletics was segregated. When the color barriers finally fell, an uneasy reality developed in recruiting—the old slave-state agricultural areas became great places to find football players. An unusually high number of speed athletes hail from Florida, especially its central part; today some Florida high school football games have dozens of scouts in the stands. When the University of Louisville surprised experts by reaching a 2013 BCS bowl, touts remarked that one reason was that this Kentucky team had thirty-four players recruited from the state of Florida.

Other former slave states also are viewed as recruiting wonder-lands. Georgia and Mississippi seem to produce big, naturally strong teens. The Tidewater area of Virginia is where to look for athletes who have reflexes and hand-eye coordination—many of Virginia Tech's most athletic players are from the Tidewater. Compared to population, Louisiana has more players in the NFL than any other state. The history of Louisiana is agriculture based on backbreaking slave labor.

Football players hail from Pennsylvania or California or Oregon too; Chicago Bears star Israel Idonije grew up in Canada. But the concentration in former Confederacy states of the physical qualities that football programs avidly seek—size, strength, speed—must have some relationship to old slave-based agricultural economies and to the ancestry of those who were brought to North America in chains. Desegregation of collegiate sports opened doors for African-Americans. But just as basketball recruiters look first in urban areas, many football recruiters look first in former slave-state agricultural areas. Nobody in football much likes to talk about this.

THEN THERE'S THE WORD *PROSPECT*. Young football players aren't athletes or students, they are prospects. Nick Saban of Alabama, reigning top recruiter in college football, invariably refers to high school students as "the prospects." Magnificent Georgetown University uses this term: an itinerary for a campus visit by high school players reads, "At the conclusion of the program, the prospects are free to leave." Grassroots, the youth league, posts a "prospects questionnaire" for nine-year-olds.

Use of *prospects* to describe young men who ostensibly are being considered as college students betrays an aspect of the football mindset. For a football coach, the prospects are meal tickets—they win games and keep the coach gainfully employed. Many college coaches do their most important work during the off-season, signing top athletes: what happens once play begins is dictated by how the recruiting class went. Viewing high school football players as *prospects*—kids eager to offer free labor that enhances the careers of adults—semantically creates a meat market.

Here is an indicator of how far as the prospect mentality has gone. When in the summer of 2012 the NCAA penalized Penn State, it said current football players at Happy Valley would be allowed to transfer without the usual one-year waiting period. Penn State had a star tailback named Silas Redd. As Tim Rohan reported, the day after the sanctions were announced, USC boosters provided a private jet to Coach Lane Kiffin so he could fly to Connecticut in the most impressive manner and give a presentation to Redd and his parents about why he should transfer to USC. Redd was coming onto the market as valuable free labor who might enhance Kiffin's career. And he was a hell of a prospect.

BEYOND THE OBSESSIVE NATURE OF football recruiting is the cult of the coach.

At high schools, many football coaches are demigod figures whom even principals are afraid to cross. Knowing they will be benched immediately if they ever dare talk back, players treat high school coaches reverentially. When a high school coach orders something irresponsible, such as sending a concussed boy back into a game, it is unrealistic to expect sixteen- or seventeen-year olds to protest, as teens are trained to obey authority figures: plus boys know that if anyone objects to cruel coaching behavior, he will instantly be thrown off the team.

Most states place on high school teachers, counselors and administrators a care-and-custody legal standard that requires them to put a child's interest first. Only a handful of states extend the same standard to football coaches: legally, coaches can put their own interests ahead of students'. In some areas, including Washington State and parts of Texas, high school coaches are not school employees, rather, work for a booster club. This means the principal or headmaster does not control their paychecks, giving the school little leverage.

High school students observe that while teachers' behavior is constrained, no rules seem to apply to the football coach: making him more like the leader of a cult than like an educator. College students observe that the football coach has special privileges—private jets, motorcades. The science building is not off-limits to students who are not science majors, yet the football facility is off-limits to students who are not members of the football program. This can make the college coach more like the leader of a cult than like an educator.

The atmospherics add to this impression. College head coaches often are flanked by security details or state troopers. When Alabama defeated the University of Georgia in December 2012 to reach its third BCS title bowl in four years, Crimson Tide coach Saban was surrounded by Alabama state troopers. The troopers were not present as security. The game was held in Georgia—local law enforcement provided any necessary security. Yet a detail of Alabama state troopers accompanied Saban on his trip and surrounded him at all times. They were present to make Saban seem a person to be revered.

One of the many likable aspects of Frank Beamer is that he has no security detail nor any detail of Virginia state troopers. Vince Howard, an armed member of the Virginia Tech Police Department, travels with the team and may stand on the sideline or at the locker room door. But Howard is present to maintain order: he does not serve as a bodyguard to Beamer. Except for police escorts of team buses, Beamer goes about his business on his own, like anyone else. Many of his peers need security details to give them an aura of importance. Beamer does not.

At the NFL level, football coaches gain standing by their public profile, high pay and the mystification of their profession. There are no deep, hidden secrets to calling a slant pass or teaching defensive backs to rotate coverages. Much of the coaching profession is guesswork—in the end, games are won by who outruns whom. But just as lawyers carry themselves as possessors of recondite knowledge, football coaches like people to think that only an exclusive elite could possibly understand what's happening at practice or on the field. During NFL games, networks constantly give viewers shots of the head coach. What is learned from these visuals is that good plays make coaches happy and bad plays make coaches scowl. But there's an image created that the head coach knows things nobody else knows. It's fine with NFL coaches if you believe that no one outside the football guild could ever grasp what they up to.

The alpha status of football coaches may be boosted by military flyovers that sometimes precede the kickoff. The Air Force's B-1 bomber and the Navy's F-18 fighters have flown over recent Rose Bowl games; the Air Force's B-2 stealth bomber has flown over an NFC play-off game in Green Bay and a University of Michigan game. As recently as the late 1990s, NATO allies were not allowed to see a B-2; now these aircraft fly above football games. Even routine games may get flyovers, for instance F-18s above the 2011 Detroit-at-Denver contest. For the Pentagon, flyovers are a recruiting tool. For the football establishment, they make it seem football has something to do with national security.

So too does the custom of broadcasting NFL and NCAA games to US troops stationed overseas, while showing soldiers cheering. On Thanksgiving Day 2012, broadcasts of the three NFL contests—Houston at Detroit, Washington at Dallas and New England at New York Jets—had live shots of soldiers in fatigues in Afghanistan, watching and applauding. It's great that military units stationed far from home can see live football. The impression given is that football is an element of national security.

Society admires soldiers and sailors who take risks in defense of freedom. To the extent football is a kind of war lite, head coaches seem like generals or admirals and may benefit from their veneer of being similar to warriors, though taking none of the risks.

FOOTBALL COACHES ENGAGE UNDUE LEVELS of public fascination to some extent for Walter Mitty reasons. There is no point in dreaming of becoming a home-run leader or a Met opera tenor or a prima ballerina or a Hollywood sex bombshell because these require physical gifts hardly anyone has. Coaches, by contrast, aren't necessarily good-looking, artistic or athletic—anyone can put on a whistle. Sitting at a desk bored, you might fantasize about winning an Oscar, but you know there is absolutely no chance you could. Fantasizing about coaching, on the other hand—why, it looks as if anyone could do that!

Coaches further represent father figures. In the contemporary United States, many actual fathers have abdicated their responsibilities to children or are absent altogether. Even a person who had a fine father knows that man will pass away, leaving a longing for someone to fill the role. In generations past, political leaders, business executives, intellectuals and clergy served as father figures. Today most politicians are oleaginous hacks who lack convictions about anything beyond power and campaign donations for themselves. Business executives seem greedy and even antisocial, eager to destroy jobs in return for a larger bonus. Intellectuals have become contemptuous of average people, while no part of society is losing standing faster than faith institutions.

Coaches still act as fathers are supposed to act—setting a stern example of tough love, and this is the best aspect of coaching. Because football coaches are iconic, it is important they set positive examples for society. Some do. Frank Beamer, Tony Dungy, John Gagliardi, Urban Meyer—if all men were like them, the world would be a better place. But instead, many football coaches abuse their positions: Joe Paterno covering up sex crimes, the married Bobby Petrino of the University of Arkansas putting a young mistress on the payroll as his assistant; there are many similar examples.

Too much football coaching is based on the notion that screaming is leadership. Saban for one is a screamer who wins games but regularly makes a bad impression in public. In the 2010 Alabama-Auburn contest, as the Crimson Tide was losing a big lead, Saban became red-faced while screaming at players on the sideline—players who in theory are college students. When the Alabama punter shanked a kick, Saban grabbed the young man as he ran off the field, shook him and screamed at him for all to see. Did he think the punter wanted to shank the kick? Saban himself made numerous errors in the game, including shoving a player out onto the field just as Auburn snapped, a substitution foul that gave the opponent a critical first down. If screaming in public is good, then one of Saban's assistants should have grabbed him and screamed at him.

POSITIVE COACHING IS THE ALTERNATIVE. When in 2011 Jim Harbaugh arrived as head coach of the San Francisco 49ers, he found a dejected team. The 49ers' previous coach, Mike Singletary, was a screamer type who publicly denigrated the player Vernon Davis, saying, "Cannot play with him, cannot coach with him, can't do it." Singletary's negative approach resulted in a losing record for San Francisco.

Harbaugh substituted the positive techniques used by Beamer, Gary Patterson of TCU, Dungy of the Colts and Gagliardi of Saint John's University of Minnesota—who retired in 2012 with the most wins of any college football coach ever. In his first season, Harbaugh took the dispirited 49ers to a 14-4 record and a title game appearance.

Positive coaching does not mean being soft—Harbaugh is strict and demanding. Positive coaching entails challenging people to improve rather than criticizing their faults, offering praise for effort, and never demeaning a player either in public or before peers. In January 2012, the 49ers made their first playoff appearance in years, and Davis, previously viewed as a screwup, caught the winning touchdown pass with seconds remaining. As Davis came to the team box, he burst into tears—an enormous, muscular man sobbing. Harbaugh hugged him joyfully, then turned to the home crowd and urged them to cheer Davis.

That's positive coaching. Far too many football coaches, and coaches in other sports, either enjoy demeaning young people they know can't talk back or view their profession in negative terms—that their role is to criticize and to punish. If professional athletes are subjected to such treatment, that may be poor coaching but there's no reason society should care, as professionals are well paid. When college players are demeaned, and especially when bully tactics are used by coaches of the large cohort of high school players, the situation is different.

Coaching has so long been associated with screaming that hundreds of thousands of high school players live in dread of the moment when the coach's volcanic temper erupts and they are assigned punishment drills. The volcanic temper, in turn, is unchecked—at most pro and college programs and at nearly all high schools, there is no one above the head coach, he must meet no standard (other than winning), and he has no oversight. The coach simply does as he pleases to young people who are powerless in his presence, and what he pleases is too often to scream. The experience, for boys and teens, can be anything from just another unpleasantness of life (there are really nasty teachers too) to child abuse. As a result, large numbers of boys are sent out into the world with an entirely negative interpretation of manhood.

Positive coaching can, in contrast, play a positive role in shaping young people's character. The football establishment is so obsessed with victory, money and coaches' prerogatives that this potential positive role is too often overlooked. Corey Moore, a player for Frank Beamer in the late 1990s, said something that struck me: "You keep learning from him even after you leave him." Great classroom teachers have that effect, as do great mentors and role models. How many football coaches have that effect? Most people—players, staffers—are relieved to get away from the football coach.

The lack of more positive coaching—and the benefits it could bring—is among the worst failings of sports in general, and football in particular. But then most cults make a point of demeaning their own members, so they don't talk back.

CULTS TEND TO WITHDRAW THEIR members from the larger society into a self-enclosed world. One of the worries about video gaming is that as technologically impressive and fun as the games may be, electronic battles withdraw gamers, mainly boys, from the worlds of education and work. As football becomes more popular and goes year-round, is football harming boys' prospects in the same way that video games do?

Decades ago the college scene was too male: women were denied entry to many of the top institutions or condescended to as "coeds." Now the gender situation has reversed. Bucknell University, where Philip Roth coined the term *Joe College*, today has more women than men. Williams College, which did not admit women until 1970, is 53 percent female, along with the Universities of Oregon, Texas and Wisconsin. USC is 55 percent women; my alma mater, Colorado College, 56 percent female. The University of Georgia is 62 percent female, which if nothing else ought to inspire thousands of boys to apply.

Across the United States, according to the College Board, 56 percent of undergraduates are female. Hanna Rosin wrote in 2012 in *The End of Men*, "Women dominate today's colleges and professional schools; for every two men who receive a BA, three women do." Richard Whitmire's 2009 book, *Why Boys Fail*, supposes the undergraduate edge for women would be greater still if many universities did not quietly employ lower admissions standards for males, attempting to keep the student body around fifty-fifty.

Surely the main reason for increasing female success in college is that girls and young women are focusing on the classroom and performing well. The secondary culprit likely is video-game addiction among teen boys. Increasing participation in football, coupled to its evolving year-round nature, is likely the third reason.

ATHLETICS THEMSELVES CANNOT BE THE cause as athletic participation is rising among teen girls and this has not detracted from their college aspirations. Studies by Betsey Stevenson, an economist at the University of Michigan, have found that since the 1970s, each 10 percent increase in girls' participation in high school sports has been accompanied by a 1 percent in increase in female college attendance. For girls, Stevenson finds, playing a sport improves college outcomes.

But there is one sport that girls do not play—football. Boys alone are devoting ever more of their youth and high school hours to football. (There are a handful of exceptions.) Ever-larger numbers of boys are getting bashed in the head during tackle football, while this is not a factor for girls. And girls are accelerating away from boys in college admission and diplomas. These facts must at least in some way be related.

PERHAPS THERE ARE INDEFINABLE EVOLUTIONARY reasons why boys fall in love with football, a team sport that feels like the hunt, which to their far forebears was a matter of life or death.

Surely there are straightforward cultural reasons. Boys click on the television and see games in which players are, to boys, men. The "men" are really overgrown adolescents: but are masculine, involved in a cool game that television treats as vitally important; they make lots of money and drive fancy cars with hot blondes in the passenger seat. What boy would not daydream of that life? Young boys and teen males can relate to playing games, which they instinctively grasp; the college-to-workplace sequence is a lot harder to relate to. Girls who follow football, and there are plenty, are not presented with anything like the fantasy package the NFL presents to boys.

Traditionally, high school football players sputtered in the classroom during the season, then made up ground in the spring. With high school football now year-round, boys on the team may have trouble with grades throughout their teen years, while doing little other than football outside the classroom. These boys send to colleges applications with a low GPA and no extracurriculars. They're competing for admissions slots against girls with better grades and a diversity of activities. Lack of college correlates to below-mean incomes and lower odds of good life outcomes, such as a successful marriage. Don Peck noted in 2011 in *The Atlantic* that marriages involving men without a college diplomas are much more likely to end in divorce than marriages in which the man is a college graduate. Part of the reason is simple economics—men without educations are less valuable than men who have them.

Football has begun to detract from boys' chances of reaching college. Of course, cults never care about harming their own members.

The next chapter: for every gleaming star, dozens of boys and men are betrayed by football.

The Price

9

USED UP AND THROWN AWAY

Michael Vick was a wonderful high school quarterback, but Ike Whitaker was better. A starter for Northwest High of Germantown, Maryland, from his sophomore year on, Whitaker led the Jaguars to the 2005 state championship in the large-school division. Whitaker threw the ball perfectly. Quicker than any tailback and stronger than any fullback, he ran through tacklers with ease, seeming to glide from place to place. He understood defenses and chose the correct receiver: arm strength is common among quarterbacks, but split-second decision-making sets the best apart. Whitaker was tall, powerfully built, broad-shouldered, as fast as Vick but noticeably bigger and stronger. Attending Northwest High games, I marveled at Whitaker's athletic prowess and grace. I remember thinking, "Move over, Michael Vick."

Every major college program wanted Whitaker; famous head coaches trekking to Germantown practically had to take a number for the chance to meet him. His play was so distinctive that Virginia Tech, the University of Maryland and other big programs began wooing Whitaker while he was fifteen years old. Whitaker boiled his choice down to two: Virginia Tech, home of Vick, his athletic hero, and the University of Florida, coached by the highly regarded Urban Meyer and coming off a national title. Then Tim Tebow committed to Florida. Tebow, who grew up near Jacksonville, was the state of Florida's best-known prep player. If Whitaker and Tebow competed for the Gators' starting job, the crowd would inevitably side with the local boy. So Whitaker chose the Hokies.

Whitaker arrived at Blacksburg just as Vick's younger brother Marcus was self-destructing. Marcus had followed his sibling's footsteps as a high school and then Virginia Tech star. Unlike Michael, who is wary in public, Marcus was wild. Like many athletic stars, he thought laws did not apply to him. Ticketed repeatedly for speeding and driving under the influence, Marcus lost his license, yet continued racing around campus until convicted for driving without a license. Then Marcus was convicted of "contributing to the delinquency of a minor," fortunate not to be charged with statutory rape. Suspended from NCAA play for a year, he seemed to bounce back, in 2005 leading the Hokies to an 11-2 finish and a bowl victory.

But old habits die hard. Twice his mother, Brenda, came to Blacksburg for awkward meetings in Frank Beamer's office; Marcus was given several second chances and ended up expelled from school. In 2008, Marcus agreed to pay a civil judgment to a woman who had been fifteen when he, as an adult, had sex with her; then he never made the payment, leading to a bench warrant for his arrest. In 2012, Marcus was jailed for failing to appear in court to answer a charge of driving with a suspended license. Michael Vick had trouble with the law, but for mistreating animals; Michael never harmed any person, was polite, reliable, a constructive member of society. Marcus was a classic fuckup, and no amount of Beamer's tough love helped.

Ultimately Marcus would go undrafted and never start an NFL game. Some scouts thought Marcus had more promise than Michael; Marcus threw that promise away because he wanted to believe he was a Big Man who could laugh at *rules* that applied to everyone else. Coaches, high school principals, college administrators, members of the sports press, do football players no favors when they excuse bad behavior. But that's the way the system works—if you're a football star, you get your own set of rules. Many athletic but immature boys and men cannot handle that. Marcus ended up with nothing, unwanted even by the CFL, texting his brother to ask for bail money.

IKE WHITAKER ARRIVED AT VIRGINIA Tech knowing his job was to make everyone forget Marcus by being the program's next red-white-and-blue all-American superstar. In athletic ability, Whitaker was equal to the task—his chances of being a college hero, followed by a high NFL draft choice, were excellent. But Ike had a secret—he had been a drunk since sophomore year of high school.

Whitaker was low-key, almost introspective, and kept his drinking to himself. Whitaker possessed so much God-given ability, he could come to practice hungover and outperform everyone else. He could drink to excess yet remain lean, fast and muscled. And he wasn't drinking for the sense of pleasure. He was drinking to overcome fear: his fear of being a quarterback.

"When I was young, I was clueless about what clique I belonged to, and drinking helped me fit in," Whitaker says. "Drinking helped me make friends. This sounds incredibly naïve, but back then I did not know that waking up unable to remember what you did the previous night is abnormal behavior. I thought this happened to everyone. By summer before my junior year in high school, I was getting media attention. My drinking got worse. There was so much pressure to live up to expectations and be a football star. I was deathly afraid people would say I squandered my talent.

"In retrospect, I should not have been a quarterback. The quarterback must be a leader in all things. I am not a natural leader. So I drank to give myself the courage to be the leader, to be the focal point of attention. If I had been a wide receiver, things might have been different. At quarterback, I heard it constantly—'You have all the potential in the world. You're going to be a wealthy star. Don't blow your chance.' I starting fearing I would blow my chance. Drinking made the fear go away."

Like many college players, Whitaker redshirted his first year. Beamer's right-hand man, John Ballein, who knows everything about every player, became aware of Whitaker's problem and quietly arranged for him to enter a detox center. "I was using the sauna before practice to sweat the alcohol out," Whitaker says. He played quarterback a little for the Hokies, but did not look like his high school self and was switched to wide receiver. There he showed what scouts call "unlimited upside"—at six feet four with strength and speed, no one could cover him. But by then his alcoholism had reached disease stage.

"Coach Beamer asked me if I wanted to go public," Whitaker says. "I knew that going public would expose me to embarrassment and ridicule because my friends back home would hear about it on ESPN. But if I did not admit my problem, it would get even worse. The Virginia Tech community showed me nothing but love when I went public. People came up to me and told me I was brave. Former Hokie players in the NFL called me to tell me about the struggles they went through with alcohol, drugs or painkillers. I felt loved."

Loved he was, but Whitaker did not get better. Eventually he was dismissed from the team, losing his NCAA funding. He stayed on campus trying to take classes, but lacked money for food and dropped from a playing weight of 220 pounds to 170, which on his tall frame made him appear skeletal. Whitaker began an unhappy journey through a variety of rehab and 12-step programs.

"Constantly I thought about how if I could just overcome this, I was still young enough to go back to Virginia Tech, play, and make the NFL. But every time I thought that, the pressure made me want to drink so the fear would go away for a few hours."

Every football factory university holds a Pro Day, a midwinter event at which professional scouts are invited to the campus to meet and time potential draft choices. In 2010, when Whitaker would have graduated, Beamer invited him to attend the Hokies' Pro Day, in hopes some NFL team would take a flier on his unlimited upside. Montreal of the Canadian Football League offered a contract. "They cut me," Whitaker says. "I had been a star at age fifteen, talked about in the same sentence with Tim Tebow, and now the CFL was cutting me. As soon as I got to the airport in Montreal to fly home, I went straight to the bar."

For a while, Whitaker hung out at his old high school, as an assistant football coach and substitute algebra teacher. "At first I loved it, getting up early in the morning with something to do," he says. "Then I kept hearing people at the high school say, 'There goes the guy who blew his chance.' It became another excuse to drink. I started calling in on Monday mornings."

Whitaker visited Blacksburg and went to see Ballein. "He came into my office drunk at eight a.m.," Ballein says. "He said he was going to kill himself. He had a gym bag and I was afraid there was a gun in it. I made him give the gym bag to me. Inside was a bottle of watermelon Mogen David." Winos drink Mogen David—"Mad Dog"—because it is cheap and the sweetness masks the ethanol.

Eventually Whitaker found a religious rehab program, became a Christian, and has been clean since. When I met him at a halfway house in 2012, he was wearing a Virginia Tech tracksuit and looked trim and fit, ready to dress for a game. "I still have the same fears about pressure and blowing my chance, but now accept that I cannot reach for a drink to make those feelings go away," he said.

His former high school coach, Randy Trivers, became head coach of a powerhouse program in Florida and invited Whitaker to be an assistant there, with the chance to earn a teaching certificate. Whitaker bought a beat-up old car and drove to Florida. The job lasted two months. "The stress was getting to me and I did not have time to attend meetings," Whitaker texted me. He returned to Maryland.

"The odd thing is that I finally have a good relationship with my mother," Whitaker says. "When I was at Virginia Tech, she could not sleep because she worried the phone would ring at three a.m. with a policeman saying I was dead. Now my own mother is not afraid of me. I can be a brother now. I went to my sister's wedding and did not drink. But I understand that I cannot be around football. Football to me is like alcohol to an alcoholic—I can't touch it, not even taste it, without thinking about what I might have become."

For addicts, the first goal is to get through the day. As part of his therapy, Whitaker sends friends text messages. Typical: "The battle is not ours. Stop taking your problem to God and start taking God to your problems. God show us the light, show us strength." Today Ike Whitaker might be a national celebrity, holding a contract with a $50 million guarantee like Peyton Manning or Tom Brady. Instead he lives in a halfway house and can't hold a job.

FOR EVERY ONE GLEAMING STORY of football success, a hundred boys and men are used up and cast aside by football. Whitaker is better off than most such casualties—his health is good, his mind is clear, he has broken no law. Perhaps Whitaker would have fallen into addiction even if he'd never heard of athletics. But football has a hidden price—those who give the game their all and end up with nothing. They are carted off and vanish. Not present to diminish the sales appeal of the sport, nor to serve as cautionary tales to the next round of young men eager to dwell as long as possible within football's Grand Illusion.

The issue is not players who were highly touted but failed to realize their potential: Tim Couch, first choice of the NFL draft in 1999, who only started a few seasons; Courtney Brown, first choice of the NFL draft in 2000, a backup for a few years, then waived; Johnathan Sullivan, sixth selection of the draft in 2003, who started a few games, then was waived; Eric Crouch, who won the Heisman Trophy in 2001 then never played in the NFL, drifting to the CFL, the United Football League and the Hamburg Sea Devils; there are many other examples. Sports lore is thick with stories of players who seemed like naturals, and then their heads became swelled or they were distracted by the club scene or they simply were overrated. The realms of business, science and the arts likewise have many examples of young phenoms who were washed up early.

But though all occupations produce people who fail, football's combination of physical danger and eminence as the most popular entertainment in the United States creates a special concern. Loggers, miners, law enforcement officers and others take unusual risks, but are paid. Less than I percent of those taking risks in organized football receive any money for doing so. Audiences are entertained, tickets and advertising are sold: Players get injured and end up with nothing.

They perform of their own free choice, but young athletes, especially at the high school level where so much of football occurs, imagine football success more likely than it is, while risk lower. Think of how the NFL is presented on television. Wealthy, celebrity athletes are the focus of coverage. Players who were harmed and then returned are idolized as comeback stories. Players who were harmed and could not return are never mentioned again.

Brain trauma, painkiller addiction, the large numbers of players who endure years of grueling training only to be waived without a paycheck—these subjects either are not mentioned because they are bad for business or are confined to public-interest shows that run in low-ratings time slots. ESPN's *Outside the Lines* public-affairs show does an outstanding job of reporting the downside of sports, but *Outside the Lines* airs in midafternoon or on Sunday mornings. ESPN's *Monday Night Football*, airing to a far larger audience, is smile-and-wave. CBS sometimes addresses the social issues of sports on *60 Minutes*, but its NFL game broadcasting is strictly happy-talk. NBC's *Sunday Night Football* discusses football safety as a regular topic, but the network rarely covers sports sociology as news; Fox rarely even attempts to offer sports journalism.

Audiences get their football commentary from former stars and coaches who moved to the broadcast booth. Most are charming, knowledgeable and exude "Q," the ineffable essence of television appeal.

They are also the winners of football's life-results contest. Players with memory loss, addiction, or whose lives fell apart do not work as football commentators for any major network. ESPN's Mark Schlereth required multiple knee operations when he was a member of the Denver Broncos and sometimes walks with difficulty. On TV he's seated and seems the picture of health. Fox's Troy Aikman had to retire from the Dallas Cowboys, and ESPN's Merril Hoge from the Chicago Bears, owing to concussions. Both recovered and are mentally sharp—unlike many former players not shown on television.

If you were choosing on-air personnel for sports broadcasting, you'd choose handsome success stories too. But the broken are not represented in the coverage of football: bad for business. This creates a distorted impression in which football is a rough game, but afterward everybody's okay and having a few laughs.

At a broader level, presentation of football to the public, by the on-air broadcast partners of the NCAA and the NFL, by *Sports Illustrated* and sports websites and by the sports sections of newspapers, generally skips over the complication that so many young men spend so many years generating entertainment as they live the Grand Illusion of wealth in the pros, then never receive a paycheck or earn some trivial amount and are sent packing, unemployed and uneducated.

When a football player can no longer generate entertainment, he no longer exists. Darron Thomas starred at quarterback for the University of Oregon in the 2011 BCS title game and was extensively hyped by the sports media, including a cover story in *Sports Illustrated*. In spring 2012, Thomas declared early for the NFL draft, skipping his senior season because he expected to be a high selection. Instead he went undrafted and was not invited to NFL training camps. By autumn 2012, he was on the practice squad of the Calgary Stampeders, hoping for football's equivalent of counter work at a McDonald's. When Oregon played Arizona State in prime time in October 2012, nothing was said about Thomas—he'd been used up and thrown away. Announcers spoke excitedly about the Ducks' new freshman quarterback.

At least Thomas is in good health. It is those who were harmed by the sport, or harmed themselves trying to succeed, whose disappearance from football coverage is troubling. Teens should hear their stories and understand the downside.

To SCRATCH THE SURFACE:

• Brian Toal, born in New Jersey, where he starred for high school powerhouse Don Bosco Prep, was among the top-rated Rivals seniors in 2004. He scored three touchdowns in the Army All-American Bowl, committed to Boston College, and was viewed as a sure-thing first-round NFL draft choice. Toal missed the 2006, 2007 and 2008 college seasons with shoulder and leg injuries, along with nerve damage to his neck. Undrafted by the NFL, he played two years for the semipro Las Vegas Locomotives. By 2011, his football days were over.

• Marlon Favorite, starter for the *USA Today* All-American team of 2003. Enrolled at LSU, where he appeared in just seventeen games. Listed at 317 pounds but believed to be at least 400 pounds—could not complete the twelve-minute run at NFL camps. Viewed by scouts as having one-in-a-million athletic ability, Favorite was invited to tryouts by the Rams, Chiefs, Seahawks, Saints, Bills, Panthers, Colts, Eagles, Redskins and Patriots, but never appeared in an NFL game. Played semipro with the Hartford Colonials, Sacramento Mountain Lions and New Orleans VooDoo.

• Albert Means, born in Memphis, Mr. Football of Tennessee in 1999 as a high school senior. Widely viewed as among the most promising linemen ever. His high school coach accepted a $200,000 bribe from a University of Alabama booster for persuading Means to commit to the Crimson Tide. The coach also arranged for someone else to take Means's college boards.

The booster, coach and another man were convicted of rack-eteering, and Alabama given a five-year NCAA probation. Means transferred to the University of Memphis, but lost focus during two years away from the sport, often testifying at trials of the booster and his former coach. Once Means was back in football, at away games crowds chanted "jailbait" or held up signs reading CAN'T SPELL KAT when his name was mentioned. Undrafted by the NFL, he became a phys ed teacher. Means has always maintained he was unaware his high school coach, who has since died, was soliciting bribes in his name. It may well be that his football career was ruined by corruption he knew nothing about.

• Fred Rouse. Born in Tallahassee, expected to be the best wide receiver since Jerry Rice, Rouse was the subject of an all-out recruiting war among college football's elite. Enrolled at Florida State University. Claiming offense that Florida State did not promote him more as a freshman, he transferred to the University of Texas–El Paso, then transferred again to Concordia College Alabama. Undrafted by the NFL, he played for the Omaha Nighthawks. In 2011, Rouse was waived by a CFL team, ending his sports days.

• Callahan Bright, born near Philadelphia, the fifth-rated player in the Rivals class of 2005, received scholarship offers from most of the country's football powers. Bright's announcement that he was choosing Florida State was carried live by ESPN.

Bright cut a lot of class in high school, resulting in a dismal GPA and low board scores. He may have bought into the urban legend that circulates among athletes—and may be true in men's basketball—that "if the college wants you, they will change your grades." Bright attended a fifth-year athletic prep academy trying to fix his GPA, then played one season of college football at Division II Shaw University. In 2011, Bright was waived by the semi-semipro Pittsburgh Power.

- Rhett Bomar. Born in Texas, he was ranked the country's number-one high school quarterback in 2004 by Rivals. Bomar became a star at the University of Oklahoma, then was ordered off the team by the NCAA when a fan website revealed he had a no-show job at a car dealership owned by a Sooners' booster. Bomar transferred to lower-division Sam Houston State, where he played well but never regained the sheen of stardom. He spent time on the practice squads of the New York Giants, Minnesota Vikings and Oakland Raiders, but never appeared in an NFL game.

  Bomar did break a rule, but the NCAA off-campus-employment regulation in effect at the time was written in a way that made a cell-phone disclaimer seem plain English. If a member of a college orchestra had a no-show job with the Steinway piano company, no one would have given a hoot.

- Madre Hill. Born in North Carolina, as a high school senior he rushed for a hard-to-believe 2,863 yards in eleven games; the NFL record is 2,105 yards in 16 games. Named High School Player of the Year in 1993 by Reebok, Hill became a star at the University of Arkansas, but tore the ACL in one knee. The following season, he tore the ACL in the other knee. Hill made the Cleveland Browns roster, but injured his neck. He performed briefly for the semipro Berlin Thunder, became an assistant coach at several universities, then left football.

- Chris Strong. In 2006, he was Mississippi's Mr. Football, subject of an intense recruiting war, and enrolled at Ole Miss. Strong flunked out of Ole Miss after a single year, and for a football star to flunk out of the University of Mississippi is not easy. Strong enrolled at Northwest Missouri Community College and flunked out again. He never had so much as a tryout with an NFL team.

- Ken Stabler. Quarterback of the Oakland Raiders' 1977 Super Bowl champions, Stabler would divorce three times, be arrested thrice for drunk driving, and see two homes foreclosed by the IRS for unpaid taxes.

- In 2009, Bernie Kosar, who when he retired from the NFL had been the highest-paid player in Cleveland Browns annals, filed for bankruptcy, having substantial debts from various "sure thing" ideas pushed by friends or relatives, plus significant unpaid taxes.

  A nonprofit called Pro Athletes Outreach estimates 70 percent of NFL players declare bankruptcy in the decade after they leave the sport, having spent wildly or been taken in by hustlers. Unsophisticated young men handed million-dollar bonus checks are obvious marks. "Financial advisers" may, in the manner of Bernard Madoff, approach young athletes with a claim to have an amazing investing secret. Madoff's amazing secret was that he was a criminal, and the amazing secret of other "financial advisers" may be the same. In 2013, Reuters reported that Everette Scott, an NFL agent certified by the NFL Players Association, was convicted in federal court of running an investment fraud. Scott and an accomplice claimed to possess an incredible secret formula for generating huge returns from low-yielding Treasury bills. Their incredible secret turned out to be that they were using their marks' money to buy themselves resort vacations. If anyone ever tells you he has an amazing investing secret, bear in mind, if he did, why would he need clients?

- Vince Young, third choice of the 2006 NFL draft, made the Pro Bowl twice, earned at least $26 million playing professional football, and by age twenty-nine was unemployed and broke. Young left the Tennessee Titans, the club that drafted him, citing psychological problems, which can be every bit as real as physical problems. He drifted to other NFL teams, brimming with talent but refusing to study the playbook. By 2011, Young had blown through his millions and taken out a reported $1.9 million high-interest loan to sustain a jet-set lifestyle a little longer; then he filed a lawsuit, trying to avoid repayment.

Young trusted his money to a self-employed money manager whose styled himself as "president and chief executive officer" of a firm whose sole officer was him. Hustlers know that athletes and music-industry figures who receive big paychecks barely out of high school are vulnerable to manipulation; may believe nonsense about amazing investment secrets or, at least, do not notice missing funds.

In 2012, two sketchy "investment advisers" were indicted for stealing $2.2 million from Indianapolis Colts star Dwight Freeney. In 2010, a "financial adviser" named Mary Wong was sentenced to prison for stealing $3 million from Michael Vick. She claimed an amazing investment secret that yielded a guaranteed 8 percent return above inflation, strikingly similar to what Madoff offered his marks. John Elway, a Super Bowl MVP and now general manager of the Broncos, lost $15 million to a Ponzi schemer later sentenced to forty years in prison. In 2012, the Securities and Exchange Commission charged former University of Georgia head football coach Jim Donnan with running a Ponzi scam aimed at defrauding football coaches and NFL players.

A football star would make a wiser choice to call the 800 number of Vanguard or T. Rowe Price or any other reputable public company and select a stock index fund available to anyone, than to deal with an "adviser" who promises instant asset growth or incredible real-estate plays. But while football stars are physically magnificent, many are psychologically infantilized. Football stars float in a culture of enablers who that tell them they are special insiders to whom normal rules do not apply. Often they lose their shirts, left with nothing but IRS invoices.

• Boobie Miles. The best-known prep football player in Texas when he was a teenager, Miles was the protagonist of H. G. Bissinger's 1990 book, *Friday Night Lights,* which spawned a decent movie and an excellent TV series. As a high school senior Miles sustained a knee injury, tried to come back too soon, and never played football again—realizing neither a college education nor income from the sport. In 2012, Bissinger went to visit Miles. The former lean, formidable athlete, Bissinger reported, at age forty-two weighed 315 pounds, had diabetes and in lived in a dump little better than a shack.

- In 2009, ESPN college scout Todd McShay predicted the first round of the next spring's NFL draft. Among his predicted first-round selections were Ciron Black of LSU, DeMarcus Granger of the University of Oklahoma, Sergio Render of Virginia Tech and Adam Ulatoski of the University of Texas. Not only did none of them become first-round choices: none ever took a snap in an NFL game. All were felled by injuries, drug problems or legal issues.

- Joe Casey. As a high school senior, Casey was a member of the *USA Today* All-USA team, the most exclusive of prep football honors. He was viewed as equal in talent to fellow high school senior Adrian Peterson. But Casey never appeared in an NCAA game, let alone an NFL contest. He had not passed enough "core" credits—science, math and English—to enroll in college, even at the junior college level. Casey attended Tilghman High School in Paducah, Kentucky, whose slogan is "A Tradition of Excellence," and somehow was ruled eligible to participate in athletics despite taking no math, science or English courses. By 2012, Adrian Peterson was the NFL's MVP. Casey was playing for the Evansville Rage of the all-but-unknown Continental Indoor Football League.

- Demar Dorsey. Born near Fort Lauderdale, in 2010 he was the twelfth-rated high school player on the ESPNU recruiting board and a *Parade* magazine all-American. Possessing seemingly unlimited physical gifts, Dorsey, a cornerback, might have been the next Deion

Sanders. He committed to the University of Michigan, then the school learned that as a teen Dorsey had been arrested three times for armed robbery. Dorsey entered a youth diversion program, where charges were sealed; the system had done him no favors by excusing his behavior. Michigan withdrew its offer, and Dorsey attended community college. Then Dorsey committed to the University of Hawaii, but was denied entry because of extremely low grades. By 2012, Dorsey was trying to hang on at another community college, his NFL dream all but a vapor.

• Maurice Clarett. As a *true freshman*, the goofy NCAA phrase, Clarett starred for the Ohio State team that won the 2003 BCS title. Extremely vain, he announced he would sue the NFL to force the league to allow him to play at age nineteen. League rules say an NFL player must be at least twenty, or three years out of high school; courts have upheld this as a bona fide occupational requirement. A retinue of hangers-on and wannabes pressured Clarett to start litigation, salivating over the thought of their shares of trebled antitrust damages against the wealthiest sport.

Clarett lost his lawsuit, then was dismissed from Ohio State for academic misconduct. Twiddling his thumbs until he turned twenty, Clarett was a high draft choice of the Denver Broncos. He arrived at the Denver training camp with Grey Goose vodka in a water bottle—that doesn't even work at high school dances! Clarett was accompanied to his first and only NFL camp by a "manager" who loudly complained to the press when Clarett was not immediately declared first-string. The Broncos waived Clarett, who never took a snap in an NFL contest. In 2006, he staged an armed robbery at a topless club in Columbus, Ohio, posted bond after his arrest, then tried to flee. After serving four years in prison, in 2010, Clarett performed briefly for the obscure Omaha Nighthawks.

Clarett's terrible life choices were his own fault—but as a football star, he had been surrounded by enablers. Because he received no bonus when signing with the Broncos, Clarett earned just a few thousand dollars from professional football.

• Willie Williams. One of the most gifted athletes ever to tape his ankles, Williams grew up in the inner-city part of Miami as a football prodigy. By his high school senior year, he was among the most heavily recruited prep players in the country. Throughout his youth Williams had repeated brushes with the law. He was often arrested, but charges always were dropped when police learned he was a football star. Williams got the message that a football star can get away with anything, and it was the wrong message.

As a teen, Williams spoke openly about what he did not grasp were recruiting violations: flights on private jets, elaborate parties, women hired by boosters to flirt with him. Williams signed with the University of Miami, every Miami athlete's dream outcome. He did not start as a freshman—and should not have, since he was behind Jon Beason, later a first-round NFL draft choice. A combination of swelled head and an entourage of street hustlers who told him he was being disrespected because he didn't start immediately caused Williams to storm away from the University of Miami, another bad judgment.

Williams began an odyssey: junior college in California, to try to fix his grades; a few weeks at the University of Louisville before being thrown out; a semester at Division II Glenville State, where he was thrown out when the NCAA, still angry Williams told the truth about recruiting, canceled his eligibility. A severe injury kept him away from athletics for a year, then Williams had one season playing at Union College, an NAIA affiliate beyond the NCAA's reach. In that year he performed magnificently, suggesting what might have been. Passed over in the NFL draft, Williams was waived by semipro teams including the Sacramento Mountain Lions. Ten points if you know what league that team is in! Williams was at a tryout for another semipro club when he was arrested for burglary. No longer protected by the glitter of stardom, he was convicted and sentenced to fifteen years.

• Corey Moore. The top performer on Virginia Tech's 1999 team that played for the national title was not Michael Vick, but Moore. A defensive end, he broke Bruce Smith's school record for sacks. Even by the standards of an androgen-driven sport, Moore played in a frenetic style, disrupting offenses by chasing quarterbacks and ballcarriers with abandon. At five feet ten inches and 235 pounds, he showed one need not be enormous to be a great football player.

Moore was a high draft choice of the Buffalo Bills, Smith's pro team, and performed well in his rookie season before injuring an ankle and being placed on injured reserve. In May 2001, he went home to Brownsville, a small town in Tennessee, to visit his mother. There he was charged with aggravated assault for striking a man over the head with a beer bottle. Two weeks later, Moore was shot in the leg. He told police his car was stopped at a Brownsville intersection at 1:00 a.m. when a man walked up, leaned in, said nothing and shot him, then ran.

The wound did not seem terrible—a glancing hit from a small-caliber weapon, Moore drove himself to a hospital, where he was treated and released. But circumstances were unclear. Charges against Moore for the fight were dropped, and no one was ever arrested for the shooting. Bills officials kept calling Moore to see if he was all right, and he would not return the calls. Buffalo placed him on injured reserve again, then waived him. The Cincinnati Bengals claimed Moore and waived him. The Miami Dolphins claimed Moore. He played a little in 2002, but his frenetic approach to the game was gone. Miami waived Moore, and just like that, his athletic career was over.

It was not easy to find Moore. One of the Virginia Tech coaches told me, "Corey is extremely intelligent but also hard to understand." Each person in Blacksburg whom I asked about Moore had the same reply: anything I wanted to know about Corey Moore, I would have to get from him. When I talked to Moore in 2012, he was in his early thirties, a single father, attending Michigan State to work on a master's degree. He agreed to be interviewed on the condition that I not ask anything about him personally—that he could comment, but I could not ask.

"I graduated fourth in my high school class," Moore said. "My mother was very strict. She would not allow me to participate in any sport unless my GPA was good. I debated whether to play college football, since I could have gone to college on academic scholarship.

"The best part of being at Virginia Tech was Coach Beamer. He has a sense of perspective about life. People say he can't win the big game, but that matters more to the alumni than to him. Coach Beamer truly does not see the lack of a national championship as mattering to his legacy. He sees helping boys become men as his legacy. When you leave his program, you are ready to be a well-rounded citizen."

I tried to get my foot in the door by inquiring if Moore liked football. "That is asking about me," he said sternly. "The ground rules were that you would ask nothing about me."

In 2010, Moore returned to Virginia Tech, stood on the sideline with Beamer during a game and watched a ceremony in which his jersey was retired. Many coaches talk about family this, loyalty that—then drop former players the instant it serves their interest to do so. Beamer does not walk that path. He had stayed in touch with Moore by annually sending an old-fashioned handwritten letter with a stamp, and was happy to have Moore back to Blacksburg to honor him, even though a cloud hangs over his name.

Or does a cloud hang over Corey Moore's name? Only he really knows. All that is certain is that Moore was a fabulous football player who left the game in the springtime of life, with only Beamer's friendship to show for it. Had things gone well, about now sportswriters would be debating Moore's place in football lore. Instead, nine out of ten football writers would not recognize his name.

THE SUICIDE OF FORMER NFL star Junior Seau was the lead item on the *CBS Evening News* in the spring of 2012. The day Seau pulled the trigger, I had been interviewing Keith McCants, who was taken one selection before Seau in the 1990 NFL draft, and who played the same position, linebacker.

In the springtime of his life, McCants was a breathtaking athlete. Born in Mobile, Alabama, as a prep star he made all-state in football and in basketball. McCants became an all-American at the University of Alabama. A feared defender, he was among the first linebackers to be both strong and fast, his 4.5 time in the 40-yard dash then unprecedented for a 260-pound man. McCants was chosen by the Tampa Bay Buccaneers with the fourth selection of the 1990 draft, signing a contract with a $4.3 million bonus, in 1990 the largest bonus ever accorded a defensive player.

When McCants arrived at the Bucs training camp, the team was struggling to sell tickets, having not made the playoffs in nearly a decade. He played well, but did not reach the Pro Bowl, leading to whispers about this top-drafted performer's being a bust. It did not help that head coaches were fired each of his first two years. Doing the firing was owner Hugh Culverhouse, whose high living caused recurrent problems with the team's finances. This was shortly before the 1993 labor-peace deal caused NFL television revenues to begin their rapid rise. Today, losing NFL teams are profitable. At the time, an NFL owner's lifestyle depended on ticket sales.

For the 1992 season, Culverhouse hired Sam Wyche as coach. Wyche was under intense pressure to win, to generate box-office results; McCants was under intense pressure to become a star. In September 1992, in a game at Detroit, McCants suffered a compound fracture of a clavicle. McCants says the injury was wrapped and injected with local anesthesia, and he returned to the contest. Tampa Bay won, improving to 3-I, with McCants playing in great pain.

A broken clavicle is not a severe injury, though normally entails several weeks of rest. McCants says he was pressured to take no time off, and the only way to do so was narcotics: "There is a fine line between pain and being injured. Football players must play hurt, that's how the sport is. But to play injured is wrong, and I should have refused."

NFL athletes are expected to "play through pain," both so their teams win and to show manhood. Players expect this of each other, as much as coaches demand this. When Chicago Bears quarterback Jay Cutler left the 2011 NFC Championship Game with an injury, then watched the second half from the Bears' sideline moving around without apparent difficulty, he was widely ridiculed, by sportswriters and by other NFL players, as not man enough. If he can't stand up, maybe he needs medical attention. If he's walking around, get his ass into the game!

The pressure to play through pain filters down from the NFL, where performers are well compensated, to college and high school, where there is only pain.

"I should not have taken painkillers the way I did, but once I started taking them, I needed more and more and went downhill," McCants says. "Narcotics like Percocet led to cocaine. I was not doing drugs to get high, I was doing drugs to control pain. A lot of NFL players fall into this trap. They know they are easily replaced, so they get injected or ask for pills. The coach can claim he was never informed, the trainer can say the player was making a voluntary choice. By the time you leave the sport, you are hooked on dope.

"No coach ever told me I was required to take narcotics," McCants says. "What they told me was that if I did not play, I would be waived. Then ten minutes later the trainer came around and offered painkillers. You figure it out."

Gulping pills, McCants tried his best to play. The Buccaneers went

2-10 for the remainder of the season, after which McCants was released, scapegoated for yet another disappointing outcome for the franchise. Over the next three seasons, McCants played sporadically for the Atlanta Falcons and the Arizona Cardinals. Frequent knee surgeries robbed Mc-Cants of his famed acceleration. He says he endured twenty-nine football-related surgeries, many at his own expense, since at the time health insurance ended the day a player was cut. With the Cardinals, McCants scored two defensive touchdowns, but did not generate sacks as a player in his position should. After the 1995 season, he was waived out of football—taking with him orthopedic problems and addiction.

McCants says that when he was in the NFL, he frequently went to trainers requesting for opioid painkillers and always received them, no questions asked. Unusual? NHL star Derek Boogaard died in 2011, at age twenty-eight, of an accidental overdose of painkillers and alcohol. In the final year of his life, Boogaard received at least thirty bottles of narcotic painkillers prescribed by team physicians.

In the years that followed football, McCants would not make smart choices. Three times he was convicted on drug charges, involving painkillers obtained illegally or cocaine, often sought by painkiller addicts. Once, McCants was arrested leaving a strip club in a bad part of town—not just an arrest, a low-class sort of arrest. McCants lost the millions he'd made and lost his Greek-god physique. By 2012, at age forty-four, McCants was obese, walked with a cane, and was in and out of halfway houses.

The benjamins—he's not even sure where they went. "Truly I wish I never made that money," McCants says. "Money brought nothing but unhappiness. I wanted to be a big man and flash a lot of money. It drew the wrong kind of people to me, pretending to be my friends." As Billie Holiday sang:

Money, you've got lots of friends
Crowdin' 'round the door.

McCants grew up in a housing project. In poor communities, if someone acquires money, word spreads; distant relatives and childhood acquaintances may appear, expecting a share or requesting a "loan." In 2012, Tyron Smith of the Cowboys, who'd recently received a large bonus, called police to ask them to remove from his home distant relatives who had, he said, let themselves in and were aggressively demanding money.

Many pro athletes want to be seen, by those who knew them back in the day, as a Big Man. This leads to their giving lavish gifts, to parties that end with guests receiving bags of hundred-dollar bills, to announcing "The champagne is on me" at crowded clubs, to "investing" in dubious "businesses" run by cousins or acquaintances. McCants acknowledges he made careless errors by giving cash to friends and relatives asking for "loans" they had no intention of repaying. But he was trying to carry himself as a Big Man.

In the end, McCants was tossed into the trash by football. He wasn't the first and won't be the last. Other athletes have faced the same set of issues and handled themselves better. But painkiller addiction colored his chance of moving on with his life.

"You're competing against players on dope, so you have to be on dope," McCants says. "The NFL absolutely does not want the public knowing the amount of narcotics used in the locker room. If the numbers were published, there would be intense pressure from Congress to reduce drug use by the NFL."

McCants has heard the cheers, been wealthy, been at the center of adulation, fulfilled the male fantasy of being chased by women. Now he's a wreck. He says, "The fans see the excitement on the field, the touchdowns and the knockout hits. They don't see that players are being pressured to ruin their bodies—offered this incredible lifestyle, but only if you are willing to destroy yourself. I made bad choices, and I blame myself for my bad choices. But I thought I joined an organization, the NFL, that would take care of its own. Turns out the minute you can't perform anymore, the NFL abandons you. They know there are a hundred fresh young men ready to fall for the same thing."

In 2012, there was a scandal in horse racing. High-end stallions at Belmont Park were being pumped with prescription drugs that improve performance but degrade health, causing the mounts to be euthanized after the last purse is won. A lengthy *New York Times* exposé read disconcertingly like descriptions of drug use in football.

"They treat us like horses," McCants had said to me a short time before. "When one breaks down, just bring in another animal. And the worst part is, we let them do it."

The next chapter: what America's love of football says about the country.

10

WITH LIBERTY AND FOOTBALL FOR ALL

Well after midnight on the morning of the 2012 Super Bowl, I stood at the city-center square of Indianapolis, before a cenotaph that commemorates sons of Indiana lost in wars. Statuary adorns the base, including a frieze titled "The Dying Soldier." A plaza with fountains surrounds the cenotaph; water spouts from the mouths of bronze bison. The monument was completed in 1901, as a remembrance of those who fell in the Revolutionary War, War of 1812, Mexican-American War, Spanish-American War and what an inscription calls the War for the Union. A sense of the march of history is communicated by the stately memorial, nearly the height of the Statue of Liberty, along with a sense of sacrifice Americans of the past endured to make possible freedoms of the present. And of the tens of thousands of Americans milling about the square in the wee hours, probably not a one had noticed.

Rock music was blasting at military-afterburner decibel levels, joined on continuous loop by the chimes and bells of the NFL's broadcast-opening musical interlude, a jingle called "Sprint Right," by

Tom Hedden. The NFL logo was being beamed around the city center by industrial-size searchlights of the type used to signal Batman. Other lights were projecting the letters XLVI, designating the Super Bowl, onto the war monument, showing not the slightest respect for its solemn purpose. Onlookers were using cell phones to take videos of towering Super Bowl Roman numerals appearing on a nineteenth-century object.

Earlier in the week, seven thousand people paid $25 a ticket, if purchased in advance, or $50, if bought from scalpers, to file into Lucas Oil Stadium and watch Super Bowl Media Day. Not to participate, merely to look on as journalists, sports agents and friends of friends milled around the field, waiting for an NFL player to wander by and submit to being hectored.

Visitors begin arriving at a Super Bowl city the week before the game and are eager for any activity that draws them, even tangentially, into the sphere of the event. Crowds start to be in evidence by Thursday, for a Sunday-evening kickoff. The ESPN, *Maxim* and *Playboy* parties, hottest invites for VIPs, are on Friday night. Boldface names have already held their parties, on Wednesday night—Shaq O'Neal typically rents a mansion for a Wednesday-night bash—so they can be out of the city, wheels-up in their private aircraft, as the unwashed begin filtering in Thursday. On Saturday night, promoters stage dance-hall parties open to the public, with NFL star names on the flyers. It was $100 a head to enter the LaDainian Tomlinson party, where there was no chance the customers actually would behold Tomlinson, who was cloistered in a private room. But paying the cover charge would let a person say, "I partied at the Super Bowl with LaDainian Tomlinson."

Some 111 million people in the United States would watch the 2012 Super Bowl, largest audience ever for an American television broadcast; in 2013, the Baltimore–San Francisco Super Bowl audience would be a 109 million, third-largest ever. Both games, like all recent Super Bowls, were viewed by tens of millions worldwide, including in the

130 nations around the globe in which the United States maintains a total of 662 military bases.

Football popularity does not stop at the games themselves. Crowds attend NFL summer training camps, where there's nothing to see but wind sprints and walk-throughs. Television audiences not only watch the NFL draft, they watch the annual NFL Combine, where potential rookies are timed and tested—the Underwear Olympics, in the deft phrase of football commentator Mike Florio. Thousands of spectators attend the annual SEC Media Days program in Hoover, Alabama, vying for a chance to have a memento signed by a brand-name coach such as Nick Saban or Steve Spurrier. In 2012, some 1,085 media credentials were issued for SEC Media Days; thirty-three radio programs aired live from Hoover for the week; the event drew more reporters and broadcasters than heads of state visiting the White House. Ten hours of press conferences were held. Softball to Spurrier, coach at the University of South Carolina: "You're starting to have quality depth all across your roster. Talk about that and how beneficial is that."

Once I was in New Orleans to take in a remarkable series of big-deal football games staged on the same field in a single week—first the Sugar Bowl, then an NFL playoff contest, then the BCS title bowl to decide the college champion. Halfway through I commented to a local resident, "A body could only take this much football once in a while."

"Oh, no," he countered. "Every day. Every day."

In the United States, football is the king of sports—the biggest thing in the strongest and richest country in the world. Why is football so popular? What does the popularity of football say about the land of red, white and blue?

ONE OF THE LEADING INTELLECTUALS of his generation is Michael Mandelbaum, a chaired professor at Johns Hopkins University. Mandelbaum has written or edited nearly two dozen books on foreign policy and is impressive both for his scholarship and for being an optimist—in intellectual affairs there is plenty of the former, precious little of the latter. A few years ago I shared a meal with him and thought we'd talk about globalization, then the number-one topic in international affairs. Instead Mandelbaum regaled me with incredible resolution of detail on athletic events of the past. As are a surprising number of smart people, Mandelbaum is a sports nut.

The professor strayed once from international subjects, for his 2005 work *The Meaning of Sports*. In the book, Mandelbaum lays out the following thesis. Once, America was a pastoral, agrarian nation. Baseball was its perfect game, acquiring the label *national pastime*. Baseball can be played on farm fields; is not strenuous, so can be played after a day's physical labor; and is untimed. A baseball game continues till someone wins, the same way maintaining a farm takes as long as it takes. And organized practices are not essential: People who've just met can choose up sides and start a baseball game.

Then America began changing to an industrial nation. Old-time farmers mainly worked alone, or with their families, for their own harvest. Factory production requires elaborately choreographed cooperation among large groups: success for the team is success for everyone. Industrial output is driven by the clock. Workers are paid based on hours, while management consultants analyze production facilities for time-and-motion.

Thus baseball, a game for a hushed era of farms, was supplanted by football, a game for a cacophonous era of factories. Add that only a stick and a ball are needed for baseball, while football requires large quantities of mass-produced equipment forged by industry. As more Americans left the cornfield or cotton field for the auto plant, Mandelbaum supposes, their preferred sport shifted to a game that is an athletic interpretation of the factory.

Taking off from Mandelbaum's thinking, part of football's appeal may be that its structure is similar to the structure of the contemporary workplace. Once most Americans were self-employed; now most are employees of corporations or government. They are given orders by a boss. The orders may be wise or foolish, but if not followed, things fall apart.

That's a football game. The coach is in charge. His orders must be followed, even if the guys in the huddle suspect the coach just called the wrong play.

National Basketball Association contests involve remarkable displays of athletic prowess, almost like modern dancing for points. But the players have guaranteed contracts and openly defy their coaches, doing as they please on the court. Who can identify with that? Football feels much more like the average person's experience. NFL players may be stronger and better paid than most Americans, but still must obey a boss and will be fired (waived) if they don't do their jobs as instructed. "Do your job" turns out to be a common locker-room saying in football.

Basketball requires God-given height and athletic ability. Size and ability help in football, but every roster has players who were born average physically and made the team through dint of effort. Two-thirds of most high school teams are boys who became football players not because they were gifted but because they worked hard in August heat. Americans identify with football's self-made aspect.

That football reflects the American self-view and feels somewhat like the workplace explains how the NFL can rely on socialist economics (television revenue evenly split regardless of victories), and the NCAA can rely on public money, yet football has a patina of political conservatism. United States society is dualistic: Americans want to talk about self-reliance but also receive subsidized benefits. That's football—looks like dynamic individualism, while grants and tax favors underlie everything.

FOOTBALL IS SET UP THE same way America is set up—a reason, surely, why cities and communities see football teams as proxies for their own fortunes. Some Midwestern towns live and die on the exploits of the

high school basketball team. In the main, football is more closely associated with civic or community fortunes than any other sport. When
the high school football team wins, that's a good omen for the town,
especially since so many more people are involved in staging a football
game than other kinds of athletic events. When the college wins—
either the local college or a person's alma mater—that's a good omen
for the local area or the alumni group, plus draws favorable national
attention.

At the largest stage, NFL teams represent cities, and the city that
wins the Super Bowl rises in national standing. This can be interpreted
as an omen, even if everyone knows such thinking is irrational. I was
born in Buffalo, New York, a city that has many virtues but has been
in decline for decades. During the decline, the Bills lost four of four
Super Bowls. Like all true sons of Buffalo, I believe that if the Bills win
the Super Bowl, a reversal of civic fortunes will occur and a Buffalo
renaissance begin. I am not just saying this—I really believe it. Of
course, the Bills may never give me a chance to be proven wrong.

This irrational feeling—NFL success reflects well on a city, and
on fans of a team—is ubiquitous in the league's thirty-two cities. Visually, NFL stadiums are principal features of the downtowns of Chicago, Denver, Pittsburgh, Seattle and other major American cities. Much
larger than downtown baseball fields, many pro football stadia are sit-
uated in a way that connects the NFL with the city's self-image. When
NFL teams fail, their supporters and the city's residents may feel it is
some judgment upon them. When NFL teams win, especially the Super Bowl, the result is civic jubilation, shared across income, race and
sociological lines.

Perhaps nothing in the NFL matches the ceremony that starts each
home soccer game for Liverpool FC: the crowd sings "You'll Never
Walk Alone." Forty-five thousand people singing together, "Though
your dreams be tossed and blown . . . walk on with hope in your heart
and you'll never walk alone," expresses a shared sense of community
increasingly absent from the American civic sphere. But among those

things that do bring Americans together for civic celebration are the fortunes of football teams, and that is among the sport's virtues.

FOOTBALL IS KING IN THE United States but nowhere else. Even Canada, which plays gridiron football—the Canadian Football League completes its season around Thanksgiving, before glaciers cover the fields—has ice hockey as sport of choice. Other nations prefer soccer, baseball or basketball. Most don't even play gridiron football.

That football is king in the United States but nowhere else may be easily explained—only the United States could pull football off. Gridiron football is the most expensive sport, the biggest sport in terms of performers and support staff, the most complex sport tactically—a sport of "mosts." Only the strongest and most affluent nation has what it takes to make football happen: every weekend in autumn, to stage sixteen pro games, hundreds of college contests and thousands of high school games, each involving at least a hundred players in costly body armor, plus dozens of coaches, trainers and equipment staff, presented in sprawling stadia before a few thousand to a hundred thousand spectators, with dozens of games telecast by well-staffed production crews backed by satellite uplink vans and power-generation trucks. Only in America!

The sheer complexity of football is part of the only-in-America appeal. All sports involve some strategy—baseball is heavy on analysis of statistics; basketball coaches study upcoming opponents. But in baseball, one or two players are making tactical choices at any moment; in basketball, two or three. In football, on each down twenty-two players must execute a range of possible assignments, then jump up from the ground and get a signal that switches them to a different assignment. Pro and college coaching staffs work year-round watching film of opponents' tendencies by down and distance, charting such details as the gaps between linemen, how many strides a receiver takes, how many steps in a quarterback's drop. Coaches study film of their own team to correct subtle "tells," such as how an offensive linemen points his feet on different types of plays. The tactics-study aspect of football is endless.

In the end, football is more about the performance of athletes than the decisions of coaches. But the complexity of football tactics has a strong appeal to the American mind-set. The country that was first to atomic fission and first to the moon; the country that invented the airplane, the photocopier and the personal computer; the country whose military exerts near-total control of the air and seas across the entire world—the most complex of team sports appeals to that country.

The postwar expansion of the US public university system coincided with the growth of football, each boosting the other. Around the same time, television was changing from a curiosity to a mainstay. Like football and college, football and television caused mutual amplification. The sport's takeover of television owes much to the single most important player in football history. As everyone knows, that man is Preston Ridlehuber.

On November 17, 1968, the New York Jets and Oakland Raiders were playing on national television, in the bygone era when just one NFL game was aired weekly. The broadcast had been hotly anticipated. Joe Namath of the Jets was then football's marquee name. New York led 32–29 with one minute remaining when the clock ticked to 7:00 p.m. eastern, then the highly formalized start of prime time. The television football scene dissolved and was replaced by a *Mädchen* yodeling. It was the *Heidi* Game.

Pre-cable and pre-Internet, fans would telephone the sports desk of newspapers to get final scores. When callers heard that Oakland gained a spectacular 43–32 victory—with the unknown Ridlehuber recording the decisive touchdown—there was a national sense of outrage. The following day, NBC announced it would never again switch away from an NFL contest in progress. This established the precedent that on television, *nothing* is more important than football. That precedent continues today. *Nothing* is more important than football. If a cure for cancer were discovered while an NFL game was in the final moments, the announcement would just have to wait.

Secure in its dominance of television, professional football has taken a strong position in new electronic enterprises such as video games, fantasy sports and online betting. The Madden video-game series debuted in 1988 for early home computers such as the sixty-four-kilobyte Commodore. By 2003, Madden games had movielike graphics and the ability to use the Internet to play against gamers in other places. This melded the NFL with technology, appealing to a generation that had never seen the Giants at the Polo Grounds or engaged in any other form of football nostalgia, and was more interested in sizzle than sports lore. When John Madden was inducted into the Pro Football Hall of Fame in 2006, it was for his achievement a video-game impresario as much as his relatively brief career as a coach.

Broadband makes fantasy football more dynamic, allowing groups of fantasy leaguers to hold trading sessions as often as they wish. Millions of people engaged in fantasy football had the unintended consequence of rendering all games interesting to someone. Even when two cellar dwellers pair off in a contest with no bearing on the standings, the stats generated can make or break some fantasy owner's season.

Wagering on sports is as old as the Roman Colosseum; online gambling, whether legal in Nevada or gray-market elsewhere, adds another level of interest to the NFL. In September 2012, when the league's regular officials were locked out in wage dispute, replacement zebras botched their call on the final down of a *Monday Night Football* game, mistakenly awarding victory to the Seattle Seahawks rather than the Green Bay Packers. An estimated $150 million changed hands on that single officiating mistake. Bettors didn't care who won—but for the error, the Packers would have covered.

Football is too loud, too manic, too extravagant. Is this necessarily a bad formula? Perhaps football is only reflecting its home. A paradox of the United States is that the country is raucous, confrontational and overstated, yet simultaneously free, fair and tolerant. NFL players slam into each other violently in publicly subsidized stadia as half-naked cheer-babes cavort—then, to cite the actual example of Baltimore Ravens linebacker Brendon Ayanbadejo, go out and campaign for gay marriage. Football is the perfect game for the cultural contradictions of the United States. Perhaps in some ineffable way, the too-big too-much nature of football helps stimulate American freedom and affluence.

Tony Dungy, who played in the NFL as an undrafted free agent, rising to become head coach for the Buccaneers and the Colts, is thoughtful about a sport not known for pensive figures. Why do football and America go together? Dungy:

"Football is America's game because it is aggressive, and Americans are aggressive people. Being aggressive is not bad, so long as it happens within a structure of rules.

"Football is a great sport for TV. The slow-motion replays allow the viewer to understand what just happened. In baseball you might want a replay to see whether the runner is safe or out, but you don't need replay to understand what's happening. Football is so fast and complicated, replay allows the average person to understand the game, and replay is only available on television. It's not a coincidence that television and football became big at about the same time.

"The once-a-week format of a football season gives people time to digest and talk about the games. And once a week makes each game memorable. I can still recall in detail the tactics and big moments of games I played in or coached in, or even just watched, from decades ago. Many fans remember specifics of games from twenty-five years in the past and still discuss them to this day. Baseball and basketball play too often for individual games to be memorable.

"And Americans like teamwork, which is a secondary factor is some sports but essential to football. Americans like to think that by pulling together as a nation, we accomplish more than we could individually. That is how football functions."

• • •

THIS VIEW IS NOT AN idealization. Football introduces young boys and teen boys to teamwork and self-discipline, which benefits the nation. All forms of athletics require self-discipline, but because football involves by far the largest total number of participants, football has the most teaching value. Done properly, football not only helps boys learn how to be men, it helps them learn how to cooperate with others and how to express their masculinity within a framework of respect for rules.

Communities can experience teamwork through football. At the high school level, where most football is played, for every one football player who steps onto the field, two people behind the scenes made the game possible. In high school, staging football games causes parents from disparate backgrounds, who might otherwise never even meet, to learn to work together. The high school drama society and the high school band have the same positive effect. But there are far more people involved in football.

Football at the pro, college and high school levels generates a shared interest that crosses racial, ethnic and economic lines. In few cultural arenas do whites, African-Americans, and Hispanics from all income classes share the same interest—football is one. Many cities and colleges have symphonies, opera houses, theaters and dance companies whose performances are excellent but which don't accomplish much to bring people together. Sports bring people together. Because football is the biggest and most popular sport, it creates the largest sphere of common interests. Common interests are precious in our fragmented, digitized world.

THOUGH COMMON INTERESTS ARE FORMED, gender and racial tensions still exist within football. The gender issue is whether success for women is propelling expansion of football. In the last generation two social transformations have happened concurrently: women have grown more powerful in employment, education and politics, while football has risen in prominence. That two changes happen at once does not prove they are related. But they might be.

Female presence in the workplace has grown from unusual to 77 percent of adult women working outside the home. By 2012, women were CEOs not just at consumer-products firms such as Yahoo! and Pepsi, but at defense contractors Lockheed Martin and General Dynamics. Nancy Pelosi had recently been Speaker of the House, the highest elected office ever held by a woman in the United States; three of the last four secretaries of state were women; three justices of the Supreme Court were female; Hillary Clinton had come within an eyelash of being the Democratic nominee for president; four of the eight Ivy League universities had female presidents; two of three bachelor's degrees were being earned by women; 70 percent of the nation's high school valedictorians were girls—and there were many other indicators of girls' and women's increasing success across American society. As this was happening, boys and men found themselves liking the artificial universe of football more and more.

A quirky 1995 book, *The Stronger Women Get, the More Men Love Football*, is worth recalling. The author, Mariah Nelson, had been captain of the women's basketball team at Stanford, where she set a record for rebounds, and has since found a niche as a motivational speaker. *The Stronger Women Get, the More Men Love Football* is thick with failed predictions, especially that men would suppress women's athletics. This turned out to be completely wrong. Not only are girls' and women's sports flourishing in high schools and colleges, broadly supported by parents and school administrators: NCAA women's basketball, volleyball and softball draw good ratings on television. Many college football and men's basketball coaches go out of their way to support women's athletics, since female athletes prove college sports is about more than male interests.

But in 1995, Nelson was right on one prediction—that as women became stronger economically and politically, men would retreat into football. Women now exert themselves in science, engineering, and other traditionally male pursuits including race-car driving; it is only a matter of time until the first female president. This, Nelson's theory holds, causes men to crave football, a macho world where women play no role, other than to look pretty and cheer for men.

In football, and perhaps only in football, boys and men can be sure that girls and women will never take over. A handful of women have worked as football officials; officiating requires poise and quick thinking but not strength. Some athletic trainers of football teams are female; at many colleges, the boys go into sports marketing and the girls go into sports medicine. But it's close to inconceivable women ever will play in the NFL; the size-and-muscles requirement gives men an overwhelming edge.

In 2012, Erin DiMeglio was a backup varsity quarterback for South Plantation High School of Florida, a football power; she got into a game late and completed a pass. But only a handful of girls have ever started in an eleven-player high school game. A few women have kicked extra points in college games, and a few girls kick in high school—in 2012, Lauren Luttrell, who had been the placekicker for her high school team, made it to the final round of cuts at Virginia Tech. But though football kickers tend to be slender and to avoid contact, they still need leg strength, and men's quadriceps are stronger. In football, even an elite female athlete would be at a huge disadvantage to a below-average male player.

This makes football the ideal place for men to retreat to—an aspect of life that will always be male, no matter how free and powerful women become.

A generation from now, women may run the White House, Congress, the Fortune 500, maybe even the Pentagon—but there is no chance, none at all, that women will be suiting up in the NFL. Football becomes, for men, a place to escape from the opposite gender. The female response may be "Let the guys have their football, we'll take everything else." Signs of this are already appearing in educational statistics.

• • •

IF WITH BARACK OBAMA THE White House became postracial, football was there first. As recently as the early 1960s, while the Southeastern Conference still banned African-American players, George Preston Marshall, racist owner of the Washington Redskins, would not sign Ernie Davis, first African-American to win the Heisman Trophy, because Marshall refused to allow blacks on his team. But since roughly the late 1960s, football has been a meritocracy: who makes the team, and who gets the precious PT—playing time—has nothing to do with race. Since roughly the early 1990s, the quarterback and head-coaching positions also have become postracial. Black head coaches have won the Super Bowl, while African-American quarterbacks regularly are chosen in the first round of the NFL draft.

Today in the states of the Old South or in South Boston, not long ago the locus of antiblack rioting, whites root for African-American football players and hold them up to their children as persons to be admired. How different from 1962, when backers of the all-white University of Mississippi football team waved thousands of Confederate battle flags at a game versus the all-white University of Kentucky team, then proceeded to riot against the admission of James Meredith as an Ole Miss undergraduate.

Any activity that causes American whites to cheer for American blacks is a positive on the social ledger. If every US institution possessed the meritocracy quotient of football, affirmative action would no longer be needed. But this hardly means all racial issues that arise from football are resolved. One concerns an underside of American psyche; the other, whether football makes black America seem to have come farther than it has. First, the issue of the national psyche.

RALPH ELLISON'S GREAT NOVEL *INVISIBLE Man* has a long, chilling section that literary critics call the Battle Royal. The narrator is a young African-American man in an unnamed Southern state of the pre-civil-rights period. He and other young black men are locked in a building where the town's white landholders are having a drunken party. The blacks are told they must fight in pairs; the last one standing will be given money. They fight savagely, brutalizing each other with their fists. Bones are broken; fighters are bloodied and fall unconscious. Finally the narrator and a much stronger young man face off as the last combatants. The rowdy assemblage is catcalling and placing bets. The narrator whispers to the stronger black that they shouldn't fight, that they are not enemies. The other black says he wants the money, and begins wildly pummeling as the crowd roars.

Ellison's point in the Battle Royal section, written in 1948 and still agonizing to read, was that some whites like to watch blacks harm each other. Civil rights laws have changed the details, but not the dynamic.

Prizefighting and mixed martial arts entice audiences to watch men savagely harm one another, with prizefights often pairing two African-Americans. But these sports, if sports they are, have little television presence and are attended in person by small numbers of people with specialized tastes, if taste they have. Football by contrast is the nation's most watched sport. It has brought the Battle Royal to prime time.

Football as played today is very different from what's described in *Invisible Man*. Participants are present of their own free will; blacks and whites participate together, sharing the same risks. And while some football fans root for limbs bent the wrong way and heads thrown backward during vicious hits, most spectators prefer a clean game. But there's no getting around that much of the action in NCAA and NFL football, and some of the action in high school football, involves African-Americans inflicting pain on each other while whites applaud.

In many respects, notably the declines of crime and of traffic deaths, the American civic sphere grows less violent. Perhaps to compensate, Americans increasingly crave violent entertainment in football, cinema and video games. But cinematic blood is fake and video games are computer animations. The harm that football players inflict on each other is disturbingly real.

Football's unsettling racial subtext would be lessened if the sport became less brutal. Some traditionalists maintain that safety enforcement will make the game sissified—but traditionalists wanted to keep the leather helmet too. There is no chance of football evolving into a timid sport. If football evolved into a sport that is aggressive without being brutal, not only would players' health be protected, audiences would no longer be offered a Battle Royal.

THE OTHER RACIAL QUESTION RAISED by football is economic. By creating a highly visible but small category of well-off black males, professional football may generate a mirage of black success, while diverting attention from the 99 percent of African-Americans who are not athletes.

The economic power and mass-media triumph of football results in a group of African-American men who are visible as millionaries and are broadly admired across US society, including by white males. So far, so good. But there may be a subconscious force here. The NFL allows America's majority to think, "See, there are black men making good money, and I root for them. So race is old news."

The NFL might be seen an as unplanned experiment in free-market reparations—where a small number of African-Americans attain wealth by their own efforts, not set-asides, and where a black executive class (coaches and general managers) is developing without government intervention. But progress is not the same as everything being all right.

Even African-American football fans avert their eyes from the large numbers of black players used up and thrown away, and from high school football's perverse impact of distracting African-American teen boys from the classroom, which offers them a better chance of a good job than sports. To the extent the NFL makes it seem black males can achieve career success without doing well in high school and college, pro football is a mirage—and a dangerous one.

•   •   •

FOOTBALL IS BOUND INTO THE American fabric. The nation loves this sport. Beyond the sociological reasons is a simple, straight-up reason—football games can be fantastic: exciting, complicated, constantly changing, and completely spontaneous. If you attend a performance of *Lohengrin*, you know when the swan boat will appear. If you attend a football game, you have no idea what's going to happen—and neither does anyone else. That's exciting.

Let's return to the Hokies to look at an exciting football game from behind the scenes and inside the locker room.

The next chapter: Virginia Tech versus Michigan.

11

INSIDE A FOOTBALL GAME

"Stay out of the French Quarter on New Year's Eve," the police officer was saying. "There's a reason New Orleans is called Sin City. Don't matter how big or strong you are. Bad things could happen tonight. Don't let bad things happen to you."

The Virginia Tech football family—players, coaches, trainers, sports-medicine majors, video crews—was gathered at the center of the Superdome, where the NFL's New Orleans Saints perform, to prepare for the Sugar Bowl, one of college football's premier events. Along the sidelines, some Virginia Tech boosters and donors were present, many with their children—young boys and girls tossing footballs and posing to have their pictures taken with the team in the background. The playing surface at the Superdome has a silver glint, as if flecks of Christmas tinsel were embedded in the turf. Football teams seeking public recognition have installed blue turf, red turf and fields with alternating stripes of color. Considering the money coming into football, it may be only a matter of time until some team has a golden playing surface.

Frank Beamer looked on as two NOPD officers addressed the players on New Year's Eve 2011. The French Quarter was an easy walk from the Hilton Riverside, where the Hokies were staying. Beamer had asked local law enforcement to put the fear of God into his players about the difference between Blacksburg, Virginia, and New Orleans, Louisiana. Liquor is everywhere in New Orleans, leading to frequent inebriated brawls. Bars open onto the streets with walk-up cocktail windows, hard stuff is for sale in pocket-size bottles at any CVS. In New Orleans, schools and churches probably sell liquor. And whiskey is the least of the city's hazards. Cops consider it a fine night if all that happens in the French Quarter is public drunkenness and scuffles. Only too happy to drop in on a visiting football team, officers regaled players with grisly accounts of crimes they'd worked on past New Year's Eves.

That night the team would watch a movie and have a fourth meal together. As midnight approached came an "optional" walk to a Mississippi River esplanade to watch fireworks welcome the New Year. Everyone attended the "optional" walk, which went in the opposite direction from the beckoning French Quarter and Harrah's casino, where high rollers were handing their Bentleys and Porsches over to valets about whose driving records they knew nothing. Fireworks, then a 12:30 a.m. bed check. DO NOT LATCH YOUR HOTEL DOORS, read an instruction sheet handed to players.

Old trick: one guy sneaks out, the other guy stays behind with the door latched. When a coach comes for bed check, the door will only crack open a bit. The wingman says, "We're both in bed, coach." The Virginia Tech coaches know this trick, perhaps having tried it themselves back in the day. Doors must remain unlatched.

Several assistant coaches have master keys to the Virginia Tech room block and check players randomly through the night. No one sneaks out, though the sounds of revelers in the French Quarter on New Year's morning drifted seductively toward the hotel. In football as in the military, sneaking out to look for drinks, parties and women makes for a great story at a get-together years hence. But if caught now, you are in trouble.

THE VIRGINIA TECH ENTOURAGE TRAVELED to New Orleans a full week before the 2012 Sugar Bowl—the bowl bonus the Hokies were at that point enjoying for the nineteenth consecutive year. The Hilton Riverside was the fanciest hotel many of the players had been in—chrome and neon lobby, a stream of beautiful people in town for the New Year's Eve rowdiness the cops warned of. Virginia Tech was out of session, so no studying. Bowl week was nearly a vacation.

Of bowl destinations, New Orleans ranks first among college football players because it combines a desirable locale with a walkable downtown. Miami, where the Orange Bowl is played, is known for South Beach nightlife; Pasadena, location of the Rose Bowl, for the trendiness of Southern California; Scottsdale, host to the Fiesta Bowl, for high-end resorts and striking Arizona girls. But Miami, Pasadena and Scottsdale require cars, and what college student can afford to rent a car? In New Orleans, the visitor is fine on foot or using the trolley.

By the second day, Logan Thomas had already located all the hungry-guy locations within a short walk of the hotel: Arby's, McDonald's and the original Popeyes. Some of the country's finest restaurants have Cajun chefs; New Orleans dining prices are intended for expense-account travelers. Team members started the bowl week with money in their pockets. By the third night, many were tapped out. Collin Carroll, the long-snapper and sports columnist for the Virginia Tech college newspaper, had just published on ESPN.com an opinion piece arguing, "Bowl games are way more pleasure than business." Carroll thought the New Orleans accommodations and bowl-sponsored activities lavish. He experienced no backlash from teammates since his comments were that antiquated written-word stuff. If he'd been interviewed on ESPN TV and the clip posted on YouTube, his teammates would have watched on their smartphones and given him a hard time.

In his commentary, Carroll noted that for the New Orleans week, each Virginia Tech player received travel, room and four meals daily, plus $450 total as per diem and about $500 in gifts—apparel and electronics—from the host committee. Not princely but not pauper-dom either. Carroll calculated that at the in-state cost of Virginia Tech tuition and assuming strict observation of NCAA practice-time rules, through their college years Hokie scholarship football players earn $38 an hour, tax-free. Not the NFL but not a bad deal.

DESPITE THE BED CHECKS AND other safeguards, during the vacation-like period that preceded the Sugar Bowl, things went wrong. Before the Hokies even departed for New Orleans, their starting placekicker, Cody Journell, was booted from the team. Journell had been arrested for breaking and entering; he would later be cleared of serious charges. But a policy Virginia Tech blandly calls the Comprehensive Action Plan mandates, among other things, that an athlete who is arrested be suspended until such time as he or she may be cleared. Though an arrest is only an accusation, not proof of wrongdoing, Virginia Tech errs on the side of caution.

Journell's suspension meant the backup placekicker, fifth-year senior Tyler Weiss, who had never hit a field goal for the Hokies would kick against Michigan in prime time. On New Year's Day, with the city sleeping off an epic hangover, Weiss missed a bed check and was caught after curfew.

Beamer ordered Weiss sent home. He was put on a bus back to Blacksburg, given 833 miles aboard a Greyhound to think about how he'd let the team down—and lost the only chance he would ever have to play football on national television. Weiss's family members had bought last-minute airfares to New Orleans and scalped Sugar Bowl tickets to be in the stands for what could have been a *Rudy*-like story of the kid who never got to play until he became the hero of his very last game. Instead the kid was on a bus home, his family's money wasted.

To open the season following its Sugar Bowl appearance, Virginia Tech would face Georgia Tech on college's equivalent of *Monday Night Football*. Cleared of the accusation, Journell would kick the winning field goal for the Hokies in overtime. Keep that fact in mind.

NORMALLY ONLY THOSE EXPECTED TO play attend away games. Bowls are different, one reason college football organizations like them so much. Not only do spouses come along for the week, so do the scout team, the redshirts and those deep on the depth chart.

Since Virginia Tech will have a full practice week in New Orleans, rather than a day-before walk-through as with most road dates, the scout team is needed to run the University of Michigan offense against the first-team defense. For many on the scout team, the Sugar Bowl is their initial experience of an away game—chartered jets, expensive hotel, fans in the lobby asking for autographs, Virginia Tech flags and logos all over a city. Scout-team members, like the starters, received tracksuits and other apparel specific to the game—someday to be treasured possessions for the Hokies unlikely to play.

Though Virginia Tech and Michigan are storied football programs, through some quirk they had never met. The Hokies entered the Sugar Bowl 11-2, the Wolverines 10-2, with Virginia Tech the highest-ranked opponent Michigan had faced in its season. Michigan's star was quarterback Denard Robinson, a lightning-reflexes player in the mold of Clemson quarterback Tajh Boyd, who had inflicted on the Hokies their sole defeats of 2011.

Both programs knew they had been selected for the Sugar Bowl over Boise State and Kansas State, higher-ranked schools backed by the touts, because Virginia Tech and Michigan "travel well"—have loyal supporters who spend freely to be present at away games. A Hokies-Wolverines pairing meant game tickets and New Orleans hotel rooms sold rapidly. The Sugar Bowl committee wasn't sure Kansas State supporters would snap up seats and suites. Because Boise State has openly denounced the BCS system—the only football power to have done so, because for years Boise State did not belong to one of the conferences that receives an automatic BCS bid—no one on a bowl committee wanted to do the Broncos any favors.

Practice during Sugar Bowl week involved using the Superdome, allowing Virginia Tech players to cavor on the same field used by the Saints, a recent Super Bowl victor. The Hokies stuck to their usual hyperspecific schedule, each phase timed down to the minute. One day's practice included thirty game-specific rehearsal phases for special teams, far more than the typical football practice. The offense elaborately repeated its presnap checks and sims, while defenders repeated their birdcalls, the hand gestures used to change alignments in response to whatever the opposition quarterback calls presnap.

Virginia Tech coaches taught so many plays, checks, sims and birdcalls that it was hard to believe the players remembered them all. A good guess is they did not. Ask any twenty-year-old male how things are going and he will say, "Good." Ask if he understands something and he will say, "Yes." Hokies players constantly told their coaches they understood everything, including clicker sessions in which the coaches would show game film rapidly forward and backward. A couple times after clicker sessions, I pulled players aside and asked if they would explain complex actions and signals to me—and to me, they admitted they could not follow what coaches had just said. During games, most of the time players knew what to do. But clearly some failed to remember assignments, and usually those were the disaster plays.

"The era of the dumb jock is over," Bud Foster says. A generation ago, a good athlete could show up having failed to study the playbook and wing it. Not today: constant study and memorization are required to avoid the embarrassing mistake that will be shown in slo-mo on *SportsCenter*. But physical performance still matters more than tactics. Several times after watching coordinators Foster and Bryan Stinespring chalk-talk their charges through complex desired reactions to tiny variations in opponents' cues, I was left thinking half as much would be twice as good.

Of course opponents were experiencing the same—Michigan players surely could not remember all the calls, either.

To relax during a Sugar Bowl practice, Beamer let the team stage an impromptu touch football game on the field of the New Orleans Saints. Asked to cite a flaw of his longtime boss's, Foster said, "He does not know how to be spontaneous." The touch football game was a rare exception.

THE PLAYERS' SCHEDULES WERE FULL, to pack in experiences and reduce the time available for getting in trouble. Meetings and game film in the mornings; practice in the afternoon; bowl-paid activities in the evening. Among the latter was dinner at Dickie Brennan's, a pricey New Orleans steak house—$66 plus tip for turtle soup, salad, house filet and a side dish—then a trip to see where the Rex Krewe builds its Mardi Gras floats. The dinner at Brennan's was at 6:00 p.m., followed by a fajita bar back in the hotel at 9:00 p.m. They are, after all, football players. The following morning, I met with a few players while most of the team luxuriated in a noon wake-up call. The early meal had been a simple continental breakfast for coaches and the travel party. Despite a gargantuan steak dinner and then fajitas the night before, the Hokies who got up early were complaining of no eggs and bacon at breakfast. They are, after all, football players.

At one smorgasbord meal served in a hotel ballroom, Beamer waited patiently behind players and graduate assistants, the interns of college-sports coaching. Beamer never cuts to the front of lines; players and staffers know not to offer him a spot at the front because he doesn't want special treatment. When Beamer finally made it to the table to present his meal request, one of the servers whispered, "Is that man someone important?" Celebrity college football coaches such as Nick Saban, Lane Kiffin or Chip Kelly would have caused a stir at the Hilton Riverside. Beamer, with more victories than Saban, Kiffin and Kelly combined, walked the hotel's halls unnoticed.

While the players practiced and saw the town, a sizable official party—Virginia Tech administrators and boosters—was present, enjoying a black-tie gala the night before the game. Bowl invitations are a bonus for the boosters too. If Division I football ultimately switches to an NFL-style playoff bracket, television audiences will grow, but for teams and the schools they represent, the resort-reward aspect will be lost.

The coaches and the better-known players were invited to daily press conferences. The coordinators, Foster and Stinespring, took a lot of the press questions, being more comfortable than Beamer exchanging banter with the media. Typical softball, to Stinespring, in a room with chairs for two hundred sports reporters: "David Wilson is such a star, does anything about his talent surprise you?"

Foster tells me he talked to Tyler Weiss's mother. There was no way to change the situation because Beamer told players beforehand that curfew violations would not be tolerated. But Foster wanted to make sure the family did not feel forgotten. It's the kind of little touch—such as sending handwritten letters to Corey Moore years later—that distinguishes the Virginia Tech approach. "College football players are so big and muscular they look like men, but inside, they are teenagers," Foster notes. "They have a teenager's understanding of the world and make the kinds of mistakes we all made as teenagers."

Beamer's son Shane is the running backs coach, and a bright light. His title is associate head coach, grander words for the office door than the title held by the two coordinators, who are far more accomplished. The younger Beamer might someday be in the running to replace his father; father-son succession often backfires in business, but might in this case receive the support of the Virginia Tech extended family. Shane already knows to greet all media questions with "That's a great question," regardless of whether it actually is. Endlessly saying "That's a great question" while thinking *How did he get in here?* is a habit of successful politicians, and of beloved coaches.

A long-snapper for the Hokies in the mid-1990s, Shane played for Virginia Tech in the same period as did linebackers coach Cornell Brown and secondary coach Torrian Gray. Together, they are the closest Virginia Tech coaching comes to a youth movement. Brown started twenty-five games in the NFL, and is the brother of Ruben Brown, one of football's best-ever offensive linemen. At Blacksburg, Brown coaches within view of the banner for his own retired jersey. Gray was a high draft choice of the Minnesota Vikings but never adjusted to the NFL and became a college assistant coach, starting at the University of Maine, when just a few years out of college himself.

On a staff that prizes quietude, Gray is the only one who cracks jokes during practice, once dropping to the ground and theatrically pretending to die when his starting secondary surrendered a long touchdown pass to the backup offense. The players pick up on the coaches' low-key. Team dinners are muted; there is no rock or rap music in the locker room; bus rides are hushed. In a day when athletes want to do something flashy to make *SportsCenter*, Virginia Tech players are remarkably reserved, more like they're looking for the library than for the field. At a Superdome practice, Wilson was the only player acting out—dancing at the center of the turf with his jersey pulled high to show off his core, which appeared to be forged from tungsten. A football player's *core* is what used to be his *abs*, which used to be his *six-pack*, which used to be *stomach muscles*.

An open secret of the coaching staff is that Stinespring and O'Cain don't speak much to each other. O'Cain is the play caller, normally a role for the offensive coordinator, so Stinespring does not have quite the duties his title implies. Because he does not call plays, Stinespring uses his extra time to coach the offensive tackles, so Curt Newsome, who works with guards and centers, isn't exactly the offensive line coach. These awkward arrangements, grounded in Beamer's desire never to fire anyone unless totally unavoidable, would end a year later with Newsome and O'Cain dismissed and Stinespring demoted.

ONE DAY A ROOM WAS SET up for interviews with Wilson, Thomas, offensive tackle Blake DeChristopher and tight end Chris Drager. Each sat on a chair placed on a riser, to create a dais; journalists' heads faced the players' knees. They are, after all, temporary royalty. Reporters crowded around the quarterback and running back, ignoring the lineman and tight end. At one point a reporter did stop at DeChristopher's podium—to ask what he thought of Wilson.

Monday before the game, the coaches met to plan final tactics. Beamer tells his assistants that if Virginia Tech faced fourth and short, he would tell Danny Coale—a wide receiver also subbing as the punter—to "rugby option." Coale would take a punt snap and roll to his right. If he thought he could reach the first-down line, he would run; if not, he would launch a rugby-style, in-motion punt. This sounds a lot easier in a meeting than at game speed.

Next, the coaches go over lineups with the medical staff. Mike Goforth, the head athletic trainer, reported that five players were scheduled for surgery the day after the team returned to Blacksburg. Usually parents come when a player needs surgery; his position coach is always at the hospital and stays until it's clear the surgery succeeded and the young man has woken up. After operations, recovering players would go home for the rest of winter break, since school would not resume for a week. Goforth consults parents or guardians if he thinks surgery is advised "because the guys always say they are fine and want to play. Nobody wants to miss the rest of the season, or even miss one game."

NCAA athletes get routine bumps-and-bruises medical attention without cost to them. For surgery, the family's health insurance pays, and a Virginia Tech secondary policy covers the out-of-pocket. The NCAA provides no insurance for long-term health complications. If football-caused brain trauma or degenerative orthopedic conditions manifest after college is over, don't bother calling the NCAA.

Goforth reported that running back Tony Gregory was one of the five scheduled for surgery on return to Blacksburg. He had a partial ACL tear: was able to play, but perhaps should not. Beamer was fond of Gregory, a special-teams ace. Goforth noted that Gregory badly wanted to be on the field because it was a BCS bowl. Beamer said he could dress.

During the meeting, Beamer nodded his head yes or shook it no on dozens of minor matters. The routine decisions regarding the rugby-option punt play, and allowing Gregory to dress, would prove essential to the outcome. Often small decisions have unexpected consequences. But you can't know in advance which small decisions will be the ones.

As THE DAY APPROACHED, VIRGINIA Tech coaches became concerned about the knock on their program—"Frank Beamer can't win the big game." This did not seem on players' minds, or if it was, none mentioned as much. "Back in my day, if we lost a game, we would be in a rage, we would smash lockers," says Brown. "Today the guys hardly react. They care, but it is important to be seen as cool and detached." Regardless of what they are feeling inside, contemporary football players feign indifference, shrugging and saying, "It is what it is." *It is what it is* has become the slogan of today's team sports, meaning anything from *I am philosophical about the situation* to *Look, we got our butts kicked, what the hell do you expect me to do about it?*

Beamer went to New Orleans with his fantastic streak of nineteen consecutive bowl seasons, but a losing bowl record. Entering the Sugar Bowl, the winningest active big-program football coach was 243-110-4 in regular-season play, just 8-10 in bowls. Virginia Tech's victory over Texas in the 1995 Sugar Bowl brought national attention to the Hokies, and by extension to the Virginia Tech admissions department. But in six appearances in the top-prestige bowls, Beamer hoisted a trophy just twice: over Texas in 1995, and over Cincinnati at the 2009 Orange Bowl.

The previous year, at the 2011 Orange Bowl, Virginia Tech played Stanford even through the early third quarter, then faded. In the college football regular season, any program that observes the NCAA limit on athletic hours, as Virginia Tech does, can't vary game plans much week to week. There just isn't time to study the next opponent, devise an original strategy and teach that strategy to players. But during the one-month layoff before a bowl game, there is time. Before the 2011 Orange Bowl, Stanford gave the microscope treatment to the Hokies' tendencies and realized Virginia Tech did not cover tight ends going deep. This was hardly an oversight: most college defenses ignore the tight end deep because college tight ends almost never go deep. Stanford sent tight end Coby Fleener deep. He responded with six catches for 173 yards and three touchdowns, breaking the Hokies' back.

This time around, Virginia Tech coaches felt confident they had prepared an original, opponent-specific game plan for Michigan. But otherwise they hadn't changed much. No extra psych-up, no special focus, the bowl week treated as a regular week. Schedules were even drawn that way. For instance, Thursday of bowl week was marked REGULAR MONDAY because players would be doing exactly what they did on any Monday.

The more I observed Beamer, the more comparisons I saw with Marv Levy, the Hall of Fame head coach of Cal, William & Mary, the Kansas City Chiefs and the Buffalo Bills. Levy is the sole football coach ever to have reached four consecutive Super Bowls, so he must have known what he was doing. Yet he lost all four. And said he slept soundly after each, which may be the key.

The farther a team advances into the postseason, the more the stress. Regular-season games can be won on the fly. In the postseason, psych-up and game-planning rise in importance.

In the first Bills' Super Bowl, Buffalo was a heavy favorite over the New York Giants. The Bills had the then-revolutionary no-huddle offense and had just cruised to a 51–3 AFC title win against the Oakland Raiders, while the Giants had a plodding offense and were lucky to win the NFC title over the 49ers on a field goal on the final down. Giants coach Bill Parcells had taken boxes of game film of Buffalo with him to San Francisco; he and his coaches flew directly from San Francisco to Tampa, where the Super Bowl would be held, and began to study Buffalo's offense aboard the charter flight late Sunday night. Levy gave his players Sunday night and Monday off. When coaches arrived in Tampa on Tuesday, he decided it was too late to study the

Giants, and they'd just use the same game plan that had destroyed the Raiders. But Parcells had spent all Monday studying that game.

Parcells wouldn't be able to sleep for a week if he lost a Super Bowl. Championships tend to be taken by driven, manic coaches with a win-at-all-costs mentality; the nice guys, who do not believe the world ends if they lose, tend to fall away at the last. Levy, a pleasant man who quotes Shakespeare and would make a fine dinner guest, was defeated in that Super Bowl by 1 point by Parcells, an angry man who often lost his temper in public. Levy's other Super Bowl losses came to Joe Gibbs, a gentleman but an obsessive perfectionist known for sleeping in his office during the season so as not to be away from game film, and to Jimmy Johnson, who as a coach had a cutthroat reputation, though mellowed after switching to sports broadcasting and buying a boat.

Bill Belichick, Nick Saban, Parcells—in sports, many ultimate trophies go to win-at-all-cost types, while nice guys such as Levy and Beamer pull up just a bit short. For his part, Beamer said, "If we were two and eleven, I would be upset. But we're eleven and two and going into a BCS bowl. Whatever happens, we have had a great year. If the program is doing okay and the university is doing okay, then you're okay. You should feel grateful." Within big-college football, that distinction was getting lost.

IN TEAM SPORTS, BOTH ATHLETIC ability and an athlete's story matter. The aware coach is not just sending bodies onto the field—rather, sending in the totality of a player's physical ability, mental acuity and life experiences. Here in alphabetical order is biographical information on Hokie players who would make marks in the 2012 Sugar Bowl, including some detail on what happened to them after their Virginia Tech years concluded:

Jarrett Boykin. A Tennessee native, Boykin would finish his Virginia Tech years as the school's all-time leader for receptions and receiving yards—then be crushed when fellow Hokies wide receiver Danny Coale was drafted by the NFL and he was not.

The all-time receiver for a major college program not drafted by anyone! But every football player knows the stories of those who refused to quit. Wes Welker was not recruited to play in college, went undrafted by the NFL—and made the Pro Bowl five times for the New England Patriots. Fred Jackson didn't start in high school, attended a Division III college, was not drafted by the NFL, and ended up as the starting tailback for the Buffalo Bills, cashing a multimillion-dollar bonus check. Cameron Wake was passed over in the NFL draft, lived in Canada to play for the British Columbia Lions when no NFL team even offered him a place on the practice squad, and made the Pro Bowl twice for the Miami Dolphins.

Undaunted, Boykin tried out for the Jacksonville Jaguars and was cut. Then he tried out for the Green Bay Packers, making the team. The Jaguars had the worst passing attack in pro football, the Packers one of the best: the bad team did not want Boykin, the good team did. Puzzling outcomes like this are not rare in athletics. By the end of his rookie season in Green Bay, Boykin was getting a bit of playing time.

Collin Carroll. From Minnesota, Carroll was the first long-snapper to attend Virginia Tech on football scholarship; most college football programs find a long-snapper among their walk-ons or backups. Though describing himself as "clumsy and unathletic," Carroll was in the Hokies' starting lineup for four years, snapping in four bowl games.

Carroll also wrote sports columns for the *Collegiate Times,* the Virginia Tech newspaper. He packed his columns with facts and statistics, and interviewed teammates about such awkward topics as their out-of-wedlock children. After graduating, Carroll enrolled in journalism school at Northwestern University, pursuing a master's degree. His future in sportswriting is bright.

Danny Coale. Every sports team has a player who leads a charmed life, and for the Hokies that player was Coale. Born in the small town of Lexington, Virginia, his parents saved to send him to Episcopal, an exclusive private boarding school in Alexandria, Virginia, just across the Potomac River from Capitol Hill. Coale's father, head of the physical education department at Virginia Military Institute, knew the quirks of the recruiting game and arranged for his son to begin Episcopal by repeating ninth grade. That ensured when Danny was being looked at by colleges, he would be a year older than his peers and performing better. Repeating a grade to get an athletic edge—grayshirting—is rarely discussed and widely practiced.

Going into high school senior year, Coale attended summer tryout camps at the University of Virginia, the University of North Carolina and North Carolina State. "After each camp," Coale says, "a coach took me aside and said, 'Who's offered you so far?' When I said no one had offered me a scholarship, they didn't want me. They only wanted players other colleges wanted." Bud Foster was Coale's recruiting coach—every college assistant coach is assigned parts of the country to recruit, and Foster had the Virginia suburbs of Washington, DC. "When I got to Virginia Tech camp, nobody asked what other schools had offered," Coale says. "Coach Foster tested me and asked to me come to Blacksburg. Compared to other colleges, Virginia Tech seemed honest and upfront."

Coale would become Virginia Tech's number-two receiver all-time for receptions and yards gained, and the first Hokie to win the Atlantic Coast Conference award for top student-athlete. In the spring of one academic year he received his undergraduate degree, in finance, then played the following autumn as a graduate student, while taking master's-degree courses. Smart, ambitious athletes work the system in that way: receiving their bachelor's, putting in one more sports season as a grad student, then departing college at Christmas with master's credits. Doing this gets a smart, ambitious athlete a bachelor's and most of a master's on a football scholarship.

Coale says, "College football for me was a dream come true, because we played in so many big games on national TV, and every year we ended the season playing for the conference championship or in a major bowl or both. But most college football players don't have that kind of experience. For many, college football leads to injury or bad outcomes. In prime time you see the successful players from the successful programs. Viewers should be reminded there's a lot of pain and unhappiness in college football too. And even as a finance major, I think the money is out of control. Money has become the beast of the BCS era. Way too much of college sports is about the money."

Leaving school immediately after the Sugar Bowl, Coale attended the NFL's annual scouting event in Indianapolis, where he ran the 40-yard dash in 4.5 seconds, defying the stereotype that white players cannot be fast. Coale was drafted in the fifth round by the Dallas Cowboys, finding himself not only at a prestige franchise but with Cowboys head coach Jason Garrett, a Princeton graduate who himself was a smart, ambitious athlete. Coale's charmed life continued.

Blake DeChristopher. Growing up in the suburbs of Richmond, Virginia, DeChristopher, an offensive tackle, was a football phenom from a young age. By the time he arrived at Virginia Tech, DeChristopher also was a giant—six feet five inches, listed at 311 pounds, able to bench-press 410 pounds while in his teens. He became a four-year starter for the Hokies—four-year starters were once the norm for the best college football players but today are increasingly rare, as the kind of athletes capable of starting for four years declare early for the NFL draft.

DeChristopher accumulated an impressive string of awards, including first-team all-ACC and an honorable-mention all-American. By senior year he'd also made his presence distinctive, growing a mountain-man beard. A diligent student, he graduated with a degree in sociology while "a junior on the field and a senior in the classroom," as someone who redshirted his first year would say, then played out his eligibility while taking master's-degree courses.

Passed over in the NFL draft, DeChristopher would end up in the camp of the Arizona Cardinals. He spent a year on the Cardinals' injured reserve, earning a token sum, then was waived. The NFL is so intensely competitive, even an unusually large, strong man with tremendous athletic ability may not make the grade.

Chris Drager. Drager grew up in Pittsburgh, grandson of a steelworker. He played both sides of the ball at Virginia Tech, tight end and defensive end, suffering several concussions. The university nominated Drager for a Rhodes Scholarship, and he advanced to the interview round in England. There, he says, "I got a lot of questions on knowledge of international economics and didn't do well on those." After the Sugar Bowl, Drager would leave college to train with a sports-performance specialist, hoping to be chosen in the pro draft. Some NFL teams want to see how a potential player performs when he does nothing all day long but train and watch football film, which simulates daily life at the NFL level.

Drager was not drafted nor signed as an undrafted free agent. His football days were over; perhaps as well, considering his concussion history. Just before the Sugar Bowl he said, "I made a point to savor senior year because I've been playing organized football since I was in fourth grade and I knew I might never do this again."

James Gayle. Born in Los Angeles, Gayle plays defensive end—once considered a power position, increasingly seen as a speed position. The spread passing offense and the zone-read rushing offense, two popular football mutations, must be countered with quick, agile defensive ends. Gayle is tall and brawny but not especially heavy—his forte is "foot speed," the ability to change directions in an instant. Defending the spread or the zone-read offense requires ends who can rush the quarterback and also run sideways into the flat.

Growing up with a single mother who worked as a prison psychologist, Gayle had on-and-off presences in his life from his father, a former Ohio State football player, and from his uncle Shaun, who started in the Chicago Bears' 1985 Super Bowl win. James Gayle did not play football until eleventh grade—"Football is a lot of work, and you get hit in the head constantly," he explains. On the latter point, James was cautioned by Shaun, who in 2012 joined a lawsuit against the NFL. At age fifty, Shaun was beginning to experience dementia and alleged his NFL playing years were the cause.

When James finally took the field in high school, he showed unusual aptitude, drawing the attention of many colleges. "In my case, football made me a better student," he says. "I was mediocre at grades until I learned that needing a good GPA was for real, that GPA would help get a scholarship. So I woke up. From the second semester of high school junior year on, I studied all the time and made honor roll."

Gayle notes, "Being at Virginia Tech, up in the mountains, it keeps you out of trouble. There's no club scene, that's for sure. If I had gone to a school like the University of Miami, there would be a lot of temptations. The Blacksburg atmosphere helps you focus on work. I decided that as a Hokie I would work out, attend class, be at practice, do my homework and go to bed early. If I was in a big-city environment, I'd probably be at clubs. My high school was mostly black, so college is a sociological adjustment for me in that respect. At first I was uncomfortable, but now I like being around many different types of people. I've come to understand that interacting with people who are different from you is part of a college education."

Unlike some in athletics, Gayle is reflective: "I know being a football star is an artificial world. There's a lot of nonsense involved. Coach Beamer says if you do the small things correctly, the big things take care of themselves. So I just work out and study and go to bed early and hope he's right."

Josh Oglesby. Coming out of high school, Oglesby was a highly recruited player, in part because his father had been a college football star, and athletic ability often runs in families. Oglesby would leave the Virginia Tech program mildly bitter that he never held the "feature" back role for the Hokies because two other strong players at his position were recruited. In 2009 and 2010, Ryan Williams was the starter at tailback, then in 2011, David Wilson won the job. Both Williams and Wilson became high NFL draft choices—what might have happened to Oglesby, if he hadn't plateaued at second-string.

"Football can set you up for failure by making you feel like the world owes you something when really you are just John Doe and you need to pull your own weight," Oglesby says. He graduated, putting himself on track for success in life. "I am fortunate because my parents are together and I grew up in an environment where education was viewed as a lot more important than sports."

Barquell Rivers. Every team has a player whose luck is bad, and for Virginia Tech in recent seasons, that was Rivers. He grew up in Wadesboro, North Carolina, which, he says, "is small and poor, there was no movie theater and no mall, playing ball was the only thing to do." Rivers's parents separated when he was young. He was raised by a grandmother, then an aunt. "My mother had to work two jobs so I only saw her on weekends," he says.

By 2009, Rivers was a star linebacker for Virginia Tech, with powerful shoulders and the fireplug build of the sport's best middle linebackers, and with an instinctual understanding of the game. The saying is "Can't coach size, speed or instincts." Rivers was drawing notice from NFL scouts.

This lasted until Max Out Day in the weight room. Rivers was attempting to power-clean 350 pounds. The maneuver requires snatching a barbell from the ground and raising the weight to the chin. The world record for this type of motion is 580 pounds, achieved at the 2004 Athens Olympics by the extremely hefty Iranian power lifter Hossein Rezazadeh, who trained for years to do nothing else. To hit 350 pounds, Rivers would need to raise almost half again his own body weight. And unlike Rezazadeh, Rivers did the power clean only once in a while.

"I didn't lock my arms correctly so put the weight back down to try again," Rivers says. "I slipped and fell awkwardly. Immediately I knew it was serious." Rivers ruptured the quadriceps tendon in one of his legs, a rare injury. Without its tendon the quadriceps muscle rolled back up into his body, making it seem a hole had appeared in his leg.

Rivers did not play in 2010, a year in which he had trouble walking. By 2011 "I could walk normally and it didn't hurt much anymore, but I couldn't plant and change direction like I used to." Changing direction quickly is essential in football. Rivers went from four-star to rarely on the field. In Rivers's senior year, most games concluded with his jersey clean, and only quarterbacks and kickers want clean jerseys. Rivers would end the season with just eight tackles, versus ninety-six in his banner 2009 season.

Rivers graduated with a degree in property management and returned to his hometown to think things through. He says, "There is no feeling like running out of the stadium tunnel to sixty-eight thousand screaming people, then hearing people chant your name in the stands. But if you are realistic, you know that one play can take everything away. When I got to Blacksburg, I chose a major that would lead to a career if the football disaster day came. Then it came. My mother did not want me to play college football because she was afraid I would get hurt."

Virginia Tech's secondary health-care insurance stays in effect only a year after an athlete's final reported injury; many colleges don't offer even that. Rivers left college football with a sports-caused condition that may lead to degenerative orthopedic conditions down the road. If health problems develop, he's on his own.

Logan Thomas. The quarterback, from Lynchburg, Virginia. Football turns on this position. Beamer said in 2012, "I will continue coaching as long as my health holds up and I have a good quarterback."

Thomas enjoys a striking physical presence: handsome, an easy smile and at six feet six inches has what scouts call "a high cut," meaning long legs and a narrow waist. Most basketball players are built like this, and in youth, Thomas favored basketball. "But in high school I began to calculate that there are a lot of six-six guys in the NBA and very few six-six guys in the NFL," he says. Cam Newton, first choice of the 2011 NFL draft, is 6-5 and high cut; Colin Kaepernick, starting quarterback for the 49ers in the 2013 Super Bowl, is 6-4 and high cut. While still in high school, Thomas correctly fathomed that quarterbacks built like basketball players could become a football fad.

"I was raised by a single mom; my grandfather was like my father," Thomas says. "There was a lot of pressure on me to become a better person, so my mother liked what she had heard about the Virginia Tech focus on respectable behavior."

Thomas is relaxed and confident, an athletic celebrity since he first walked on turf. Raised in a media culture, he feels the loss of privacy: "Everywhere I go, I must represent the university, even though I am not an employee and receive no pay. I enjoy privileges other Virginia Tech students do not, but also have obligations they don't. If I screw up, like with a DUI, the entire country would know. If the typical college student screwed up with a DUI, only his parents would find out."

Some colleges talked to Thomas about being a tight end, but Beamer saw him as a quarterback. "This shows Coach Beamer really knows what he's doing," Thomas said with a twinkle in his eye. "Plus quarterbacks are paid more in the pros and get hit in the head a lot less."

David Wilson. From Danville, Virginia, a rural burg in the same area as Frank Beamer's hometown, Wilson is a born tailback: fast, strong, ideal build to run the ball. As a high school senior he rushed for 2,291 yards and thirty-five touchdowns, remarkable numbers. Virginia Tech badly wanted him and had the inside track, being about a hundred miles away. Most star-rated prep players end up at a university close to home. The close-by program has the proximity to scout and woo, while offering a stadium in driving distance for friends and relatives.

Wilson would be chosen in the first round of the 2012 NFL draft by the New York Giants, then defending Super Bowl champions. He fumbled on his first NFL carry. While it's impossible to play football without fumbling once in a while, a rookie who fumbles in his first outing lands in the coach's doghouse. This happened to Wilson, who barely saw the field for months. Then in a December 2012 contest against the New Orleans Saints, Giants head coach Tom Coughlin would give Wilson a second chance; he responded with three touchdowns and 327 all-purpose yards, best in the Giants' nearly century-long annals. Entering the 2013 NFL season, Wilson was seen as a potential star.

WAKE-UP CALL FOR PLAYERS was 11:00 a.m. on the morning of the Sugar Bowl, for a scheduled 7:38 p.m. kickoff, local time—8:38 eastern. Football ratings are higher on the East Coast than the West Coast, so networks are conscious of not starting games so late that half the nation will head to bed by the fourth quarter. Basketball ratings are higher on the West Coast than in the East, which is why the NBA doesn't worry about starting playoff contests after 10:00 p.m. eastern.

The Hokies had breakfast, then chapel, which was held in the dining area right after the meal. Most players stayed, though chapel is unusual in being an optional football activity that actually is optional.

Johnny Shelton had been the team chaplain at Elon University, a liberal arts college in North Carolina, till by chance he sat next to Beamer on a plane flight. They got to talking, and Shelton says Beamer told him, "All these wins are great, but I worry about the futures of my players. So many young men on the football team come from fatherless homes; we are teaching them how to play, but are we teaching them how to live?"

At chapel, Shelton reads from the Paul's letter to the Philippians: "For God has graciously granted you the privilege not only of believing in Christ, but of suffering for him as well." Playing a football game entails a kind of suffering, though it's hard to see what this has to do with the Christian hope for humanity. In the locker room before kickoff, several players will come to Shelton to be blessed. He offers the traditional prayer that the Lord place a hand upon the shoulder of the faithful and keep them from harm. Though none ever say so, football players are keenly aware that once the game starts, one of them may get badly hurt. Safety Antone Exum—sporting a high-tech Mohawk cut, dyed gold—would kneel before Shelton in a pose little different, except for cleats, from a medieval devotional painting.

At 5:00 p.m., buses began departing for the Superdome. First three buses with the dress squad, those who would play, plus coaches. Then three buses with the scout teamers and athletic department staff. Then three buses with the official party from the president's office, the top Virginia Tech officers and boosters.

Putting on the football gear took the better part of an hour; taping ankles was the least of it. Virginia Tech has a chiropractor in the trainers' area before games, to "manipulate" players' spines and limbs, in hopes that looseness before contact will reduce injuries. Many players waited in line to lie on their stomach and have the backs of their legs repeatedly kneaded with massagers that look like science-fiction waffle irons. The goal is to loosen muscles and tendons so they don't cramp, especially the hamstrings, which are made cramp-prone by weight lifting and speed training. "Once this kind of preparation was viewed as soft," Goforth says. "Now it's all about whatever gives you a competitive edge. Massages, yoga—whatever works."

The locker room is quiet, almost still—no shouting, no exhortations. I say, "Good luck tonight," to David Wilson in a whisper, as no one's speaking loudly. The appropriate thing to say to an athlete before a contest is "Good luck." Perhaps "break a leg" is the right thing to say to an actress before she steps on stage. In sports, it's "Good luck tonight."

Because sporting events are sometimes presented as morality plays, fans and sportscasters like the notion that triumph stems from personal heroism. Players and coaches are conscious of the role of luck in sports outcomes. After a loss, saying "we had bad luck" sounds like excuse-making, after a win saying "we had good luck" sounds like false modesty. But whenever a game is close, Lady Luck chooses the victor. Players and coaches get this; audiences and sports commentators may not.

That luck is discounted as a factor in sports mirrors the discounting of luck in society. Americans tend to believe one person became wealthy, and another poor, based entirely on each person's merit. Few want to think that a major influence on life outcomes is simple luck. The rich don't want to think that because it implies greater obligations to the poor, who don't want to think that because it implies less hope they will rise from present circumstances.

The quiet turns to shouting as the players reach the tunnel. By the time they arrive at the sideline, the Hokies are pumped. O'Cain and Gray ascend to the press box; Foster and Stinespring stay on the sideline. Whether an assistant should coach from the sideline or the press box has long been debated. The press box affords an aerial view, what coaches call the A22 perspective—all twenty-two men on the field. But on the sideline a coach can ask players what they observed during the action, and players have a perspective available to no one else. Sometimes simply asking a player, "When we ran X, what did you see?" is the key that unlocks a game-winning call.

Because O'Cain relays the play call down to Stinespring, who relays it to the backup quarterbacks, who give hand signals to relay the call to Thomas, who relays the play to his teammates, the Virginia Tech system is clunky.

FINALLY, KICKOFF. ANYONE WHO ISN'T excited by a game of this import doesn't like football.

Michigan plays a "zone read" offense, a football meme—unknown a decade ago, now common even in high school. In the basic zone read, the quarterback stands deep in the shotgun; one defensive lineman is deliberately left unblocked, allowing an extra blocker for other defenders; the quarterback holds the ball out to a running back; if the unblocked lineman goes for the running back, the quarterback keeps the ball and runs sideways; if the unblocked lineman keys on the quarterback, he hands the ball to the running back. When the zone-read option first appeared—many coaches claim paternity—it was unstoppable.

Now defenses know how to handle this offense. But it's still effective, especially with an elusive quarterback.

Michigan receives the opening kickoff and goes three and out, Virginia Tech stopping a series of zone-read runs. The Hokies take over at their 37, and eight plays later have first and goal on the Wolverines' 4. This is a good omen. Virginia Tech is more comfortable playing with the lead—jumping ahead early, then applying defensive pressure—than coming back. Though any sports team would rather have the lead, some angle to exhaust opponents by the fourth quarter; Virginia Tech angles to strike early, then hold on.

On first and goal, Wilson takes a handoff and is hemmed in for what should have been a short loss. He has a brain freeze and sprints backward more than ten yards, trying to find a place to reverse field. Any purist in the stands covered his or her eyes, thinking, *Never run backwards!* Jim Brown, Barry Sanders and punt returner Dante Hall could profit by running backward; that is the entire historical inventory of football players who benefited by running toward their own goals. Earlier in the season, Wilson had been hemmed in, gone the wrong way, found a spot to reverse field and ended up with a 20-yard gain. Shane Beamer, Wilson's position coach, winces as he sees Wilson try the same again: the Hokies were in first and goal, and now their top offensive player is sprinting in the wrong direction. Wilson wants to "make a play," to do something flashy, and instead commits an error. The result is a 22-yard loss.

Now it's second and goal on the 26—effectively, second and 26. Not many offenses have a play for that down and distance. The drive ends with a field goal, as third-string placekicker Justin Myer connects. Virginia Tech 3, Michigan 0.

Michigan takes the kickoff, and soon Robinson throws an interception to Kyle Fuller, who makes a stellar play. A gifted athlete, he is of average stature. You wouldn't notice him if he walked by on the street.

Kyle's older brother Vincent was a star for the Hokies and then played six seasons for the Tennessee Titans. Kyle's older brother Corey is on the present Virginia Tech squad, later to be drafted by the Detroit Lions. Their younger brother Kendall, a much-sought high school senior, would commit to the Hokies. College coaches like to recruit brothers: once one brother has been in a program, he can help siblings prepare. Brothers Antoine and Derrick Hopkins are playing defensive tackle for Virginia Tech in the Sugar Bowl. They are nicknamed Hop and Skip; the Hokies hope to recruit their third brother, nicknamed Jump.

Virginia Tech moves the ball but is guilty of two penalties and soon faces third and 20. The Hokies rush to the line to quick-snap, and Thomas hits a 27-yard pass to Coale on a deep turn-in. Michigan seems surprised when the Hokies quick-snap on third and long. The Wolverine defensive back seems surprised by a white guy who attended a snobby private prep school—okay, he didn't know the private prep school part—accelerating past.

Late on the possession, Thomas converts another third-and-long pass, but two runs gain little; the first quarter ends. Thomas tries a quarterback draw on third and 7 and is stopped. Myer hits a 43-yard field goal. In the NFL, 43 yards is viewed as routine; in college play, any field goal attempt beyond the 40 is an adventure. Virginia Tech 6, Michigan 0.

On the next Wolverines drive, Virginia Tech's line gets a big sack on first down. Coaches call sacks and penalties "drive killers"—it's hard to score on a drive with a negative-yardage play. Michigan punts, and Virginia Tech takes possession on its 26-yard line, leading by 6.

So far everything is going the Hokies' way. Enthusiasm is high. I am standing on the sideline with two distinguished former Virginia Tech players, Bruce Smith, the Hall of Fame defensive end, and Antonio Freeman, a Pro Bowl wide receiver who started for the 1997 Packers team that won the Super Bowl. "This is going to be the Hokies' night," Smith says. "After this, no more talk about how Coach Beamer can't win the big one."

Thomas connects with Coale for another long gain. Josh Oglesby, the backup tailback, enters the game and snaps off two nice runs. That Wilson, a special talent, sometimes expects special treatment, while Oglesby is a straight-up team player, has led to slight tension in the locker room. Some of the Hokies would rather see Oglesby carry the ball.

Leading 6–0, the Hokies reach fourth and 1 on the Michigan 4. A field goal here makes the margin two scores, but a first down followed by a touchdown would be the early roundhouse punch that Virginia Tech seeks. There's a 75 percent chance of converting a fourth and 1, so going for it is not a "huge gamble," as sportscasters say, rather, playing the percentages. Besides if a team tries and fails in this situation, the opponent is pinned against his goal line.

On most football teams, the head coach makes the fourth-down decisions. Beamer decides to go for it. Seeing a specific hand signal, Thomas immediately breaks the huddle and runs the Hokies fast to the line of scrimmage. The call is the Brady sneak. On fourth and 1, Belichick, Yoda of NFL coaches, has been having Tom Brady rush the New England Patriots up to the line and quick-snap for a quarterback sneak, catching the defense not set. Thomas quick-snaps, dives forward and is stuffed for no gain.

Every previous time Virginia Tech had run this action during the season, it worked. But Michigan coaches had a month to put the microscope on Hokie game film and detected the Brady-sneak tendency. Virginia Tech coaches failed to anticipate this tendency would be noticed and had not designed a different fourth-and-1 play.

The stop invigorates the Wolverines. Michigan reaches midfield, where a sack creates third and 17. On this down, when all Virginia Tech needs is an incompletion, Robinson hits a 45-yard touchdown pass against a busted coverage. The Hokies' secondary was confused about who had whom and left a man unguarded. Busted coverages occurred on the killer plays in the Clemson losses too. All teams, including the best NFL clubs, occasionally have busted coverages. When defenses try to create confusion by changing alignments one second before the opponent's snap, the result may be that the defense confuses itself. Michigan 7, Virginia Tech 6.

The Wolverines kick off, and the ball sails to Tony Gregory, the player with the partial ACL tear. Michigan does not know that, but the play unfolds as if Michigan did. Gregory fields the kick, starts to run, is hit on his injured knee and fumbles: Wolverine recovery. Virginia Tech holds, and the Wolverines kick a field goal. Halftime score: Michigan 10, Virginia Tech 6.

IN THE LOCKER ROOM AT intermission, Goforth tells Gregory to take his pads off: he is done for the night. Gregory feels awful, having touched the ball exactly once and fumbled on national television. Teammates say nothing to him. No one yells nor consoles; they just say nothing.

The coaches huddle in a separate room for a few minutes, deciding on second-half tactics, then meet with players, by their positions. Foster, always emotional, is fired up and uses a chalkboard to show the defensive front how to foil Michigan's blocking. But he speaks the clipped code of football so rapidly, it's not clear if his charges can follow him. Newsome stands at the center of a circle of offensive linemen who are seated on folding chairs. He does not say much and looks worried. At halftime, coaches may be full of bluster or red-faced angry— these are standard conditions. When a coach simply looks worried, that's not good.

Danny Coale, a senior and a leader, gives an agitated oration, reminding seniors this is the last time they will wear the Virginia Tech uniform, extolling them to go out as winners. "People remember the last thing that happens," Beamer told me earlier. "If we win eleven games but lose the Sugar Bowl, all we will ever hear about is 'Why didn't you win that last game?'"

Coale shouts, "Never! Seniors, you will never wear these colors again! We need to finish this fight!"

A network stage manager sticks his head in the door to announce the teams are due back on the field.

FOR ALL THE ELECTRICITY AND testosterone of a big football game, teams can get drowsy at halftime. The signature play of the 2010 Super Bowl was the New Orleans Saints' surprise onside kick to start the second half. The Indianapolis Colts seemed a bit drowsy and, for a critical instant, did not react. The Who had been the halftime act—multimillionaires who arrived by private jet screeching into the microphone, "Out here in the fields / I fight for my meals." The Who's sets were being rolled out the tunnel on the Colts' end just before the second-half kickoff. Several Indianapolis players were watching the sets, not the Saints. It was a great time to call an onside.

Maybe Michigan is drowsy. Virginia Tech gets the second-half kickoff and soon faces fourth and 2 on its own 37. Beamer said in pre-game meetings that he would call a fake punt in this situation, and considering halftime torpor on the Michigan side, this seems the perfect place. But with the Hokies defense performing well, Beamer decides to kick. Exum sacks the Michigan quarterback on a safety blitz—a high-risk, high-reward tactic—and soon Virginia Tech has the ball again.

Thomas throws an interception, his only mistake of the night. Interceptions temporarily demoralize a team. They not only cost possession of the ball, they broadcast the word *mistake*—the quarterback threw poorly, or the receiver went to the wrong place. Making a big, obvious mistake saps a team's energy for a moment: Interceptions often result in a quick touchdown the other way. That happens. Michigan 17, Virginia Tech 6.

Mistakes can lead to resolve, and that also happens. The eyes of the Hokies' players flash. David Wilson springs a long kickoff return, then the offense pounds the ball into the Michigan red zone. The drive leads to Virginia Tech facing fourth and 1. That's the very down on which a quick sneak failed in the first half. Human nature makes coaches prone to think that whatever happened on fourth and 1 last time will happen again this time, though if a coin comes up heads ten times in a row, this tells nothing about what will happen on the next flip. Beamer doesn't want to risk not scoring, and sends in the field-goal team. Michigan 17, Virginia Tech 9.

The eyes of defenders are flashing too: the Hokies force a Michigan three and out. Momentum—impossible to quantify, unmistakable when present—is a central aspect of team sports. The momentum has swung back to Virginia Tech.

The Hokies drive to the Michigan 35, where it's fourth and 11. Sportscasters talk about the red zone; the opponent's 35 is in the maroon zone, where it's too far for a field goal but too close to punt. Beamer keeps his offense on the field, to go for the first down. Thomas drops back to pass, spies a lane where there are no defenders and takes off running. He's hemmed in a few yards short of the line to gain, but uses his large frame to bull his way to the Michigan 22 for a first down.

The Virginia Tech sideline erupts. At its core, football is about muscle and determination. When a player makes a crucial first down on sheer effort, his teammates become emotional. Even Smith and Freeman, decades removed from wearing burnt orange and Chicago maroon, are fired up. The Hokies call their dark color Chicago maroon because when Virginia Tech's predecessor school was established in the late nineteenth century, the University of Chicago was an athletic powerhouse, its maroon widely known as a symbol of sports prowess.

Virginia Tech reaches first and goal; consecutive rushes by Wilson and Thomas punch the ball across. Now trailing by 2, Beamer decides to go for a deuce. Marcus Davis—a junior wide receiver in the shadows of seniors Coale and Jarrett Boykin—snags a diving catch. Virginia Tech 17, Michigan 17.

The defense forces another quick Michigan three and out. For the night, Virginia Tech would outgain Michigan, 377 yards to 184 yards, and make ten more first downs. Both are significant edges.

Three snaps later, the Hokies face fourth and 1 on the Michigan 48—fourth and 1 for the third time in the contest. The game is tied with eight minutes showing in the fourth quarter.

Going for a first down is tempting—a strong chance of maintaining possession, with possession of the ball being more important to football success than field position. Plus a punt might roll into the end zone, netting not much in field position. Beamer decides to go for it, but makes a major miscalculation. He calls time-out, gathers the punt unit over to him, and heatedly gives instructions.

Fourth and 1 at midfield in the fourth quarter of a tie game—Michigan head coach Brady Hoke already suspects fake punt. In this situation, most head coaches in Hoke's position would signal "safe," calling a defense against a fake rather than setting up a return. With Beamer using a time-out to tell things to his punt unit, he has telegraphed that the play will be a fake. For a fake kick to work, the coach needs a poker face, acting as though nothing is happening.

Coale takes the snap on "rugby option," starts to run and is surrounded so rapidly he can't give up on the fake and just punt. Beamer should have left the offense on the field and let the regulars gain a yard. The Michigan sideline is jubilant. Momentum has shifted their way.

THE WOLVERINES DRIVE TO THE Virginia Tech 24. There the defense stiffens. Michigan goes short gain, short gain, incompletion, field goal. Michigan 20, Virginia Tech 17.

During the ensuing kickoff—the word *ensue* would fall out of usage were it not for sports events—Virginia Tech is called for holding. The result is Hokies' ball on their 9, four minutes remaining in the fourth quarter. "The team is up against it," as was said, or perhaps was said, in Knute Rockne's perhaps-apocryphal 1928 speech about the Gipper.

Showing determination, Virginia Tech stages an 83-yard drive. Coale makes a dazzling 30-yard catch. Tight end Chris Drager catches for a first down. Tight ends are central to NFL offenses, especially at New England and New Orleans, but in college they rarely see the ball—Drager would end a fourteen-game season with sixteen receptions. Tight ends do their work short over the middle, and only expert quarterbacks, such as Tom Brady and Drew Brees, have the green light to throw short over the middle, where the danger of interception is high. College quarterbacks are coached to throw outs, quick screens and "fade" routes, where interceptions are less likely.

With the clock nearly expired, Thomas hits Boykin, who struggles toward a first down but is stopped at the Wolverines' 8-yard line. Virginia Tech uses its final time-out.

The situation: fourth and 2 on the Michigan 8, five seconds remaining. The choice: kick a field goal to force overtime or go for the touchdown, one play to win or lose.

One play to gain eight yards is not a high-percentage call, especially inside the 10: the closer a football team gets to the goal line, the less territory the defense needs to protect. Near the goal line, with too little space for other kinds of patterns, football teams often run fades. The fade—what the San Francisco 49ers tried on fourth and goal from the Baltimore 5 at the end of the 2013 Super Bowl—is the hardest pass in football to defend. But it's also the hardest pass to complete; few college offenses reliably can execute a goal-line fade.

Proceeding to overtime is a fifty-fifty proposition. Michigan has just defensed ten Virginia Tech snaps in rapid succession, from a fast-paced no-huddle. Wolverine defenders are visibly tired, chests heaving—"sucking air," in sports slang. There's a decent chance Virginia Tech could score a touchdown, and the clock would expire during the play, giving the Hokies their biggest bowl win in many moons.

Beamer decides to kick. He sees the choice as the near certainty of an overtime, versus wagering everything on one play to gain 8 yards.

Nearly all college and NFL head coaches would kick in this situation, either owing to their calculation of the odds or to the knowledge that if they do the expected thing and kick, then the team loses later, the players will be blamed, while if they roll the dice for victory and fail, the head coach will be blamed. Myer drills the field goal: the third-string placekicker quietly has gone 4-for-4. Overtime at Virginia Tech 20, Michigan 20.

THE NFL LONG USED THE morbid phrase *sudden death* for overtime. Sudden victory would be better. The third (or sixth, depending on who's counting) *Stars Wars* movie originally was titled *Revenge of the Jedi,* then rechristened *Return of the Jedi,* since the just do not seek revenge. Overtime needs the same kind of retitling.

But even a positive spin such as sudden victory sells short the intense pressure of overtime. Every once in a while, a football game is won on the final play; overtime games are always won on the final play, with one side jubilant, the other crushed. One side will know joy, and the other unhappiness, though when a football game goes to overtime, either might have prevailed on a different bounce of the ball. But all anyone will remember is the last thing that happens, who wins and who loses.

The college overtime format gives each side an equal number of possessions starting at the "downhill" 25, taking possession in range for a field goal. If the first team with the ball scores a touchdown the second must also score a touchdown, forcing another overtime, or the first wins. If the first team with the ball scores a field goal, the second wins by scoring a touchdown, or forces another overtime with a field goal. If the first team with the ball fails to score, the second team wins with a field goal. (On paper a safety also would do the trick, but a safety is nearly impossible in the NCAA overtime format; safeties have won overtime games in the NFL format.)

Captains go back out to the center of the field. There's a new coin flip. Michigan wins and elects to make Virginia Tech take the ball first. Owing to different formats, NFL teams winning an overtime coin flip almost always choose first possession. In college, coaches would rather go second. That way, when their turn comes, they know whether they must score a touchdown or can settle for a field goal. Whoever goes first does not know this.

Unlike the game opening, with building music, then a kickoff, the Hokies simply line up on the Wolverines' 25 and the referee gives the ready-to-play signal.

Two Wilson runs advance the ball to the 20. Now it's third and 5. Conservative tactics would focus on the first down. But O'Cain calls a deep crossing pass, hoping to put the game away.

Coale makes a magnificent lunging catch at the back corner of the end zone. The line judge and the side judge, bracketing the play, have perfect position to see Coale's hands and feet. Both signal touchdown. The building shakes.

WHEN THE TEAM WITH FIRST possession scores a touchdown in overtime, odds of victory are high. Freeman, the former Pro Bowl wide receiver, was standing on the play side at the team-box limit—the closest to the end zone that officials will allow those on the sideline—and had a clear view. He runs excitedly to the coaches, crying, "He caught it! Good catch! He was in bounds!"

The Virginia Tech point-after team is heading onto the field when the referee waves his arms and announces the dreaded phrase "The ruling on the previous play is under further review." That redundant wording—"further review," when there's been no prior review—is for some reason mandated by the NCAA rulebook.

Bruce Smith, Virginia Tech's member of the Pro Football Hall of Fame, shouts at the referee that the catch was good. He's partial, of course, but has some experience in these matters. Freeman, who has made many tiptoe sideline receptions, declares, "The key thing is both officials on the play said touchdown." If one official signals touchdown and the other signals out of bounds, or one looks to the other unsure, anything might happen on review. When officials awarded victory to the Seahawks instead of the Packers on the final snap of the infamous 2012 *Monday Night Football* game, the whole mess began with one official signaling touchdown and the other signaling interception. But when two officials on the spot have clean views and both give the same signal, Freeman says, they're always right.

Fans and boosters in the seats behind the Virginia Tech team bench are celebrating. During the live broadcast, the play was shown in slow motion five times, and each time announcers Brad Nessler and Todd Blackledge—the latter the seventh choice of the 1983 NFL draft—said the catch was good. "They're not going to overturn this, it's a touchdown," Blackledge declared. But the Virginia Tech coaches are wary, knowing reviews can result in nasty surprises.

In the NFL, the referee—the head official, distinguished by a white cap—looks at replays from a monitor near the field and decides whether to uphold or reverse. In the NCAA, an extra official in the press box makes the review, then calls his decision down to the field; the referee has no role, other than announcing the booth official's judgment. An NFL referee can factor what he saw on the field, at game speed, into his review of a challenged call. An NCAA booth official watches from high above, seeing a distant mass of bodies.

The review is taking a long time, which makes the Virginia Tech coaches nervous—sometimes a long review means the booth is first ruling on the result of the play, then determining where to spot the ball. If it's a touchdown, there is no spot to determine. Referee Jay Stricherz walks onto the field and flips on his microphone: "After further review, the receiver did not maintain control of the ball as he hit the ground."

Danny Coale seemed to make one of the best touchdowns in college football annals, a spectacular catch in the end zone in overtime of a BCS bowl. His catch would have been talked about by football aficionados for decades—given a nickname, added to every highlight reel.

Suddenly it's just a failed pass, listed in the game book as "Thomas incomplete to Coale," the overturned touchdown not even mentioned.

BOTH CUSTOM AND THE RULEBOOK say that a call on the field should be overturned only if clearly wrong. If the call only might be wrong, the call should stand. Supposing a play is ruled a touchdown on the field, and it's not certain that ruling is correct, the touchdown should stand. Supposing the same play had, with equal uncertainty, been ruled out-of-bounds on the field, then the call of incompletion should stand. The NCAA rulebook reads: "To reverse an on-field ruling, the replay official must be convinced beyond all doubt by indisputable video evidence." Of the present and former NCAA coaches and players with no connection to Virginia Tech to whom I have shown Coale's play, two-thirds said it was a touchdown, one-third said the ball was bobbled. Because there was no "indisputable" evidence "beyond all doubt," the call on the field should have stood.

The next morning Beamer would tell me, "The game happens so fast, officiating mistakes at game speed are inevitable. What bothered me was that the mistake was on a replay. The call was made correctly at game speed by both linesmen who were right where the play happened, then changed into a mistake by a replay guy who's watching a tiny monitor. That's what bothered me."

NOW THE DOWN IS FOURTH and 5 on the Michigan 20. Beamer sends out the field-goal team, and Myer misses the short kick.

On the night, Myer hit four of five, and 80 percent accuracy is good for a college placekicker. But though Myer connected the first four times, he missed his last try—and what happens last is what gets remembered. Kyle Brotzman of Boise State kicked sixty-seven field goals, one of the best career totals ever in Division I. All anyone remembers is that in 2010, he missed a short attempt in overtime, disqualifying Boise State from a BCS bowl game.

Michigan runs into the line three times to improve position, then launches a short field goal from exactly the spot on the field where Virginia Tech just missed. Final: Michigan 23, Virginia Tech 20.

THE PLAYERS LOOK AS IF they've been hit by a truck. They wear stunned expressions; some are crying. Men should cry: about love, family, or fate—not about sports. But this is different. The Hokies thought they'd won a BCS bowl, and a faceless zebra locked in a booth took their triumph away. The players know they outperformed Michigan statistically by a wide margin. The scoreboard tells the only story anyone will remember.

In the locker room, Beamer walks from senior to senior, shaking hands. They will never wear the Virginia Tech colors again. A stage manager announces whom the media have requested for the interview area—this requires a rapid shower and change into nice clothes. After victory, it's a thrill to be asked to the media area. After defeat, a burden.

Beamer moves to the center. In this commodious NFL locker room, there's space to step back and form a circle. The players fall silent.

"Tonight, I am proud to stand with you and proud that you are part of my family," Beamer says. "You gave your best—the rest was beyond your control. Each one of you will always be part of the Virginia Tech family. No matter what the future holds, I will always be proud of every one of you."

That was his speech. No raised voice, no histrionics, no thrown chairs. Just an expression of father-figure pride.

At first I thought: If only the touchdown had counted, this would have been a perfect night for Frank Beamer. On reflection I realized it *was* a perfect night for Beamer. He'd coached a terrific winning season; his players and assistants abided by the rules, doing everything with their heads held high; in the spring, 75 percent of the senior players would graduate. Behaving conscientiously, the Hokies pulled up exactly one snap shy of a monster victory in one of the premier events in college athletics.

If every football program were run to values and standards shown by Virginia Tech's, the sport would be just as exciting and popular, but no longer notorious.

The team had a few hours of fitful rest at the Hilton, then went to the airport to board a charter flight that touched down in Roanoke, closest field to Blacksburg with a runway long enough for a large jet. Buses arrived at Virginia Tech in late afternoon. The campus was quiet, with Christmas break in progress. Players could enjoy a few days without class, while the next morning, coaches would report to the athletic complex to watch film of potential high school recruits. The winter sun was already declining and fresh snow had fallen, accentuating the stillness. They were safely back in football's Brigadoon.

The final chapter: The future of football.

Putting a Sport into Perspective

12

THE FUTURE OF FOOTBALL

The best football games your writer has ever attended were the two Super Bowls that paired the Patriots versus the Giants, in 2008 in Glendale, Arizona, and in 2012 in Indianapolis, Indiana. Each contest was well played by both teams. Each was tense, thrilling and decided on the final snap. Each was a huge ratings success, with much of the country watching intently. Each had the quality, increasingly rare in an amped-up society, of being memorable: sports fans will be talking about those games, the tactics and the big plays, for decades. And though there was plenty of aggression in both games, including crunching hits, there was no brutal helmet-to-helmet contact, no extreme violence, in either.

The future of football is written in those two Super Bowls.

The sport must be reformed so that vicious contact declines but excitement remains. Other reforms are needed too, in many areas. But reducing the severity of contact must come first—not so much to protect professionals at the top of football but to protect the far larger number at the bottom, in youth leagues and high school.

As the science of brain trauma improves, and the long-term effects of repetitive head contact become better understood, the combination of legal liability and social disapproval could mean the end of football. With each passing year, the American prospect hinges more on brainpower and education. For that future to work, the nation's most popular sport cannot be one in which millions of young boys and teen males systematically injury their heads. Those who say "leave football exactly as it is" are in effect saying "put football on a path to abolition." Better that the game be reformed.

To the extent the NFL is attempting to moderate helmet-to-helmet contact, there's no evidence that this is because the league's corporate-welfare ownership royalty cares about the health of their players or about the much larger number of youth and high school football participants. In 2012 and 2013, the NFL pledged a total of $90 million over four years to support research into brain harm from contact sports. Sound impressive? The pledge is less than one-fifth of I percent of the revenue the league expects in that period. By appearances, the NFL is taking baby steps toward change solely because its owners fear liability judgments cutting into their net worth. Reform must go much further.

HERE ARE REFORMS THAT COULD make football less dangerous, less subsidized and less harmful to education. First, on the college game:

• Division I football players should receive six-year scholarships, with a maximum of five years in athletics. That way once eligibility expires and the NFL does not come calling, Division I football players will have a final year as regular students—time to complete their credit hours, and graduate. The extra year of college, at the school's expense, would both advance education for athletes and allow colleges to repay football players for the revenue and publicity they produced on the field. (Department of Education Title IX regulations would need to be tweaked so that six-year scholarships applied only to football and men's basketball, the sports that make money at the expense of athletes' educations.)

• All colleges and universities should be required to present clear, prominent disclosures of the portion of tuition costs or "activity fees" that goes to the athletic department. Publicly funded colleges and universities should be required to disclose detailed athletic budgets, including details of coaches' pay and perks. Consumers deserve to know what they are buying: tuition bills should itemize the amounts that are diverted to NCAA sports. Taxpayers should know what they are supporting: at public colleges and universities, line items in the athletic department should be public information.

Such disclosures might be required by the new federal Consumer Financial Protection Bureau. Alternatively, the Department of Education could mandate that any college or university that accepts federal aid must disclose athletic spending and athletic department subsidies. Tying federal aid to public-interest reform has worked with colleges and universities before.

• The college football rankings formulas—for the media rankings published by the Associated Press and by *USA Today*, for the BCS rankings and for whatever supplants them when the expected Division I championship playoff is finalized—should give one-quarter weight to team graduation rates. By extending recognition to graduation rates, the BCS organization and the big-school football playoff organization could show they are more than just business ventures. Media companies should voluntarily adopt this standard for college football polls, as they have voluntarily adopted many other standards for what and how they report.

Today, schools jockey over the second and third decimal places of poll rankings. If graduation rates were a factor, coaches would ensure their players were in class. This reform would not be a panacea, but making graduation rates part of the all-important rankings would create a real incentive for college athletic departments to get serious about education. All give lip service to the classroom; few care, because their reward structure is based on wins. Changing the reward structure would add accountability to the collegiate sports system.

In 2012, the major college sports conferences agreed to a "framework" of a future football playoff system, under which 10 percent of playoff revenue would be distributed based on the academic performance of football programs. This is a classic sham reform. Ninety percent of the emphasis remains on wins, while the educational money would be distributed in so many slices that any one college's incentive would be slight. Distribution would be based on the Academic Progress Rate, itself a sham. This plan is designed to create the appearance of progress while locking into place the status quo.

By contrast, factoring graduation rates into bowl rankings would revolutionize college football. The games would remain exciting and popular, but the players would become more likely to focus on class and finish their degrees. To oppose the idea, one must say, "College football is only about victory, not about education." Of course that is the reality in many places. Stating that reality makes the entire NCAA system into a sham.

• Sanctions and related penalties should follow a head coach. Head coaches say they deserve high pay because the buck stops with them—but when violations occur, usually the head coach is not held responsible. In 2010, University of Tennessee head coach Lane Kiffin left to become head coach at USC, in part because he knew sanctions were about to be imposed on the Tennessee program, owing to events during his leadership. The Volunteers were put on four years' probation, while Kiffin signed a rich new contract at a new school and whistled a merry tune.

One reason college football coaches break NCAA rules is that the reward is great (victories lead to multimillion-dollar contracts and endorsement deals) while the risk is low (most violations result in wrist slaps, or no action at all). Ohio State head coach Urban Meyer, known as one of football's progressive thinkers, has noted that if an eighteen-year-old freshman breaks an NCAA rule he did not understand, the roof falls on him; "But when a forty-five-year-old coach does something wrong on purpose, that's called a 'secondary violation' and nothing happens. The coach should receive a serious penalty."

If head coaches knew an NCAA sanction to their old employer would mean they couldn't work in NCAA sports for the same number of years, they would have a self-interest in running clean programs.

• One-year suspension for the head coach of any football program whose players graduate below the rate of the student body as a whole; adjusting for players who transfer and for players who depart early for the NFL, both of these always small numbers. The suspension would follow the coach. If the low graduation rate was at School A and the coach jumped to School B, he would be suspended there.

True, literature professors are not penalized if lit majors graduate at below the rate of the student body as a whole. But professors do not control their students' schedules and scholarships, as do Division I head coaches. College coaches ostentatiously claim to be educators of student-athletes. It is time they were held accountable as educators.

• NCAA coaches should receive bonuses only for academic results, not for victories, conference titles or bowl invitations. There is plenty of incentive to win already.

Is education-based pay impractical, as a coach or athletic director might claim? In 2013, Mitch Daniels, the former governor of Indiana, became president of Purdue University. At his own request, he received a contract with lower base pay than that of the previous president, along with generous bonuses based on metrics of the university's core mission—including graduation rates and keeping the school affordable to students. Daniels's contract provides him ample motivation to perform, but his pay increases only if he serves the interests of education. Daniels is setting an excellent example, one that college coaching should follow.

• Bowl committees, athletic-booster funds and stadium-construction funds should lose their nonprofit or tax-deductible status. Only donations to the academic mission of a college or university should be tax-deductible.

REFORMS FOR SAFETY:

• At all levels of football, an unnecessary-roughness penalty for a deliberate helmet-to-helmet hit should bring with it an automatic one-game suspension. If players were suspended for vicious hits, behavior would rapidly change.

In 2013 the NFL, having forbid defensive players from deliberately leading with their helmets, forbid offensive players from doing the same. Traditionalists protested, Hall of Famer wide receiver Jerry Rice saying restrictions on contact will cause "powderpuff football." But Rice wouldn't be in the Hall of Fame if traditionalists of prior generations had been heeded: they opposed the forward pass, claiming it would sissify the game.

Stricter regulation of contact is essential to the future of football. The 2013 NFL rule change helps but does not go far enough: drawing a flag does not penalize the player personally, while most flags are forgotten before the contest even ends. If any deliberate lead-with-the-helmet play led to automatic suspension, for the first few weeks that this new standard was in effect, players and coaches would moan while spectators booed the officials. Then behavior would change, making the game safer.

• The three-point stance should be prohibited, so linemen and full-backs do not begin plays with their heads down, ensuring helmet-to-helmet contact. All sports rules fundamentally are arbitrary. Why is a touchdown 6 points? Once a touchdown was 4 points. Why are there twenty-four seconds to shoot a basketball, instead of twenty-three or twenty-five? There is no inherent reason why linemen need to start plays with their heads down. Altering the rules so action begins with the linemen's heads up will decrease brain trauma.

• State and local laws should be amended so the care-and-custody standards that pertain to high school teachers also pertain to coaches, in football and in other sports. Nearly all high school athletes are, legally, children under the care of an adult. Coaches need to approach them as children to be protected—not as miniature NFL players to be mistreated for the coach's ego and victory record.

   Changing the legal standard would alter coaching behavior, making sports safer for high school students. The games would be just as exciting. If such a change led to a high school football coach's being prosecuted for child abuse, this would only need to happen once, and all other football coaches would get the message.

• Advanced helmets and Type 3 mouthguards should be mandatory from high school football on up. Many NFL and NCAA teams already use only advanced helmets and Type 3 mouthguards; all should. Some public school systems will have trouble funding purchases of advanced helmets—an order for a school's entire varsity and JV can cost $15,000. But should a school system's budget troubles ever justify exposing its students to brain damage?

- Year-round high school football should end. From Christmas till the end of the spring semester, high school football teams should have no meetings, including no off-campus events such as seven-on-seven tournaments. This is how it was in high school football for decades, and come autumn, the games were well played.

  With more than a hundred public and private sanctioning bodies for high school athletics across the country, getting them to agree to return football practice to its traditional seasonal basis won't be easy. But it won't be impossible either.

- Tackle football should not be played until age thirteen, or until eighth grade.

  It is cynical of the NFL to sponsor youth leagues that risk brain trauma to 3 million young people, in order to sell equipment and increase the fan base. At the least, sponsoring organizations for youth tackle should lose their tax exemptions: the public should not subsidize activity that causes head injuries.

  Flag football is a fine alternative to tackle at the youth level, and is lots of fun to play. The NFL should sponsor flag leagues for youth players, but not sponsor, and thus glamorize, youth tackle.

REFORMS FOR PROFESSIONAL FOOTBALL:

- NFL headquarters should lose its nonprofit status. Public funding for NFL stadiums should end.

- NFL press guides, websites, and similar media should list only the last school from which a player actually has graduated—if that is high school, then no college listing.

  Estimates are that only about 50 percent of NFL players have graduated from college. Yet every press guide, roster and the league's annual *NFL Record and Fact Book* lists a college after each player's name. For example, since he entered the league in 2004,

Steelers press guides, NFL.com and ESPN.com rosters and the *NFL Record and Fact Book* have listed Steelers star Ben Roethlisberger as a graduate of Miami University. But Roethlisberger did not actually complete his degree until 2012. He's a college graduate today. He was presented to the public as one when he was not.

Implying that NFL players have graduated from college makes pro football seem practically civic-minded: get a scholarship, get a sheepskin, then take your college fight song into the NFL. But when the NFL, and NFL game announcers, talk on television about a player's college, roughly half the time they are deceiving the audience.

If NFL players who did not graduate from college were listed by high school, young boys and their parents would have a more accurate understanding of what football at the top level entails—and there would be pressure for reform.

• Use levels of prescription narcotics, painkillers and injected anesthesia should be disclosed by all NFL teams.

• Congress should direct that any professional sports images created in facilities built with public funds belong to the public. That would mean the NFL could not sell television license rights from games played in stadia that were funded by taxpayers; such images would become "public domain," like images from a national park.

Currently there is no federal law on this point. An individual state could enact a law placing images from taxpayer-funded stadia within its borders into the public domain. National legislation that levels the playing field, as it were, across the country would be preferable. The devil is always in the details of legislation that impacts interest-groups, so drawing this law would be a challenge. But if the United States can regulate health care, a $3 trillion industry, then Congress can fix a problem regarding football broadcast rights. The Communications Act of 1934 grants Congress broad authority regarding interstate communication.

Ending the practice of images from public stadia becoming private property for private profit rapidly would result in the NFL and its owners paying the full cost of any new stadium construction, while repaying the taxpayer-funded gifts they have received for existing NFL fields. Large sums would be transferred from the NFL's aristocratic owners to the public that made the wealth possible. This would be a healthy development for society and the sport. NFL owners and executives often mouth empty words about "giving back." This reform would result in actual giving back, while preventing any more situations in which taxpayers are forced to finance NFL facilities.

BEYOND THESE REFORMS IS THE need to place football into perspective. During interviews for this book, I asked dozens of players and coaches what one thing they would change about the sport. The most reflective answer came from Tony Dungy:

"If I could change one thing about football, it would be that we need more time away from the game—as players and as a society.

"Young boys and teens should not be doing football year-round. Year-round football may be good for promoters; it is not good for the players. Injuries such as sports hernias are becoming more common because young people's bodies don't get the resting time, away from athletics, they once got. That is a medical warning society needs to pay attention to.

"There is an educational warning too. High school boys who play football should be trying other sports, or participating in the school musical or other extracurriculars in order to become well-rounded. They need to do things that broaden their horizons and teach them how to interact with all the different kinds of people in our world. Football can be a positive experience for a boy. But if the price is damaging his body or neglecting his education, then the price is too high.

"As for society, it's great that America loves football. But now with the Internet, the mock drafts, the fantasy leagues and recruiting mania going year-round, with colleges and high schools playing more often and the NFL talking about an even longer schedule—we need time off, away from the game.

"The price of football needs to be lower—in money, in health harm, in young people's time, in the country's focus. Football is wonderful, but the price has gotten too high."

FOR HALF A CENTURY, FOOTBALL has gotten bigger and bigger. Each time the NFL or a major college conference signs a new broadcast contract, it's assumed the limit has been reached; yet each time the numbers get larger. This dynamic, driven partly by the nation's rising prosperity, can make it seem football can only get bigger. But no law of nature says football must remain the king of sports.

Seemingly secure companies go out of business; products fall out of favor; needs cease being needed. Once the leaders of the Western world sat up at night fretting about running out of coal—now coal producers practically give the stuff away. Today it seems as though football can only be bigger, but no law of nature protects football from decline.

The United States faces many challenges far more important than reforming football. Income inequality, the national debt, climate change, a fragile global economy, gridlocked politics—there is a daunting list. If the United States can't come to grips with the relatively small task of cleaning up its national sport, how will the country ever achieve progress on grand issues?

EIGHT REMARKABLE WORDS ARE ETCHED into stone on the grandstand at Whittier Field of Bowdoin College, in Brunswick, Maine, a place where football has been played since 1896. Above the tunnel to a very old locker room are the words:

FAIR PLAY AND MAY THE BEST MAN WIN.

The noun choice may be antiquated. Joan Benoit Samuelson, first woman to win an Olympic gold medal in the marathon, trained at

Whittier Field, running past the "best man" etching thousands of times. But the sentiment expressed is entirely up-to-date. Fair play will always be a lesson men and women need to learn.

Standing on Whittier Field at dawn when all is quiet, a person who strains can hear the distant echoes of cheering and brass bands playing, of shouts of exhortation, dismay and triumph, from 1896. If all goes well, football still will be played on that field in 2096 and far into the future, as fields all across the nation host football games for many generations to come. This will happen only if the king of sports is reformed.

ACKNOWLEDGMENTS

Thanks are due to Greg Aiello, Jonathan Alter, Bobby Azarbayejani, John Ballein, James Bennet, Greg Bishop, Jackson Bowling, Anne Brewer, Lisa Brooks, Jerry Carle, David Caputi, Michael Carlisle, Diana Clark, John Clayton, Robert Cole, James Collins, Chandos Culleen, Larry Culleen, Lucinda DeCastro, Vince Doria, Thomas Dunne, Rich Eisen, Josh Elliott, Maureen Elliott, Mike Florio, Olga Grlic, Jeff Harding, Justin Havens, Eric Heckman, Billy Hite, Lynn Hoppes, Arianna Huffington, Kevin Jackson, Robert Jauron, Tom Jolly, Ned Jovanovich, Kevin Kelley, Jimmy Kemp, Brian Kenny, Prodige Kikwata, Rob King, Michael Kinsley, Mel Kiper Jr., Michael Knisley, John Kosner, Charles Kristich, Darrien Locke, Abbey Lostrom, Jay Lovinger, Bill McGregor, Thomas McKean, Bob Milloy, Greg Neuendorf, Thomas Neumann, Joe Nocera, Jeff Norman, Tina Pagano, Denise Pellegrini, Mike Philbrick, Chris Russo, Mary Sadanaga, Aaron Schatz, David Schoenfield, Jack Shafer, Katherine Sharp, Bob Sickles, Michael Signora, Kenneth J. Silver, Mark Simon, John Skipper, Dave Smith, Kurt Snibbe, Chris Sprow, Patrick Stiegman, Clarence Thomas, Roman

Vejmelka, John Walsh, Eric Weinberger, Bram Weinstein, Matt Wilansky, Jim Wilkie, Willie Williams, Matt Willis, David Wilson, Ralph Wilson Jr., Peter Wolverton, Jules Yakapovich and Mark Zimmerman; to my siblings Frank, Neil and Nancy; to my children Grant, Mara and Spenser; and to my wife, Nan Kennelly.

If only I could place this book into the hands of my father, George Edmund Easterbrook, born in Toronto in 1918, who in 2012 passed away in his sleep at the conclusion of a long, accomplished life. And if only I could place this book into the hands of a very smart sports enthusiast whose light shone in this world too briefly: Reuben Mitrani, 1992–2012.

SOURCES

Books, studies, and articles referred to in *The King of Sports*, plus a few books on athletics that should not be overlooked.

BOOKS

American Football Coaches Association. *The Football Coaching Bible.* Champaign, IL: Human Kinetics Books, 2002.

Archibald, Robert, and David Feldman. *Why Does College Cost So Much?* Oxford: Oxford University Press, 2011.

Bacon, John. *Three and Out.* New York: Farrar, Straus & Giroux, 2011.

Bissinger, H. G. *Friday Night Lights.* Boston: Addison-Wesley, 1990.

Blount, Roy. *About Three Bricks Shy of a Load.* New York: Ballantine, 1986.

Bowen, William, and Sarah Levin. *Reclaiming the Game: College Sports and Educational Values.* Princeton, NJ: Princeton University Press, 2002.

Cantu, Robert, and Mark Hyman. *Concussions and Our Kids.* New York: Houghton Mifflin Harcourt, 2012.

Carroll, Linda, and David Rosner. *The Concussion Crisis.* New York: Simon & Schuster, 2011.

Clotfelter, Charles. *Big-Time Sports in American Universities*. Cambridge: Cambridge University Press, 2011.

Dungy, Tony. *The Mentor Leader*. Carol Stream, IL: Tyndale House, 2010.

Ellison, Ralph. *Invisible Man*. New York: Random House, 1952.

Farrey, Tom. *Game On*. New York: ESPN Books, 2008.

Feldman, Bruce. *Meat Market: Inside the World of College Football Recruiting*. New York: ESPN Books, 2006.

Gumbrecht, Hans. *In Praise of Athletic Beauty*. Cambridge, MA: Harvard University Press, 2006.

Halberstam, David. *The Education of a Coach*. New York: Hyperion Books, 2005.

Hanson, Mary Ellen. *Go! Fight! Win! Cheerleading in American Culture*. Bowling Green, OH: Bowling Green University Popular Press, 1995.

Hawkins, Billy. *The New Plantation*. New York: Palgrave Macmillan, 2010.

Hyman, Mark. *Until It Hurts*. Boston: Beacon Press, 2011.

Layden, Timothy. *Blood, Sweat and Chalk*. New York: Time Home Entertainment, 2010.

Lewis, Michael. *The Blind Side*. New York: W. W. Norton, 2007.

Long, Judith Grant. *Public-Private Partnerships for Major League Sports Facilities*. Oxford: Routledge, 2012.

MacCambridge, Michael. *America's Game*. New York: Random House, 2004.

Mandelbaum, Michael. *The Meaning of Sports*. New York: Public Affairs Books, 2005.

Meyer, Dutch. *Spread Formation Football*. Saddle River, NJ: Prentice Hall, 1952. (Written in the late 1940s, this book describes tactics that today's sportswriters treat as brand-new.)

Nelson, Mariah. *The Stronger Women Get, the More Men Love Football*. Boston: Harcourt Brace, 1995.

NFL Record and Fact Book. New York: Time Home Entertainment, annual.

Nowinski, Christopher. *Head Games*. Plymouth, MA: Drummond Publishing, 2007.

Rosin, Hanna. *The End of Men*. New York: Riverhead, 2012.

Saint John, Warren. *Rammer Jammer Yellow Hammer.* New York: Crown, 2004.

Schatz, Aaron, lead author. *Football Outsiders Almanac.* CreateSpace Independent Publishing, annual. (By a huge margin the best annual on the NFL and college football.)

Smith, Ronald. *Pay for Play.* Urbana: University of Illinois Press, 2010.

————. *Sports and Freedom.* Oxford: Oxford University Press, 1987.

Sweeney, Walt, with Bill Swank. *Off Guard.* Self-published, 2012.

Walters, Guy. *Berlin Games.* London: John Murray, 2006.

Whitmire, Richard. *Why Boys Fail.* New York: Amacon, 2010.

Wildavski, Ben. *The Great Brain Race.* Princeton, NJ: Princeton University Press, 2010.

Yakapovich, Jules. *The Radar Defense for Winning Football.* Saddle River, NJ: Prentice Hall, 1970. (I include this book because it's by my high school football coach.)

STUDIES

Anderson, Michael. "The Benefits of College Athletic Success." National Bureau of Economic Research, 2012.

Bailey, Martha and Susan Dynarski. *Inequality in Postsecondary Education.* University of Michigan. 2013.

Borchers, James, et al. "Risks for Football Players Go Beyond Impact." Indianapolis, IN: American College of Sports Medicine, April 2011.

Brenner, Joel. "Overuse Injuries, Overtraining and Burnout in Child and Adolescent Athletes," *Pediatrics,* June 1, 2007.

Broglio, Steven. "Head Impacts During High School Football." *Journal of Athletic Training,* July–August 2009.

Carnevale, Andrew, et al. "The College Payoff." Washington, DC: Georgetown University Center on Education and the Workforce, 2011.

Cavassin, Tacey, et al. "The Role of Age and Sex in Symptoms and Postural Stability in Athletes After Concussions." *Sports Medicine,* April 26, 2012.

Chai, Grace, et al. "Trends of Outpatient Prescription Drug Utilization in US Children, 2002–2010." *Pediatrics,* March 19, 2012.

Collin, Mickey. "Examining Concussion Rates and Return to Play in High School Football." *Neurosurgery,* February 2006.

Cottler, Linda, et al. "Injury, Pain and Prescription Opioid Use Among Former National Football League Players." *Drug and Alcohol Dependence,* July 1, 2011.

David, Jesse. "Downing Concussions." Washington, DC: Edgeworth Economics, August 2012.

Digest of Education Statistics 2012. National Center for Education Statistics, 2012.

Echlin, Paul, et al. "A Prospective Study of Physician-Observed Concussions During Junior Ice Hockey." *Journal of Neurosurgery,* November 2010.

"Estimate of Motor Vehicle Traffic Fatalities in 2011." National Highway Traffic Safety Administration, May 2012.

"Final Report of the Counsel to the Special Committee of the Board of Directors of the Fiesta Bowl." March 2011.

Garrett, Thomas. "The Distributional Burden of Instant Lottery Ticket Expenditures." Federal Reserve Bank of St. Louis, January 2012.

Gilchrist, Julie, et al. "Nonfatal Traumatic Brain Injuries Related to Sports and Recreation Activities Among Persons Aged 19 Years or Less." Centers for Disease Control and Prevention, 2011.

Hartlyn, Jonathan, and William Andrews. "Review of Courses in the Department of African and African American Studies." University of North Carolina, May 2, 2012.

Hess, Frederick, lead author. *Diplomas and Dropouts: What Colleges Actually Graduate Their Students.* Washington, DC: American Enterprise Institute, 2009.

Huma, Ramogi, and Ellen Staurowsky. "The Price of Poverty in Big Time College Sports." National College Players Association, 2011.

Jones, Christopher, et al. "Pharmaceutical Overdose Deaths, United States." *Journal of the American Medical Association,* February 20, 2013.

Lapchick, Richard. "Keeping Score When It Counts." Orlando, FL: Institute for Diversity and Ethics in Sport, March 2011.

Laurson, Kelly, and Joey Eisenmann. "Prevalence of Overweight Among High School Football Linemen." *Journal of the American Medical Association*, April 4, 2007.

Lee, John, and Anita Rawls. "The College Completion Agenda 2010." College Board, 2010.

Matava, Matthew, et al. "Recommendations of the NFL Physician Society Task Force on the Use of Toradol." *Sports Health*, September–October 2012.

May, Ashleigh, et al. "Prevalence of Cardiovascular Disease Risk Factors Among US Adolescents." *Pediatrics*, May 12, 2012.

Report of the National Commission on Terrorist Attacks Upon the United States. Washington, D.C. 2004.

NCAA. "Binding Consent Decree Imposed by the NCAA and Accepted by Penn State." July 23, 1012.

———. "Division I Graduation Rates." http://www.ncaa.org/wps/wcm/connect/public/NCAA/Resources/Research/Graduation+Rates.

———. "Revenues and Expenses 2004–2011: Division I Intercollegiate Athletic Programs Report." NCAA, 2012.

NCAA versus Board of Regents of Oklahoma University. Supreme Court. 1984.

"Organized Sports for Children and Preadolescents." Policy statement of the Committee on Sports Medicine, American Academy of Pediatrics. *Pediatrics*, June 1, 2001.

"Prescription Drug Abuse: The Public Health Perspective." White House Office of Drug Control Policy, 2012.

Restoring the Balance: Dollars, Values, and the Future of College Sports. Knight Commission on Intercollegiate Athletics, 2010.

Schatz, Philip, et al. "Early Indicators of Enduring Symptoms in High School Athletes with Multiple Previous Concussions." *Neurosurgery*, June 2011.

Stephenson, Betsey. "Beyond the Classroom: Using Title IX to Measure the Return to High School Sports." National Bureau of Economic Research, 2010.

"Summary of NFL Helmet Testing Study." National Football League, July 23, 2010.

US Department of Education. "The Equity in Athletics Data Analysis Cutting Tool." http://ope.ed.gov/athletics.

Zeitler, Phil, et al. "A Clinical Trial to Maintain Glycemic Control in Youth with Type 2 Diabetes." *New England Journal of Medicine*, June 14, 2012.

ARTICLES AND DOCUMENTARIES

Alexander, Raquel, and James Gentry. "From the Sideline to the Bottom Line." *New York Times*, January 1, 2012.

Bachman, Rachel. "The College Football Grid of Shame." *Wall Street Journal*, August 30, 2012.

————. "The Revenue Bowl." *Wall Street Journal*, January 6, 2012.

Belson, Ken. "As Stadiums Vanish, Debt Lives On." *New York Times*, September 7, 2010.

Bishop, Greg. "For New Ohio State Coach, It's First Down and $4 Million." *New York Times*, November 28, 2011.

Bissinger, Buzz. "After Friday Night Lights." *Byliner*, 2012.

Bogdanich, Walt, Joe Drape, and Rebecca Ruiz. "Racing Economics Collide with Veterinarians' Oath." *New York Times*, September 21, 2012.

Branch, Taylor. "The Shame of College Sports." *The Atlantic*, October 2011.

Cantu, Rick. "Refugio Quarterback's State Passing Record Leaves a Bad Taste." *Austin American Statesman*. October 15, 2012.

Carroll, Collin. "Eliminate Bowl Week." ESPN.com. January 2, 2012.

Corben, Bill. *Broke*. ESPN documentary, 2012.

deVise, Daniel. "Athletic Fees—a Large, Hidden Cost of College." *Washington Post*, October 24, 2011.

Dretzin, Rachel, and Caitlin McNally. *Football High*. PBS documentary, 2011.

Duncan, Arne. "Missing from March Madness: Better Academics." *Washington Post,* March 16, 2011.

Easterbrook, Gregg. "Two Misconceptions in College Sports." ESPN .com, December 15, 2009.

————. "Virginia Tech Helmet Research Crucial." ESPN.com, July 19, 2011.

Eichelberger, Curtis. "College Sports Gifts Rise 24 Percent." Bloomberg .com, September 15, 2011.

Eichelberger, Curtis, and Elise Young. "College Football Fails Profit Test as Students Pay $1,000." Bloomberg.com, May 3, 2012.

"Ex-College Football Star Found Guilty of Burglary." *Cincinnati Enquirer.* March 29, 2012.

Farrey, Tom. "Seminoles Helped by LD Diagnosis." ESPN.com, December 18, 2009.

Gayle, Tim. "Fans Gave Saban Warm Welcome in Tuscaloosa." *Montgomery Advertiser,* January 3, 2007.

Goodwyn, Wade. "Undefeated Horned Frogs Leap to Title Contention." NPR, December 4, 2009.

Grasgreen, Allie. "Another Round at Rutgers." *Inside Higher Ed,* August 24, 2011.

————. "Stanford, Notre Dame . . . and Miami?" *Inside Higher Ed,* September 1, 2011.

Greenburg, Ross. *Star Spangled Sundays.* NFL Films documentary, 2013.

Greenstein, Teddy. "Big Ten Told It's Safe to Expand Horizons." *Chicago Tribune,* March 1, 2010.

Harris, Amy. "Stanford Athletes Had List of Easy Classes." *Stanford Daily,* March 9, 2011.

Herman, Peter. "Police Escorts Under Scrutiny." *Baltimore Sun.* September 14, 2011.

Jenkins, Sally. "NCAA Athletes Deserve Respect More Than Money." *Washington Post,* November 23, 2011.

Kane, Dan. "Report Finds Academic Fraud Evidence." *Raleigh News & Observer,* May 4, 2012.

Karp, Hannah. "Former Players Say Saban Twisted the Truth." *Wall Street Journal*, November 26, 2010.

Keating, Peter. "Doctor Yes." *ESPN The Magazine*, April 2006.

Kuriloff, Aaron, and Darrell Preston. "In Stadium Building Spree, Taxpayers Lose $4 Billion." Bloomberg Businessweek, September 5, 2012.

Lederman, Doug. "Winning Football, Failing Grades." *Inside Higher Ed*, December 20, 2011.

Lombardi, John. "Sports Subsidies and Library Spending." *Inside Higher Ed*, June 1, 2012.

Lopresti, Mike. "Steelers Quarterback Graduates at Thirty." *USA Today*, May 7, 2012.

McGrath, Ben. "Does Football Have a Future?" *New Yorker*, January 31, 2011.

———. "Head Start." *New Yorker*, October 15, 2012.

———. "Will High-School Football Become a Big-Money Sport?" *New Yorker*, January 2, 2012.

Moltz, David. "Tax-Exempt Pedicures." *Inside Higher Ed*, January 5, 2011.

Nocera, Joe. "Academic Counseling Racket," *New York Times*, February 4, 2013.

———. "Standing Up to the NCAA." *New York Times*, March 23, 2012.

Outside the Lines. ESPN, air date May 9, 2012.

Ozanian, Mike, lead author. "Football's Most Valuable Teams." *Forbes*, September 5, 2012.

———. "Vikings Stadium Not Likely to Help Minnesota Economy." *Forbes.* May 4, 2012.

Palaima, Thomas. "The NCAA and the Athletes It Fails." *Chronicle of Higher Education*, April 17, 2011.

Peck, Don. "Can the Middle Class Be Saved?" *The Atlantic.* September 2011.

Rose, Stephen. "How We Spend." *The Atlantic*, April 2012.

Ryman, Richard. "Super Bowl Winning Season Led to Record Profits." *Green Bay Press Gazette*, July 11, 2012.

Sander, Libby. "NCAA Punishes an Ivy." *Chronicle of Higher Education*, September 8, 2010.

Smith, Erick. "Assistant Football Coaches See Surge in Pay." *USA Today*, December 21, 2010.

Thamel, Pete. "Tebow Studies Xs and Os." *New York Times*, October 30, 2008.

———. "Top Grades and No Class Time for Auburn Players." *New York Times*, July 14, 2006.

Thamel, Pete, and Kyle Whitmire. "Auburn's Kingmaker." *New York Times*, January 8, 2011.

Trotter, Jim. "What's Next for Johnny?" *Sports Illustrated*, March 6, 2013.

Tsitsos, William, and Howard Nixon. "The Star Wars Arms Race in College Athletics." *Journal of Sport and Social Issues*, February 2012.

"*USA Today* College Football Coaches Salary Database." (Running Internet feature with data on public-university coaches. *USA Today* maintains similar databases for assistant coaches and athletic directors.)

Weiberg, Steve, lead author. "Texas Athletics Overwhelm Rivals in Revenue and Spending." *USA Today*, May 15, 2012.

Weissmann, Jordan. "Penn State's Fine Is Less Than the NCAA Wants You to Think." *The Atlantic*, June 2012.

Wilson, Duff. "NFL Executives Hope to Keep Salaries Secret." *New York Times*, August 11, 2008.

Yost, Mark. "The Price of Football That Even Nonfans Pay." *Wall Street Journal*, February 3, 2011.

INDEX